deeply regrets
to do what
proposed.

WITHDRAWN

Pryce-Jones, David
Evelyn Waugh and his
world

World

EVELYN WAUGH AND HIS WORLD

edited by David Pryce-Jones

Little, Brown and Company
Boston   Toronto

Designed and produced for George Weidenfeld and
Nicolson Limited, London
Printed and bound in Great Britain

Library of Congress Catalog Card No. 73-5746

First American Edition

Contents

List of Illustrations | | vi

Introduction | David Pryce-Jones | 1

1 Escape from Golders Green | Alan Pryce-Jones | 7

2 At Lancing | Roger Fulford | 15

3 A Kingdom of Cokayne | Peter Quennell | 23

4 He-Evelyn and She-Evelyn | Dudley Carew | 39

5 Madresfield and Brideshead | Lady Dorothy Lygon | 49

6 The Religion of Evelyn Waugh | Father Martin D'Arcy S. J. | 59

7 Lush Places | Eric Newby | 81

8 Recollections | Penelope Chetwode | 97

9 'Judge and Jury Must Decide' | Douglas Woodruff | 103

10 Captain Waugh | Fitzroy Maclean | 133

11 Fiery Particles | The Earl of Birkenhead | 137

12 America and the Comic Vision | Malcolm Bradbury | 165

13 The Fugitive Art of Letters | David Lodge | 183

14 His Bookseller's View | Handasyde Buchanan | 219

15 What's in a Name? | John Jolliffe | 229

16 Yours affec: Evelyn | Anne Fleming | 235

Index | | 242

Illustrations

PARENTS: CHILDHOOD: OXFORD *pages 25 to 32*

Catherine Charlotte Raban, *Private Collection*
Arthur Waugh, *Private Collection*
Evelyn Waugh, *Private Collection*
Alec Waugh, *Private Collection*
Drawing by Evelyn Waugh, *Private Collection*
Evelyn Waugh with his mother, *Private Collection*
School photograph, *Lancing College*
Programme for a play by Evelyn Waugh, *Private Collection*
Detail from school photograph, *Lancing College*
Photograph inscribed for Terence Greenidge, *Private Collection*
Evelyn Waugh on Magdalen Bridge, *Private Collection*
Portrait of Evelyn Waugh by Henry Lamb, *Private Collection*
Pen-drawing for the Oxford Union, *Private Collection*
Caricature of Harold Acton, *Private Collection*
'The woeful state of the Kingdom of England', *Private Collection*

ARTIST *pages 65 to 72*

Caricature of Alec Waugh, *Private Collection*
Watercolour by Evelyn Waugh, *Private Collection*
Woodcuts, *Private Collection*
Jacket design for *Circular Saws*, by Evelyn Waugh, *Private Collection*
Christmas cards, *Private Collection*
Bookplates, *Private Collection*
Frontispiece for *Vile Bodies, Chapman & Hall*
Frontispiece for *Love Among the Ruins, Chapman & Hall*

FIRST WIFE: CANONBURY SQUARE: CONTEMPORARIES *pages 105 to 120*

Evelyn Gardner, *Private Collection*

Sitting-room of the Waughs' house, *Private Collection*
Police Summons, *Private Collection*
With Patrick Balfour, from *The Tatler*, 1930, *Private Collection*
At Alec Waugh's wedding, with Patrick Balfour, *Private Collection*
With Isobel Strachey, *Private Collection*
At Madresfield, from *The Latler* *Private Collection*
At Madresfield, *Private Collection*
With Lady Mary Lygon and Lady Dorothy Lygon, *Private Collection*
At Captain Hance's riding school, *Private Collection*
At Madresfield, beside the bust of Emperor Vitellius, *Private Collection*
With Alec Waugh at Villefranche, *Private Collection*
Alastair Graham, *Private Collection*
With Lady Rosebery and Lord Berners, *Radio Times Hulton Picture Library*
Drawing of Nancy Mitford by Cecil Beaton, *Private Collection*
'The Romance Reader' a postcard sent to Nancy Mitford, *Private Collection*
Inscription on the back of the postcard, *Private Collection*
The Railway Club, Oxford, 1925, *Private Collection*
The last meeting of the Railway Club, *Private Collection*
At Mells with Osbert Sitwell and Lord David Cecil, *Private Collection*
Opening ceremony at Campion Hall, *Private Collection*

TRAVEL: WAUGH AT WAR *pages 153 to 160*

Frontispiece to *Labels, A Mediterranean Journey*, 1929, *Chapman & Hall*
HIM Seth of Azania, *Columbia University Library, NY*
Drawing for *Black Mischief*, *Columbia University Library, NY*
Painting presented to Campion Hall by Evelyn Waugh; photographer Thomas Photos, Oxford. *Campion Hall, Oxford*
Bathroom at Combe Florey, *Private Collection*
In Kenya, 1930, *Private Collection*
Evelyn Waugh with the Infanta Beatrice of Spain, *Private Collection*
In Palestine, 1935, *Private Collection*
In the Royal Marine Corps, 1939–40, *Private Collection*
With Randolph Churchill, *Private Collection*

LETTERS *pages 185 to 188*

Letter, 1928, *Private Collection*
Postcard from Abyssinia, 1930, *Private Collection*
Inscription on postcard, *Private Collection*
Letter from Piers Court, *Private Collection*
Letter from Combe Florey, *Private Collection*
Letter from Ethiopia, *Private Collection*
Evelyn Waugh receiving the Hawthornden Prize, 1936, *Private Collection*

SECOND MARRIAGE: FAMILY: AMERICA: AT HOME: COMBE FLOREY *pages 197 to 212*

Marriage to Laura Herbert, *Private Collection*
Evelyn Waugh with his wife in St James's, *Private Collection*
Wife, mother and first-born, *Private Collection*
Arrival in New York, *Associated Press*
In Hollywood, *Private Collection*
Return to Plymouth, *Popperfoto*
Garden at Piers Court, *Private Collection*
Garden at Piers Court, *Radio Times Hulton Picture Library*
With Alec Waugh, *Madame Yevonde*
Cartoon of Evelyn Waugh by Osbert Lancaster, *Private Collection*
Evelyn Waugh with five children and retainers, *Private Collection*
Family group, *Private Collection*
Family group; photographer Mark Gerson. *Camera Press*
Teresa reading, *Madame Yevonde*
In the garden at Combe Florey; photographer Mark Gerson. *Camera Press*
Wash-stand by William Burges; photographer Mark Gerson. *Camera Press*
Library; photographer Mark Gerson, *Camera Press*
The Perils of Travel, eighteenth century; artist Robert Musgrave Joy. *Private Collection*
The Perils of Travel, nineteenth century; artist Richard Eurich. *Private Collection*
Evelyn Waugh in the library; photographer Mark Gerson. *Camera Press*
In the entrance hall of Combe Florey; photographer Mark Gerson
'No Admittance on Business;' photographer Mark Gerson
Hand-out for the Edinburgh University Rectorial Campaign, *Private Collection*
Poster for a garden fete at Piers Court, *Private Collection*
'Mr Evelyn Waugh . . .', *Private Collection*

OLD AGE *pages 221 to 224*

With the Duchess of Devonshire, *Keystone Press*
Interview on the BBC 'Face to Face' programme, *BBC*
At Auberon Waugh's wedding, *London Express*

Photographic work by Angelo Hornak and A. C. Cooper
Picture research by Philippa Lewis

INTRODUCTION

David Pryce-Jones

THOUGH

Evelyn Waugh used to complain sometimes that his books were ignored or stupidly dismissed, he was content to leave his reputation to the Parsnips and Pimpernells who hold the literary line. He gave few interviews, and when he did, as on the television programme *Face to Face* in 1962, he was uncompromising, implacably so. Yet it was not exactly aloofness for he often went out of his way to introduce or promote other writers: Father Thomas Merton, for instance, Jessica Mitford, Muriel Spark, Eric Newby. 'An act of Homage and Reparation' was the title of the essay he published in *The Sunday Times* in 1961 about P. G. Wodehouse, who for years had been very shabbily treated because of some broadcasts he had given while a prisoner in Germany during the war. He sent a letter to the *Spectator* to defend one of Angus Wilson's novels from its hostile reviewers. 'I like to write for the *Spectator*,' he wrote to me when I was its literary editor, 'when there is some writer who seems to be getting too little or too much praise, or when there is an expensive book on Victorian painting or architecture which I want for my library.'

Had Parsnip and Pimpernell contributed to this volume, they would have argued that the early novels retain their anarchic charm, *A Handful of Dust* being a minor classic; that the later books, especially *Brideshead Revisited*, are best passed over in embarrassed silence, except for the scenes of battle in *Sword of Honour*. Edmund Wilson found *Brideshead Revisited* 'a bitter blow' and almost all critics since then have followed suit: John Betjeman was one of the very few with courage enough to say that it was 'his greatest achievement'. But the enchanted circle of Evelyn Waugh's lasting world, of Captain Grimes and Prendy, Lord Copper, William Boot, Basil Seal, even Drs Parsnip and Pimpernell, had been at once recognised for what it was.

'His development has taken him steadily from the Left towards the Right, and Right Wing Satire is always weak – and he is a satirist': Cyril Connolly in 1936. ('Somebody's been tickling up Cyril's class consciousness . . .', I read in one of Evelyn Waugh's letters). The following year, the lines were drawn properly when Evelyn Waugh was asked for the purposes of a propaganda book, *Authors Take Sides on the Spanish War*, 'Are you for, or against, the loyal government and the People of Republican Spain? Are you for, or against, Franco and Fascism?' His complete answer was:

I know Spain only as a tourist and a reader of the newspapers. I am no more impressed by the 'legality' of the Valencia Government than are English Communists by the legality of the Crown, Lords and Commons. I believe it was a bad government, rapidly deteriorating. If I were a Spaniard, I should be fighting for General Franco. As an Englishman I am not in the predicament of choosing between two evils. I am not a Fascist nor shall I become one unless it were the only alternative to Marxism. It is mischievous to suggest that such a choice is imminent.

Several writers – Sir Fitzroy Maclean and Lord Birkenhead are witnesses – have helped to explain how deeply the politics of the world war disillusioned Evelyn Waugh. His sense of disgust that the modern age would always be in arms arose from it, and so did his response to America, complex but representative too, as Malcolm Bradbury shows it to be. Afterwards, the jeering tone was often in his prose, and David Lodge describes how wounding and provocative this could be, although when directed in letters or personal feuds against friends of long standing like Cyril Connolly or Peter Quennell, it went deeper still. That he had critics and enemies was in many ways his own fault; he welcomed them, he teased them to keep boredom at bay but was usually met with no humour at all. Literature at the time had come to be narrowly, almost exclusively, valued for its social purpose, as though imagination had nothing to do with it. It was not his later novels which were under review but Evelyn Waugh himself, caricatured as every sort of ideological villain – a presence to whom the writers of England would succumb if they did not ward him off. All the same, he can hardly have expected that J. B. Priestley would charge him with insanity, writing in the *New Statesman* (31 August, 1957) ostensibly about Gilbert Pinfold and his hallucinations: 'He will break down again, and next time may never find a way back to his study. The central self he is trying to deny, that self which grew up among books and authors and not among partridges and hunters, that self which even now desperately seeks expression in ideas and words, will crack if it is walled up again within a false style of life.' And more besides. The Emperor Seth of Azania, one recalls, was modern enough to have read Priestley.

Most of the contributors to this book knew Evelyn Waugh well at different times or for most of his life, like Douglas Woodruff, Penelope Chetwode – and Father D'Arcy who received him into the Catholic Church. In general, they make it clear that he was denying nothing to a central self; that as he got older his ideas and words were expressed with particular lucidity, not desperately at all. Dudley Carew, like

4 David Pryce-Jones

Roger Fulford, was a school friend, and his essay is from a longer manuscript so far unpublished and called 'A Fragment of Friendship', and he has been kind enough to let me select from it the more touch-and-go bits.

How fierce and final is the nostalgia in the three letters written from Yugoslavia, quoted by Lady Dorothy Lygon; that same passion which fires Brideshead, forever out of reach. It is impossible to doubt of his loyalties to places or to chosen people such as Anne Fleming or Lady Diana Cooper (see her memoirs), but somehow reality was never quite up to imagination. Wreckers were everywhere. Towards the end of his life he was stout, a little deaf, with that famous ear-trumpet, and thoroughly intimidating. There was something phenomenal about the apparition of England's most distinguished contemporary novelist, this cham, this sacred monster. At a dinner given for him once by his eldest daughter in the Randolph Hotel at Oxford, I sat one away from him. Within minutes, the girl between us had been reduced to tears. He waved the ear-trumpet at her. Diverted at last by a question, he began to talk about the children of homosexuals, but loudly enough for everyone in the room to hear. On another occasion, I was introduced to him for about the fifth time, so I told him that he knew perfectly well who I was. He started back, eyes a-bulge, trumpet up. 'Ah, I used to know your poor dear father' (who here gets his word in first). You were not sure if you were in the grip of his fantasy, or of your own.

Around such a figure, so publicly private, as it were, stories sparked like summer lightning, and for the first time many of them are now authenticated and collected, I am glad to say – all the more so because the Humanities Research Center of the University of Texas now possesses Evelyn Waugh's papers and apparently takes a cue from Mr Joyboy himself towards that unregenerate corpus of writing. A great many people, however, did help me, and first among them are Christopher Sykes and the late A. D. Peters, Evelyn Waugh's literary executor. Miss Philippa Lewis took a lot of trouble over the illustrations. My thanks are due to Harold Acton for allowing me to reproduce the wood-cuts and drawings in his possession; to Lady Helen Asquith; Lord Baldwin of Bewdley; Cyril Connolly; Lady Diana Cooper; Mrs Teresa Cuthbertson; F. W. D. Deakin; Richard Eurich for permission to reproduce his painting in 'The Pleasures of Travel' tryptich, and to Mrs Teresa D'Arms whose pictures they are; Sir Roy and Lady Harrod; Lord Kinross; Osbert Lancaster for permission to reproduce his cartoon; to Lancing College and the Head-master's secretary, Miss Ruth Hollis; Lady Mary Lygon; Nancy Mitford; Lord Moyne, for permission to reproduce the portrait by Henry Lamb; John Sutro; and Alec Waugh. I wish also to thank the publishers Chapman & Hall, for their kind permission to quote extracts from Evelyn Waugh's books, and from the Evelyn Waugh Estate for permission to quote extracts from Mr. Waugh's letters.

1

ESCAPE FROM GOLDERS GREEN

Alan Pryce-Jones

SOME years ago, my solicitor fell in the fire and died. His remains, appropriately enough, were cremated in Golders Green, and I happened to leave the crematorium with Alec Waugh, who had for many years shared with me the surprises and reversals of fortune (seldom for the better) which came from taking the old gentleman's advice.

Alec took me on a walk in the neighbourhood. We turned into a quiet road, and stopped by a gate: not a lodge-gate, not, I think, even a carriage-gate, but a small barrier at the end of a footpath. It led to a house: nothing remarkable, the kind of house a child draws in crayon. 'Look at it well', Alec said. 'That is the house where Evelyn spent his formative years. He doesn't care to be reminded of it.'

I thought back a quarter century. In those days we made jokes about Evelyn toiling up the hill to Hampstead so that his letters might bear a more distinguished postmark than Golders Green. This is the kind of jest, I should add, that gets into circulation when people make jokes against themselves – a propensity of Evelyn's when he was young. The jest rebounds: more stupid friends take it for the truth. It is, however, a fact that Evelyn's attitude to social nuances was both prim and subtle. It would be absurd to call him a snob. On the other hand, it would be absurd to echo on his behalf Sir Walter Raleigh's celebrated verses beginning, 'I wish I loved the Human Race.' Evelyn had no wish to do anything of the kind, but his disinclination was not rooted in anything so simplistic as snobbery.

I did not know him in his Golders Green period; indeed, the only time I ever knew him with any degree of intimacy was in his twenties, at the time of his first marriage: a time he did not care later to remember.

But I did know his brother Alec, and to a lesser degree his father. When I left Oxford, my first job was as assistant editor under J. C. Squire on *The London Mercury*. Squire was a cricketing editor, of a stamp now fallen from fashion. Alec, also a cricketer, used to join him, from time to time, at our local, the Temple Bar. So, in the course of his work as managing director of Chapman and Hall, did Arthur Waugh, though much less often.

At that time, Evelyn was a faunlike observer – the epithet is Harold Acton's – of the London life finally immortalised in *Vile Bodies*. In order to understand his attitude to Lady Metroland, say, it is essential to put Evelyn's own life into perspective first; to understand a little of his personal background.

Arthur and Alec Waugh were anything but faunlike. Born in 1903, and thus by five years the younger of two sons, Evelyn depended for love and companionship during his nursery years on his mother and on Lucy, the nanny. His father, he says, remained a 'figure of minor importance and interest', who seldom entered the nursery except on a routine evening visit. Alec was soon away at school.

In *A Little Learning*, the first volume of an autobiography, Evelyn writes of his own childhood with affection. But it is easy to discern a certain exasperation with the minutiae of family life. He would hear his father's key turn in the lock and a voice from the hall cry 'Kay! Kay! Where's my wife?' 'That', he observes coldly, 'was the end of my mother's company for the evening.' Worse, there was a scene at Hampstead Heath Fair when Evelyn, aged four or five, was led home to luncheon – too early in his view – and rolled on the path, abusing his father as 'You brute, you beast, you hideous ass' – a phrase 'which became part of our family language': not very serious – after all, family languages are a mark of mutual affection – but at least an indication that Evelyn took after his paternal grandfather more closely than after his somewhat Pickwickian father.

The grandfather in question was a country doctor, who practised for over forty years at Midsomer Norton, near Bath. Evelyn's immediate family is well-documented. Not only he but his brother and his father wrote autobiographies, and it is to the point that the manner in which they describe the same incidents differs substantially. Arthur Waugh did not wish to disparage his own father. Himself a family man, he hesitated to describe Dr Alexander Waugh as the tyrant he in fact had been. Subject to rages, parsimonious, happy to hurt those close to him, he presented a very different front to the public, who found him a genial and hospitable sportsman, an excellent shot and an understanding practitioner.

He left his son Arthur a legacy of fear. Not that Arthur lacked courage in face of life, but he was a pessimist, an asthmatic, a rather shy man, as I remember him, who offset these disadvantages by extreme joviality. He was a play-actor by nature, taking up one part after another: the martyr, the business man, the man of instant decision, the amateur comedy star. He excelled at paper-games, and fancied himself as a lyric writer after the school of W. S. Gilbert.

Evelyn found him immensely old – he had been thirty-seven at Evelyn's birth – and slightly absurd into the bargain, though, as time passed, their affection deepened, for Evelyn possessed his grandfather's dual nature, only in reverse. Where Dr Waugh had shone publicly and reserved his faults for his family, Evelyn did the opposite. He was much at his best with those closest to him, and at his worst with strangers: a tendency aggravated by the passing of time.

Indeed, the Waughs turn out to be surprisingly volatile. Evelyn notes that they 'grew shorter throughout the nineteenth century, perhaps because it suited their bossiness to marry small wives'. They are not easy to pin down. Their ancestors were small farmers in the Border country; they developed a clerical streak as they shrank, first as Dissenters, then in the Anglican Ministry: Evelyn's great-grandfather was, for forty-one years, rector of Corsley in the West Country, and by all accounts a most amiable patriarch.

From his mother's side, Evelyn inherited the blood of Lord Cockburn, the distinguished Scottish lawyer and memorialist of the early nineteenth century, and also a single dash of Catholicism in the person of his own great-grandmother, Theodosia Mahon, who, to make matters worse, was a convert. Her sisters-in-law, shocked by this apostasy, removed Evelyn's grandfather from her care, and forbade him to meet his popish half-brothers and -sisters when later she remarried: an attitude which recalls to me the situation of a great-aunt of my own who lived, when I was a child, among the ruins of Beckford's Fonthill. She too, went over to Rome, taking her daughters but leaving her sons to Canterbury after the fashion of her period; and my mother, knowing that a Jesuit chaplain was installed at Fonthill, always gave me a strict warning when I was asked to stay there: 'Be careful,' she would say, 'or Aunt May will get you.' Aunt May, a most genial old lady, evinced no interest whatever in my spiritual future. And similarly, it took three generations for Theodosia's decision to be repeated within her family circle.

There was also, on the Waugh side of Evelyn's family, an eminent man of letters, Edmund Gosse, who had greatly helped Arthur Waugh in his literary beginnings, and was held in contempt by Evelyn. To a child who confessed to loving panache, Gosse seemed drab and a toady, however exhilarating to the older generation.

Already, as childhood ended, Evelyn betrayed an odd ambivalence to the life which surrounded him, a life on which he ended by bestowing its brightest lustre. Men of letters were all around. His father's publishing firm was small but distinguished, and even though Arthur Waugh had little personal ambition, he had, in his day, won the Newdigate, and contributed to *The Yellow Book*. Alec, before

Evelyn had reached his teens, found fame with a sensational novel, *The Loom of Youth*, an unvarnished account of school life which had the immediate effect, on Evelyn, of banning him from Sherborne, the school in question, for which his father had an obsessional affection.

The atmosphere of his home, then, was bookish: in no self-conscious sense, and with no leaning to the new or the intellectually fashionable. Dickens, Trollope, Arnold, Tennyson, Browning represented (not unfairly) the mainstream of literature as it flowed through North End Road – not Pound, Eliot or Proust. Books, and the love of books, were taken for granted; and so it was as a draughtsman that Evelyn first brushed with the creative arts – his own illustrations to *Decline and Fall* are delightful.

Debarred from Sherborne, he went to Lancing: hardly an Athenian academy, but one at which, having overcome a personal unpopularity which surprised him, after years of happiness at home, he grew into an aesthete rather than a hearty, and from there on took his place at a jogtrot Oxford college, Hertford, among the bloods from Christ Church and Magdalen.

The value of Oxford to Evelyn was that it removed him for good from Golders Green – not the Golders Green of reality but the bourgeois citadel of legend. He discovered the uses of idleness and alcohol, the velvet glove which hid the iron hand of Etonian contemporaries, the puzzling friendliness (for in the Oxford of the Twenties things were never quite what they seemed) of exceptional dons like Maurice Bowra, 'Sligger' Urquhart and R. M. Dawkins. He had always attracted the interest of clever and ambiguous elders – in his autobiography, he writes with detached sympathy of J. F. Roxburgh, later headmaster of Stowe, but a House-master in the Lancing of Evelyn's day. At Oxford, he moved into the company of those contemporaries whom he calls, without hostility, 'mad, bad and dangerous to know'.

To him they presented no danger. Fauns are immune, by their nature, from corruption, and whether he liked it or not, Evelyn was far too much of a Waugh to escape from a family pattern which embraced a wife, a child – better, many children – and a settled home. But he was attracted to the eccentrics of his day, who later, barely caricatured, so accurately are they depicted, made up the cast-list of *Decline and Fall* and *Vile Bodies*.

And as a legacy of this period, he displayed a remarkable sense of loyalty. After years passed, Evelyn could be censorious to a degree. He reigned most powerfully in the kingdom of disapproval. But his old friends, however disreputable, commanded his total loyalty. One, of whom he has written under the pseudonym of Hamish Lennox, presented his acquaintance with a series of problems almost impossible to surmount; others went to jail for sex offences, or attracted scandal as heather collects honeybees. Evelyn never failed them in friendship. Even when they became bores – a deterioration he must always have been among the first to note – he preferred them to attractive strangers; so that, although it is easy to find harsh critics of the Evelyn who survived to write *Officers and Gentlemen*, those who had known the faun seldom lost their affection for the portly figure of later years.

It was some time before he came to think of himself as writer rather than draughtsman. The act of writing belonged, in his young eyes, to Golders Green. He discerned in it a certain ignobility. When he was born, had not his elder brother hailed his arrival by exclaiming, 'At last we have a wicket-keeper'? Paradoxically, it was, I think, the need to express revulsion from, agreeably mixed with love for, the different layers of existence which marked his beginnings, that moved him to set up first as satirist, and later as chronicler of his own experience.

He had been happy in the nursery, bored or unhappy at school, dizzied by Oxford, cast down by academic semi-failure, horrified by the rigours of teaching at second-rate schools as a means to earning a living. During these first decades, he had continually been reminded of a father's presence by admonition, and finally (as promise seemed to evaporate more quickly) by a despair none the less trying for being laid out in theatrical phrase and gesture. Into the bargain, his elder brother, having found a wicket-keeper elsewhere, was doing very well. To cap all, an early marriage, to which he had pinned unlimited hopes, failed through no fault of his own.

That his first novel met with immediate success was no consolation. As a matter of plain fact, Evelyn was the most professional of writers, with an exact care for the English language, a marvellous ear and a fastidious sense of what to avoid. There are, among his works, no pot-boilers.

But he was also a romantic and an old-fashioned one at that. Friends like Hugh Lygon, and Hugh's sisters, were sought out not because they were the children of Lord Beauchamp and lived in large houses beautifully run, but because they appealed to the anti-Golders Green strain in him, much as the pious have been dazed by the wonders of a Heavenly City. Luckily, the Heavenly City oi the Lygons and their like was perfectly accessible. Nothing had to be taken on faith; the pleasures of citizenship could be tasted and maintained. Was it unkind to laugh at Evelyn for taking riding lessons, with Captain Hance, in an almost vocational spirit? Was it absurd for him to make an increasing fuss about the quality of the champagne offered, and the unsuitability of the guests assembled to drink it? No; because in order to write, Evelyn had to build a persona for himself utterly unlike that with which he had been born; he had to protect himself against demons – not only the hallucinatory demons which harassed Gilbert Pinfold, but enemies implanted by heredity and environment.

It would be over-dramatic to see his writing simply as a form of exorcism, but it would not be wholly untrue. Just as he had to travel at one period of his life, to play (very effectively) the soldier at another, to reproduce, in Gloucestershire or the West Country, a laird's concept of living passed down from Berwick in the late eighteenth century, so his mission was to interweave restlessness and repose, in order to make books very different in kind but surprisingly constant in quality.

It is a measure of the sheer niceness of Arthur Waugh that he accepted Evelyn's approach to writing as tolerantly as he did. The single book of his own which survives, *One Man's Road*, is at the opposite pole of literature. Chatty, affectionate, slightly fatuous, bathed in nostalgic sunlight, it tells the story of a pleasant life from which the mad, the bad and the dangerous were excluded as far as possible. If Evelyn grew up an aesthete, his father remained a hearty through and through.

Having so little in common with his nearest relations did not sour Evelyn's judgment of them. Of Alec, he insisted in print that, though antithetical, they were not antipathetic to one another. His tribute to his father was positively cordial. 'There were times', he wrote, 'when I was inclined to regard his achievements as rather humdrum. Now I know that the gratitude I owe him for the warm stability he created, which I only dimly apprehended, can best be measured by those less fortunate than myself.'

These are the considered verdicts of middle age. While still a faun, Evelyn was more severe. He grew up, be it remembered, in a very special society, and a heady one at that. The middle Twenties in London combined several revolutions in one: political, social, financial, sexual. As an escape from Golders Green, the London of the Cavendish Hotel and of Mrs Arthur Bendir's welcoming house in Grosvenor Square was total. Evelyn had very little money at that time, like most of the friends among whom he moved, but somebody always had money. The mauve-and-beige drawing rooms of the period were lavishly equipped for the delectation of charming young strangers on their way to Rector's or the Embassy, to the Eiffel Tower (where nobody ever seemed to pay the bill anyway) or, for the more dissolute, the Blue Lantern.

By the time I came on the scene, the great days were fading. But it was still clear that Evelyn had no need to stretch his powers of invention to write those early novels: they might have been taken straight from an observant diary; and the characters, suitably remoulded for purposes of fiction, were still easily recognisable in daily life.

The romantic in Evelyn loved them, as did the amateur of the eccentric upper classes. But Evelyn was not for nothing descended from the Rector of Corsley, the James Hay Waugh who had impressed his descendants 'as the embodiment of patriarchal authority'. A Calvinist streak surviving in Evelyn, derived from the dissenting forbears whose progeny abandoned Scotland for the softer West Country of England, bred in him a severity which took over as soon as he stopped laughing at folly. He had the makings in him of a Savonarola and of a Lord George Hell: finally, the manifold masks he wore came to hide his real face except from the very few who had known him over the years well enough to remember a faun still sometimes visible under the integuments of the patriarch.

The closing paragraphs of *A Little Learning* describe a moment in Evelyn's young manhood when no hope remained. He half decided to kill himself; and, with a tag from Euripides pinned to his clothing, swam out to sea by moonlight with no firm intention to return. A jelly-fish stung him; then another. Prudently he swam back to shore, tore up the tag, dressed and 'climbed the sharp hill that led to all the years ahead'. It is typical of the paradoxes which surround him that it should be a jelly-fish which made actual the vocation of that tough, vulnerable little man.

2
AT LANCING

Roger Fulford

I should not talk so much about Lancing. If you weren't at Eton or Harrow or Winchester or Rugby no-one minds much where you were.' That was advice given to me by Evelyn when I arrived as an undergraduate at Oxford, in 1923, where he had been established for eighteen months. Superficially, those words may seem harsh and, considering that we were both Old Lancians, a shade disagreeable. That might be the obvious interpretation but it would be completely wrong. The words have always stuck in my memory because they sprang from kindness not from harshness; they were factual not fashionable, cautionary not admonitory. Indeed, they can be compared with something Carlyle once said – though more bluntly – to his friend William Allingham – 'Allingham, let me tell 'ee a thing; you're in danger of becoming a bore.'

In order to see Evelyn in his setting as a school-boy, the background of Lancing when he was there must be noticed. In *Decline and Fall* he calls a school, which is clearly Lancing, 'a small public school of ecclesiastical temper on the South Downs'. That was correct but limited. With the end of the nineteenth century, the school had emerged from obscurity and religious difficulties. Under Henry Bowlby – a fashionable Eton House-master and a great Headmaster of Lancing – who had been appointed in 1909, the school was firmly established in the second rank of English public schools. Its reputation was further helped during Henry Bowlby's time by a remarkable team of young masters – 'Dick' Harris, who was our House-master when we arrived, E. B. Gordon, a man of discriminating taste and a typographer of distinction who was to become our House-master, J. F. Roxburgh, whose achievements are to be found in Lord Annan's magnificent biography of him, Brent-Smith, a musician of renown, and Adam Fox, who endeared himself to us all by combining the priesthood with command of the OTC. The progress of the school, coupled with its success at games and at Bisley, and the reputation of its OTC, fostered among the boys a certain swagger and a certain intolerance for those who could not contribute to its forward march. The Head's House to which Evelyn and I were sent, though not differing in austerity from the other Houses, had certain distinguishing features. The Headmaster was our House-master, occasionally limped round the dormitories and always took prayers on Sunday evenings. His children's nurse was our matron, and the baize door by which she entered our stark surroundings from the comforts of the Bowlby home seemed to link us with feminine society – society which was completely lacking in the masculine House by which we were surrounded. People in the Head's House had to pay an extra fee and, as there was no obvious return for this levy, it gave the impression that our House was a little pocket of affluence and indulgence.

For the two new boys in the summer of 1917, Evelyn and myself, any indulgence was not noticeable. Regimentation was the thing. Scholarship, skill in athletics and good looks made regimentation possible to bear and opened the door to popularity. Now Evelyn, in those days, was clever but not a scholarship-boy, courageous but no games-player, pleasant-featured but not good-looking. On arrival, he therefore sank to a low place in the esteem of House and school. In the narrow setting of the Head's House and in the wider setting of Lancing College, he was too independent, too prone to notice oddities and comment on them, to be popular. How often in those early days did I hear those ominous words 'that awful little tick Waugh'. And over certain things the little tick did not make things easier for himself; he was never a conformist. At that time, before getting into bed, we used to fall on our knees to use the chamber-pot and to address a brief word to the Almighty. Long after the pot was used, Evelyn would remain plunged in prayer by his bedside; similarly, in chapel his devotion was pronounced. Such practices were not unnoticed by our companions. They were not liked. He had in those days a strange and ungainly walk – more of a trudge than anything else. It was whispered behind his back, and I am afraid to his face, that he was a martyr to trench-feet. Blake's 'Jerusalem' was much sung in Lancing Chapel during the First War and when we came to the lines

> And did those feet in ancient time
> Walk upon England's mountains green?

there was much spluttering, tittering and staring at poor Waugh. He showed neither by the flicker of an eyelid nor by a brave smile that he noticed or minded.

In the early decades of this century, convention and formality were powerful even in school-life: boys kept to the company of their contemporaries; time governed friendship; the chance of propinquity made companionship. Consequently, Evelyn and I were inevitably thrown together. We were in the same House, started in the same form, were seated next to each other for meals and knelt next to each other for worship. Perhaps each of us felt rather like Mr Gladstone in Sicily: he was conscious of what he owed to the mule which carried him on all his journeys over the island but he could not rouse even a flicker of affection for it. Yet I can not remember that we ever quarrelled and, searching back, I realise that even then I fully enjoyed Evelyn's wit. At the end of our first term, we were companions in adversity – victims of mumps when we should have started our summer holidays. We were in the sick-wing in charge of a matron with a masculine face, a splendid moustache and the general air of a warrior. I can remember Evelyn's delight when he told me that she had said to him, with the joy of battle in her eyes, 'I think that poor little Fulford is going to have complications.' Poor little Fulford disappointed her. But it was long a jest between us.

After about a year, when we were able to mix with the large number of new boys who came in the term after us, and with those just senior to us* we moved from joint isolation into a more voluntary and more agreeable companionship. For the next two years – that is to say, from 1918 to 1920 – Evelyn as a school-boy would not have been particularly remarked. He moved steadily up the school in work, won admiration for fighting a boy on the Downs because of 'what he said about my brother'. (Alec Waugh was execrated in some circles for a book which he had written about school-life, *The Loom of Youth*, and Evelyn's antagonist had hinted that the natural corollary to such a book was to capitulate to the enemy. Alec had just been made a prisoner-of-war.) He took part in the gruelling five-mile cross-country race up the Downs, through the thickets and over the Sussex dykes. Far from coming in last, as we, his friends, expected and (in the cruel fashion of the day) half hoped – he finished respectably. He was, as I have said, never a popular boy but, from this time, he began to enjoy a certain repute. Among his intimates, he was their leader in jests and gibes against masters and boys. Two examples illustrate this. One evening, we were all caught ragging in the dormitory; a boy who had been in the thick of things was heard to say in cringing tones 'I was on my bed-mat all the time.' It was Evelyn who gave the degrading sentence an additional twist by

---

* These included Emlyn Bevan whom we rudely and absurdly nicknamed 'Buttocks', as readers of *A Little Learning* will remember. The identity of 'Buttocks' was a matter of rather ludicrous curiosity to Mr Randolph Churchill, and his correspondence with Evelyn on this and kindred matters was published in *Encounter* in the summer of 1968. Had Evelyn been alive, I feel sure that he would not have agreed to the publication of this passage because he was scrupulous to avoid hurting the feelings of old friends, and would have disliked anything which could have identified our transient ribaldry with the distinguished man, well-liked and greatly respected in Lombard Street.

adding the prefect's name to it, and then setting it to one of the tunes in 'Chu Chin Chow'. He was, as we were ready to admit, always a determined rather than a musical singer. At this time, 1918, we had a singularly lethargic House-master, and Evelyn and I developed the innocent habit of going to his room to run through his correspondence. Our choicest discovery was a letter from a teacher of mathematics – he was the gentleman in *Decline and Fall* who inspired the observation that, during his classes, it was going too far to eat pineapple chunks – reporting that a boy in our House, justly famous for original impertinences, had behaved in an unseemly way. After reprimanding him, the master complained, 'he was pleased to belch rudely in my face'. Evelyn was delighted by the well-chosen 'pleased' and 'rudely', and the words echoed round our circle to the end of our time. Without his forceful sense of the ridiculous, the spirit of our House would have been unworthy of recall.

It must have been throughout 1920 that Evelyn moved into a wider world. He formed friendships outside our House, particularly with Hugh Molson, who won all our hearts by creating himself as an *Il Pomposo* and then leading the laughter against his own creation, and also with Tom Driberg, who was then, as always, a storehouse of learning and erudition, and also with Dudley Carew – novelist and sports-writer – who worshipped Evelyn and even copied his habit of never writing a lower-case r but always R. With them and others Evelyn moved somewhat out of the world of the conventional school-boy into a circle drawing its strength from the arts and from intellect. With them, he saw something of the holy fathers at Cowfold, of Francis Crease who encouraged his interest in wood-carving and lettering and of Roxburgh his form-master. But he never kept his Head's House friends and his new friends apart. I remember that on one afternoon he and I entertained Mr Roxburgh to tea in my pit (study). It was an enormous success. We had bought some China tea which tasted as if it had been steeped in a boatswain's rope, and we were disappointed that our guest never commented on this delicacy. I remember Evelyn saying afterwards 'You see how considerate he is. He never commented on the tea because he wanted us to believe that he knew perfectly well that we always drank it.'

Perhaps it was the impact of these out-of-House friends which fostered in him a certain fatigue with the prejudices and loyalties inside the Heads. (Out of respect for the preoccupations of the present, I explain that he was neither courted by older boys nor, when he grew older, did he pursue younger ones. From knowledge I confirm what he says on page 135 of *A Little Learning*.) Our House excelled neither at soccer nor at cricket; we certainly did not glory in failure but equally we were not distressed by it. The practice then at Lancing was for the victor in any inter-House games or athletics competition to hold a silver cup for the year. The House which won it next year fetched it away from the holder in a Triumph marked by running and shouting. This, in the elegant language of the school, was know as 'a jerry run'. Evelyn conceived the idea that our House should win the cup given for the smartest House on the OTC parade – a contest in which we had a fine, unbroken record of last place. Every effort was made by polishing boot and button and by surreptitious drilling, to reverse the order. We failed, because one platoon commander had not realised the new doctrine and clung to the outmoded slovenliness. We had made up our minds, if we won, to rag the 'jerry run', and make it a funeral progress; news of this reached the prefect responsible – a ludicrous personage from a Sussex rectory; he sent for us and said 'Well, gentlemen, we intend to fight your decision.' This was the sort of occasion which was never wasted on Evelyn. The apostrophe particularly struck him because at Lancing we were always 'you men' and never addressed in the more courteous form; I remember his pointing out that this usage meant that the threat was being taken seriously, and we long ruminated on the clash of power between the orthodox and the unorthodox. This particular episode deserves emphasis because it illustrates the authority which Evelyn's personality stamped on his fellows. Virtually the entire House followed his leadership; anyone can follow their leader but, when following entails behaving like a guardsman, we realise that the leader is a man of character.

Looking back on Evelyn as I knew him then, I am of course conscious of his humour – a mordaunt wit which was unusual in a boy of that age but made him always a stimulating companion. I grew to respect and possibly a little to fear his mind; he was in the Sixth, I was not; we both went in for a prize essay – Pope I think – he won it, I did not; he wrote a brilliant House-play attended by the Bowlbys in all their feminine splendour; I played a part, he produced it. As a new boy, I was reading *Little Dorrit*, he was deep in *The Time-machine*. I do not think that I was jealous of his renown in the school, but I could have envied it. But for him his success never made the slightest difference to our friendship; it was perhaps deeper than in 1917 but I would say that, throughout all our time at Lancing, his relationship with me was uniform in tolerance and understanding.

3

A KINGDOM OF COKAYNE

Peter Quennell

IN his autobiographical narrative *A Little Learning*, which unfolds the story of his life as far as the moment at which he finally decided that he must abandon any attempt to become a private school-master, Evelyn Waugh devotes only forty-five pages, less than a fifth of the whole book, to his experiences at Oxford. They are pleasant pages. He enjoyed himself there, he tells us, and made some very good friends; and, though he was idle, often fairly riotous, like most of his contemporaries lived beyond his means and eventually went down with a modest Third, he does not regret his years of residence.

It surprises him that others were less fortunate; and he attributes their failure either to their exotic origins or to the fact that they 'had been oddly educated'. Thus, his friend Hubert Duggan was 'part American, part Irish-Argentine. He languished at the House without feminine company and went into the Household Cavalry after two terms complaining of damp sheets and an immature society. Mr Peter Quennell, whom I have met since from time to time, had been at a day-school. He, too, despaired of the place. To me it was a Kingdom of Cokayne. . . .'

As the author suggests in a characteristic phrase, once we had both left Oxford, we ceased gradually to meet on amicable terms; and at length I joined the ranks of favourite bugbears – the 'boobies' and the 'fuddyduddies' – who excited now his taste for ludicrous imagery, now his remarkable talent for invective. At Oxford, however, I can claim, I think, to have known him pretty well; and Evelyn was among the first to call on me in my gaunt and lofty Balliol rooms, where my bedroom looked out across the Broad and my sitting-room over St Giles's churchyard.

I had met him earlier, in very different surroundings. The 'day-school' I had attended was Berkhamsted – it included, by the way, a large proportion of 'boarders' – a grammar-school, or minor public school of which the Headmaster, Charles Greene, was the father of the famous novelist. Berkhamsted itself, an over-grown country-town, had an interesting population: George Macaulay Trevelyan lived on its outskirts, as, in a big, ugly late-Victorian house, did the large family of the then-celebrated comic story-teller W. W. Jacobs. Seldom can a renowned humorist have looked more woebegone and ill-tempered – yellow and pinched, with thin, sharply contracted lips and a reddish, watering eye.

His children, on the other hand, were notably active and exuberant;

Catherine Charlotte Raban before her marriage to Arthur Waugh.

Arthur Waugh.

Childhood

Evelyn   *Alec*

Suffragettes – the earliest drawing by Evelyn Waugh to have survived.

Evelyn, aged about five, with his mother.

Lancing School group. Evelyn Waugh is sitting on the ground, second from the left.

THE HEADMASTER'S HOUSE
requests the honour of your company
on Sunday, June 19th. at 7·45 p.m. in
the Great School at a performance of

CONVERSION

the tragedy of Youth in three burlesques,
by
EVELYN WAUGH.

Act I. School, as maiden Aunts think it is.
Act II. School, as modern authors say it is
Act III. School, as we all know it is.

R.S.V.P., F.E.Ford.

The programme of a play of his, performed in his House at school.

An enlargement from the picture on the left.

Oxford

Photograph inscribed for Terence Greenidge.

On Magdalen Bridge, Oxford, as an undergraduate.

Evelyn Waugh aged twenty-six,
painted by Henry Lamb.

The Oxford Union in the Twenties. A pen-drawing by Evelyn Waugh.

Evelyn Waugh's caricature of Harol Acton, then editor of The Oxford Br

EUROPE LISTENS WHERE OXFORD SLEEPS

AT THE SIGN OF THE UNICORN.
MR HAROLD ACTON
THE LAST OF THE POETS.

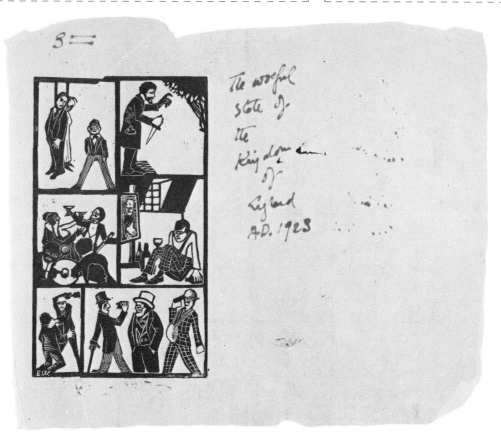

The woeful state of the Kingdom of England A.D. 1923

'The woeful state of the Kingdom of England AD 1923.'
Evelyn Waugh has marked his work Beta double-minus.

and I presently heard that his graceful elder daughter had become engaged to the brilliant young man who had recently published a somewhat shocking novel, *The Loom of Youth*, an exposure of the moral corruption and mental stagnation of an English public school. Never before had I come face to face with so controversial a literary personage. Alec Waugh proved rubicund, jolly and easy-going, completely lacking in pretension; but his brother Evelyn, whom he afterwards brought to the house – all the younger Jacobs were my friends at the time – possessed a more distinctive sense of style. Evelyn Waugh was a dandified schoolboy, just about to leave Lancing, who affected, I think, a yellow waistcoat and, I seem to remember, a fashionably-cut pearl-grey suit.

He was dapper and curly-haired, cheerful and talkative; and no less elegant was his appearance when he visited me at Balliol. His own college, he told me, was Hertford, which, in *A Little Learning*, he describes as 'respectable but rather dreary. . . . In my time there was no scholar of importance among the Dons; among the under-graduates no member of the Bullingdon, no President of the Union, or of the OUDS, no Blue. . . .' Hertford was a placid retreat 'agreeably free both from the schoolboyish "college spirit" which was the bane of many small colleges and of the hooliganism which on occasion broke out against eccentrics in the larger'; but at least it provided the future satirist with a splendid object for his ridicule.

Evelyn, in those days, was a generally good-natured man. His gift of invective still lay dormant; and it was the Dean of Hertford, C.R.M.F. Cruttwell, who first aroused it from the depths, and provoked some early flashes of that *saeva indignatio* which glows and sparkles through his stories. In *A Little Learning*, he draws a ferocious portrait of this clumsy and unhappy don:

He was tall, almost loutish, with the face of a petulant baby.

He smoked a pipe which was usually attached to his blubber-lips by a thread of slime. As he removed the stem, waving it to emphasise his indistinct speech, this glittering connection extended until finally it broke leaving a dribble on his chin. When he spoke to me I found myself so distracted by the speculation of how far this line could be attenuated that I was often inattentive to his words.

The Dean, Evelyn writes, 'had written me a cordial letter of congratulation and welcome when I was elected scholar'; and for some while all went smoothly. Then the crisis occurred. During Evelyn's third term, after a 'freshers' blind' at which the promising undergraduate had grown 'conspicuously drunk', the Dean harangued him in a solemn lecture, 'warning me that I had not chosen the best way of ingratiating myself with the college'. It was ill-received: 'I became fatuously haughty, saying I regretted my excesses but that (as was true) they had not been committed with any wish for popularity. I added that I was quite indifferent to college opinion. I think it was then that our mutual dislike became incurable.' From that moment, Cruttwell headed the list – before he died, it was to be a very long list – of Evelyn's literary and conversational victims; and, as time went on, even at Oxford, it included many other characters whose names he now and then introduced into the pages of his novels. I have forgotten exactly who 'Philbrick' was; he may, I believe, have been a bellicose moralist whom Evelyn had once derided and who had immediately knocked him down. But 'Prendergast' – 'poor Prendy' – had incurred his displeasure in my own rooms by some slighting reference, as he bade me goodbye, to the kind of bohemian company I now frequented – not that there was the smallest resemblance between Evelyn's legendary villain and my entirely blameless visitor. He merely borrowed a name that had acquired provocative associations.

Yet Evelyn at Oxford, though sometimes unruly – as when he hurled a champagne bottle from my sitting-room window at an astonished passer-by, a feat that cost me a rather heavy fine – was no iconoclast or revolutionary spirit. Still less was he a social snob. Oxford, in the mid-Twenties, was an extremely snobbish place; but again to quote from his autobiography, 'my absurdities were those of exuberance and naivety, not of spurious sophistication'. He wanted 'to do everything and know everyone, not with any ambition to insinuate myself into fashionable London or make influential friends ... nor to cut a figure among the intellectual hierarchy', who then assembled at Garsington Manor round Lady Ottoline Morrell, or round Lady Keble on the slopes of Boars Hill. Evelyn would afterwards be accused of having become a self-elected member of the English upper classes; but, as an undergraduate and, later, the author of *Decline and Fall*, he still observed them from a certain distance; and, depicting Paul Pennyfeather's first catastrophe, he would poke delightful fun at their more unseemly antics: 'A shriller note could now be heard ... any who have heard that sound will shrink at the recollection of it; it is the sound of the English county families baying for broken glass. Soon they would all be tumbling into the quad, crimson and roaring in their bottle-green evening coats, for the real romp of the evening.'

The Oxford society that Evelyn knew was a complex social microcosm, with a *Guermantes* layer made up of grand young men (whose débutante friends bore such romantically Tennysonian names as Lettice Lygon, Daphne Vivian and Rosemary Hope-Vere, and who afterwards developed into bluff, weather-beaten landowners) superimposed on a high bohemian world of pleasure-loving *dilettanti*, which itself rested on a world of a more genuinely bohemian kind, the frequenters of the raffish Hypocrites' Club, a kind of early-twentieth-century Hell Fire Club, established at the shabbier end of St Aldate's.

Evelyn enjoyed the Hypocrites' revels; but, very sensibly, he did not frequent the rich; and, so far as I know, his only patrician friends were the amiable Lord Clonmore, a lively but unusually well-conducted member of the Hypocrites who, when he inherited his father's title, most regrettably disappeared to Dublin, and Hugh Lygon – the 'original', if any of his characters can be said to have an original, of the sweet-tempered, sympathetic young man he drew in *Brideshead Revisited* – and Hugh's monumental brother, Lord Elmley. Evelyn preferred bohemian misfits, and one of his closest associates was the wild eccentric Terence Greenidge. Among other equally strange habits, purloining random ink-pots, hair-brushes and nail-scissors – Terence had a passion for collected scraps of dirty paper, which he gathered from the Oxford pavements and stuffed in his coat-pockets, preparatory to scattering them on Evelyn's carpet – a whim his host did not discourage.

Social arbiter of the Oxford *Côté de Guermantes* was the ill-fated Brian Howard, who played Beau Brummell to the good-natured grandees whom he thought it worth his while to educate, instructing them in the secrets of modern art, lecturing them about the clothes they wore, or urging that, like himself, they should have their racing colours designed by the Parisian firm of Charvet. Evelyn detested Brian, and took some hints from his character when he created the personage of 'Anthony Blanche', though he could not help denying that this blend of Brummell and Disraeli – Brian was of Jewish-American descent – did not lack a curious fascination: 'he had dash and insolence . . . a kind of ferocity of elegance that belonged to the romantic era of a century before our own'. But there were other members, or part-time members, of the Oxford *beau-monde* who inspired in Evelyn a warm affection, which he retained until the end.

Both John Sutro and Harold Acton were at home on many different levels – John, a privileged court-jester and extraordinarily accomplished mimic; Harold, the 'aesthete' *par excellence*, poet, raconteur and man of taste. When he first reached Oxford, he was regarded by Christ Church 'hearties' as a highly suspect figure and obliged to barricade his door against assailants. Latterly, however, he achieved the status of a distinguished local institution, and even the Bullingdon Club were proud to entertain so witty and so blithe a guest.

He had a romantic, yet fatherly attachment to Evelyn, and Evelyn enjoyed his splendid luncheons. Harold occupied rooms in the Victorian annexe of Christ Church Meadows; and from this balcony, after an opulent meal, accompanied by draughts of steaming mulled claret, he would declaim his own verses through a megaphone to the crocodiles of school-children who passed beneath. Some critics, writes the autobiographer, 'to his annoyance and mine', have attempted to identify those two diverting *dramatis personae* 'Ambrose Silk' and 'Anthony Blanche' with the well-known Oxford poet. There are, indeed, he agrees, 'a few incidental similarities. . . . But in neither of the characters mentioned did I attempt a portrait of Harold.'

Though an exception should be probably made for 'Captain Grimes', Evelyn was far too good a novelist, even at his earliest period, to produce a photographic likeness. All his characters are composite productions, as are those of Marcel Proust; and 'Basil Seal', for instance, owes a great deal to both Peter Rodd and Basil Murray, each a bizarre adventurer who, before he went down, had become the focus of many fantastic legends, which their admirers were still busily circulating when I first arrived in Oxford. Of Peter Rodd, said to be another Rimbaud – he had the same handsome, sulky, rather spotty face – I was told that, having left the University, he had almost at once master-minded a revolution against some tyrannical South-American government.

Evelyn always appreciated bold, extravagant characters; but one of his oddest contemporaries, a neighbour of mine at Balliol, he never employed for an imaginative purpose. Alfred Duggan, brother to the Hubert Duggan described above, was a dashing Restoration rake, who, having at length been converted to Catholicism, developed into a successful and prolific historical novelist. At Oxford, Alfred 'was very rich. . . . He was, moreover, the stepson of the Chancellor of the University, Lord Curzon. This connection irked the authorities, who otherwise would have summarily sent him down. We were often drunk, Alfred almost always.' And not only did he keep a string of hunters, but every night of his life, wearing full evening dress, he would have himself driven off to London, and there spend the next three or four hours at a then-notorious Soho night-club. Driven back again, he would scale the façade of the college and struggle through his first-floor window. The bribes that he paid his scout, I remember him telling me, ran into several hundred pounds a year. But, drunk or sober, he was always polite and impassive; and his starched shirt-front, with its lustrous pearl studs, seldom showed a crease or dent.

Such panache was greatly admired at Oxford; whatever the state of our bank balances, we most of us bought expensive clothes, and Evelyn, during the earliest stages of his career, was himself a modern dandy. The rooms he first occupied were decoratively furnished with Lovat Fraser prints and Nonesuch editions of the English poets. But then a startling change took place: having overspent his allowance, he held an uproarious private auction of all his more valuable books and pictures, and retired to the smallest, darkest and gloomiest set of rooms that Hertford College could provide. Thereupon he exchanged his earlier dandyism for a somewhat truculent bohemianism. He took to drinking beer, eating bread and cheese and, at night, carrying a heavy stick, fresh from his jollifications at some dusky riverside pub, would roam around the streets and quadrangles.

The Dean of Balliol, during our joint residence, was the celebrated 'Sligger' Urquhart, who kept a quiet intellectual salon in his sitting-room above a college-gate. 'Sligger' was fond of handsome young men, whom he also welcomed to his uncomfortable Alpine chalet. But, although he had a deep affection for clever, attractive youths, he remained, I think, a natural innocent, and did not deserve the sinister reputation that was sometimes bestowed upon him by his enemies. Evelyn was an especially vociferous critic; and, when he visited Balliol after dark, the walls would echo to his chantings. *'The Dean of Balliol sleeps with men! – the Dean of Balliol sleeps with men!!'* he would assure the college in a voice of thunder.

The young Evelyn Waugh, as I have suggested, showed now and then a violent side. But, if he was often noisy and obstreperous, I cannot recollect that he was ever ill-tempered. He loved his friends and, while he still had money to burn, he was a lavish host and the source of uncommonly generous presents. Alas, I have long ago lost the noble manuscript book – a solid quarto volume, beautifully bound – that he once had made for me, and into which I immediately transcribed an entirely worthless epic poem. But I remember its rich and heavy pages, and the title, *Peter Quennell: his Book*, inscribed upon its leather spine.

Evelyn Waugh at Oxford was a carefree and good-natured character, with an exuberant sense of fun and taste for human absurdities, but no trace of underlying bitterness. The origins of the transformation that latterly overtook him cannot be discussed here. In later life, he was a difficult man to know; he himself drew a cruel self-portrait when he depicted the personality of Gilbert Pinfold, the secluded and embittered novelist, tormented by ill-health and a strain of overwhelming *accidie*, who wonders why it is that 'everyone except me finds it so easy to be nice', and, whenever he looks at his watch, notices, 'always with disappointment', that the hour is earlier than he hoped, and reflects how much of his mortal existence still lies before him like an untracked desert.

I prefer to remember Evelyn in the 'Kingdom of Cokayne' – Oxford about 1925 – drinking among the Hypocrites, stumping from pub to pub, or proclaiming the fictitious sins of 'Sligger' Urquhart. He was happy then. But happiness unalloyed is not a climate in which genius flourishes; and it was under a very different and much more baleful star that he produced his adult books, which have now established him as one of the greatest imaginative novelists of the present generation.

4

HE–EVELYN
AND SHE–EVELYN

Dudley Carew

OLIVIA

OLIVIA Plunket-Greene has had a bad press, a phrase which would have amused and puzzled her. There was Harold Acton, in his *Memoirs of an Aesthete*, who mentions her as possessing 'minute pursed lips and great goo-goo eyes' and, as Evelyn implies in *A Little Learning*, that was by no means adequate. Barbara Cartland, describing in *Follow My Leader* a game through Selfridges played by what the gossip columns of the day called 'the Bright Young People', wrote of her as having a 'dead-white expressionless face made up like a mask'.

More important, C. M. Bowra, I suspect, had her in his sights when he wrote of Evelyn's fatal habit of gravitating towards women who were of no possible use to him. Certainly, it is difficult to think of Olivia as a person who would go about forwarding any man's career. Evelyn, I am sure, was much in love with her and she, in her turn, was deeply attached to him. At the same time, that common sense which found an incongruous place in an eccentric, delicate and fundamentally unworldly personality, weighed and found wanting any question of marriage. Her affection for Evelyn was, then, precious to her, but it worried her and, when I came on the scene, it was my perception of this that led her to lower the barriers she normally kept erected against the world outside her family – to them, her mother, Gwen, that is, and her two brothers, Richard and David, she was devoted.

She was frequently the centre of uproar and outrage – she could, in fact, herself represent uproar and outrage – yet the quality that comes back most clearly to me across the years is her gift for sudden silence, a passive sort of stillness. Shaw makes his Archbishop say to St Joan that she was in love with religion, and I think Olivia was, even in those days (she was then, in 1927, about twenty) although I doubt whether Evelyn or I fully recognised the fact at the time.

How, then, would it be possible to be in love with a girl who was at one and the same time a ghost with a glass of gin in her hand, a *religieuse* and a Bright Young Person, sometimes wilful and silly? I do not think that there is any harm, after all these years, in bringing up the question of drink. We all drank too much. I remember that, when I would go up to Oxford to see Evelyn during his early days there, his cry concerning alcohol was 'sustain the mood', but even Evelyn found that more difficult to do than to say. In those days, he used to reproach me for my moderation; there was no need for him to do that any more.

It was a period in which the graph of Evelyn's fortunes was turning ominously down. There was, I know, an emotional turmoil going on within him, with Olivia not primarily involved; outwardly, it was the near-disastrous time of the art school and the preposterous Welsh prep-school. Evelyn was taking a relish (which Byron would have appreciated) in the wreck he seemed to be making of his life – those who see him only through his books and the biting edge of satire that shaped them will find it hard to realise that the romanticism on which he fed in his early youth was not dead in him. Olivia would have fitted easily as a counter-balancing figure in a Byronic exercise in excessive self-disgust, such as Evelyn was capable of, although she would have been tart indeed in her expression of disapproval at so incongruous a role.

More important for the immediate sequence of events was the fact that Evelyn and I were once more in touch with one another. It was natural, therefore, in the new, or rather, the old, order of things, that I should hear one morning on the telephone that mock-gruff voice asking me how I dared write a tolerably good novel. This was my third, and Evelyn was right – it was tolerably good, and it shared the fate of the others, admirable reviews and deplorable sales. It was once more natural for me to be asked up to 'Underhill' or to parties involving Evelyn in one way or another, and natural for me to think of Evelyn in the same terms. At any rate, when I did give a small party at my Red Lion Square flat, I asked Evelyn, and there he met the girl who was to become his first wife.

That girl was the Honourable Evelyn Gardner, and I spell out the courtesy title in full, because it should be given its due weight, neither more nor less, in the curious equation which finally resolved itself in the marriage of the two sharply contrasting Evelyns. It is difficult without the aid of diaries to pin-point exact dates, but I think I introduced the two Evelyns to one another some time in the autumn of 1927.

I myself had known Evelyn Gardner for some little time before that, and here Call Boy's 1927 Derby helps to plot the time schedule. Evelyn Gardner and myself were fellow guests on a bus hired by the White Rajah of Sarawak for that particular Derby, and it was through the Sarawaks that I met her. She was a friend of – I think she was half engaged to – the Rajah's secretary, Barry Gifford, and somewhere or other I had met Barry Gifford and he himself introduced me to the Sarawak house in Portland Place. I went there fairly often, partly because the Ranee, a Brett and a vivacious personality with generous instincts, had an interest in the young and the 'arts', and partly because Noni, the eldest daughter, then about twelve and as lovely in face as she was in mind, decided that she liked me.

There, at any rate, was Evelyn Gardner and a most pleasant, simple (the word here has its more attractive overtones) girl she was, with a small up-turned nose and an engaging ingenuous manner. A typical English miss? A typical English rose? Yes, perhaps. On the surface, certainly. She was sharing a flat at that time with Lady Pansy Pakenham over a tobacconist's shop off Sloane Square, and when I got to know them better, I thought how lucky Evelyn was to have Pansy to 'look after' her. I do not suppose that Pansy was more than a year or so older than Evelyn, but she was a person of such calm authority that it was natural to think of her in this 'looking after' capacity. She probably did no such thing, but there she was, as decorative as she was dependable, entirely, or so it seemed to me, certain of herself and where she was going – she was going, as it happened, to marry Henry Lamb, and I for one had no doubt of the success of her marriage.

To return to Evelyn Gardner: there she was, with a kind of puppyish eagerness to appreciate and embrace everything and everybody – I think that I underrated at that time a certain strain of toughness and sophistication in her. She was a girl it was impossible to dislike or, rather, I could imagine only one person who might, no, who in my own mind I was sure, would dislike her, and that was Evelyn Waugh. One reason for this conviction was, I suppose, the fact that she was so completely unlike Olivia, although better psychology would have realised that the very contrast she made with Olivia and all the things that that elusive girl stood for, might well have been an attraction.

And again, there was that in Evelyn Waugh, at that period of his life, which was itself ready to respond to the simple and uncomplicated. There were, of course, sombre moods; there was the restlessness of his brain; there was the satire which was soon to express itself on paper; there was a seeming collapse in his life, but there was a side to him that rejoiced in the less exacting forms of humour. He delighted in fantastic exaggeration, in acting out to the full his repertoire of burlesque ferocity, and he would roar with laughter at his own jokes. Evelyn Waugh could make a good deal of noise.

Meanwhile, Evelyn and I were proceeding by roughly parallel

paths towards our respective marriages, although Evelyn's lacked the touches of fantastic extravaganza that illuminated my own (to Anthea Gamble). Fantastic is the right word, and that element was heightened by a liberal attitude towards drink. But men, young men, at times are sober and think by fits and starts, and these occasional bouts of sober contemplation were painful.

I remember that once I was alone with Pansy in her Sloane Square flat and I said that of our three approaching marriages, I was certain that hers with Henry Lamb would be a success, I thought mine had a fifty-fifty chance (the coin was destined, in tragic circumstances, to fall against me) while I was convinced that that of the two Evelyns would fail. I do not think she went so far as to disagree.

And now comes perhaps the most precious of all my memories concerning Evelyn. The time must have been early in January 1928 – Evelyn was to go back to that prep-school for the spring term. At any rate, I was staying the night at 'Underhill', and after Arthur and Kate had gone to bed, he told me that he had something to show, or rather to read, to me. He had already finished his *Rossetti* (I have a presentation copy dated 19 April 1928, but whether that was the actual publication date or not I would not like to say) but I do not think he had any great hopes that it would make him famous overnight.

What he read to me that night sitting in the chair in which Arthur was wont to proclaim that beautiful Evelyn Hope was dead were the first fifty or so pages of *Decline and Fall* which are, as I think, among the best he ever wrote. I shall never forget the happiness, the hilarity, that sustained him that night, and I was back giving him my unstinted admiration as I did at Lancing. It was marvellously funny and he knew that it was. As was his habit on those old innocent days, he roared with laughter at his own comic invention and both of us at times were in hysterics.

But there was nothing hysterical about Evelyn's attitude towards the book or my appreciation of it. It was quite time Evelyn produced something to prove to the world that he was the remarkable person his friends knew him to be. It was unthinkable, especially in view of his forthcoming marriage, that he should go on teaching at that prep school. He knew, as I did, that he had a winner in *Decline and Fall*, but when he had finished reading and laughing, he became serious enough. All would be well once it was published, but *would* it ever be published? He foresaw difficulties with publishers who were fearful in those days of anything 'daring', let alone comedy which could be construed as indecent. He was justified in his fear – Duckworth, who were bringing out his *Rossetti*, refused to handle it. There was always Chapman & Hall, of course, but I remember Evelyn on that night saying that he knew Arthur would not like it and that he was reluctant to saddle his father with what was bound to be to him, Arthur, that is, a painful choice.

Evelyn always showed a reckless inclination to go to extremes, to involve himself totally in his immediate preoccupations. What is more, he was, for one of his acute intelligence and formidable brain, surprisingly lacking in the compass directions provided by theory and thought. He loved the excesses of absurdity; to him people were perpetually playing parts in some wild extravaganza of his own imagining – anybody less like an intellectual I have seldom met. Thus I can never remember him engaging in any long and coherent discussion of ideas on why he liked certain plays or pictures or poems or whatever it was – he was capable of remarkably shrewd snap judgments, and that was that. In our play-going days, he 'liked' *R.U.R.*, for instance, and 'disliked' *Abraham Lincoln*; the criticism seldom rose above that level.

This tendency, especially in the company of comparative strangers, to confine himself to platitudes went back to the earlier days of our friendship and to the time at which Evelyn was still in his 'teens. I remember that in those days the Waughs would give a kind of combination of an 'At Home' and a cocktail party, at which people like St John Ervine, so prickly and contentious in print, so kindly in conversation, G. B. Stern, Sylvia Gosse, the booming Bourchier whom Evelyn has so admirably described in *A Little Learning*, and many others, would gather and then it was Evelyn's custom to sink himself into the background and to become, to all intents and purposes, anonymous.

Again – and once more this runs counter to the conventional idea of the prodigy – he disliked music, and so had my sympathy in that particular matter, and, again like myself, had no interest in the ballet and yet we would find ourselves walking quietly, as though in homage, when we passed Pavlova's house in Hampstead. And when Diaghilev and his Russian Ballet appeared on the scene we were both of us bowled over. But I do not think that it ever occurred to Evelyn to analyse the reason. The days of his absurd enthusiasm for James Branch Cabell were, of course, in the past and I remember him insisting that I buy *The Wasteland*. His reactions were still subjective and instinctive and he was at all times extreme in his response to his friends and the ideas they represented – or those he fancied they represented.

A little time before this, we had found ourselves at a party given by two artists, one, I believe, admirable, who were rather older than we were. I had heard them called pansies and although my continuing innocence on this subject prevented me from understanding precisely what the word meant, I disliked it and its implications. I had had enough to drink that evening to declare that my hosts and, as far as I could guess, the majority of his guests, fell into the pansy category and that therefore I found them distasteful.

The elder of the two artists behaved perfectly. He told me that I did not know what I was talking about, that I had been guilty of disgraceful discourtesy and would I kindly leave the house. Some of his guests, however, seemed disinclined for the matter to be resolved in so undramatic and civilised a way. They thought that I should be taught a lesson – and a painful one. It was at this moment, ringed round with a circle of menacing young men, that I caught sight of Evelyn at the far end of the studio. '*À moi*, Evelyn' I called out with the theatricality of the tipsy, '*à moi*' and at once he came charging down the long room like a rugger forward with the line in sight. He did not know what the quarrel was about and cared less. It was less a question of standing by me than of getting involved in physical action. For a moment or two, there was a real prospect of a stand-up fight with the odds heavily against us, but somehow or other the first blow was never struck and we found ourselves out in the street with the door closed behind us.

I was sober enough immediately to be remorseful both at my own outrageous conduct and at having cut short the party for Evelyn. He did not see it at all that way, and if he had any regrets, it was for the fact that he had been cheated out of a stand-up fight.

Direct action was what Evelyn revelled in, and this was never more obvious than in his relationship with alcohol. That evening, while we were talking about the possibility of *Decline and Fall* never being published, I remember thinking in rather more than a vague sort of way that rejection of it might be especially catastrophic. He could not go on declining into obscurity and failure; indeed he went so far as to attempt suicide, an effort foiled in the best Evelyn Waugh tradition by a swarm of jellyfish. This, of course, he recounts in *A*

Little Learning; I knew nothing about it and I do not think anybody else did either.

What I was contemplating that evening was the possiblity of a more prolonged form of suicide through drink. Evelyn went at the bottle as though he was engaged in a desperate, murderous struggle with one who was at the same time deadly enemy and devoted comrade. It was almost a combat on a physical level, Evelyn's own favourite field, with seconds out. In this connection, I remember a curious and disquieting incident. For some reason or other, Audrey Lucas, the daughter of 'E.V.' who was one of Arthur's most intimate friends, and I were to meet Evelyn at lunch-time at a little pub near the British Museum. When we got there Evelyn was on the verge of passing out into unconsciousness, but what I remember even more than his swaying figure, like a boxer who is still on his feet but who has received a knock-out blow, was the awed expression of the land-lord who looked fearfully at him and told us again and again that he had 'never seen anything like it'. We were too preoccupied with the task of finding a taxi and getting Evelyn into it to worry about asking him what he meant, but I suppose Evelyn had not been waiting for us for more than twenty minutes or so and that what so impressed the landlord was the way Evelyn had so ferociously gone about the task of drinking himself insensible.

Evelyn's drinking at that time was not, then, the sort of part-time vice in which most of us indulged; it was a serious, not to say deadly business, and it was this aspect of affairs which was so disturbing should *Decline and Fall* fail to find a publisher, or if it did, if it were to meet with the tepid kind of reception that greeted his *Rossetti*. Evelyn needed success at that time, and he needed it badly and by no means solely for the normal material reasons, although they naturally came into it. I was very conscious that evening that Evelyn's whole future was in the balance, and that the brilliance – – and brilliant it was – of what he had read to me would make it harder for him to bear if fate tilted it the wrong way. Things did not work out that way, although success, as it happened, was destined to provide Evelyn with almost as many problems as failure would have done, but then at that particular stage in his life he was at his most dangerous and unpredictable.

On the credit side in Evelyn's immediate future was the fact that *Vile Bodies* was destined to be an even greater success than *Decline and Fall*; on the debit, the collapse of his marriage. I have never been able to convince myself that this disaster – for disaster, of course, it must have been – had such traumatic consequences for Evelyn as those who knew him afterwards seem inclined to believe, but then that was, perhaps, because the two Evelyns had always appeared to me so unsuited to one another that I could never believe in the possibility of a life-long union between them.

There is one final incident. At the end of our honeymoon, Anthea and I came back to London and stayed a few nights at 'Underhill'. When we got down to breakfast the first morning – it must have been rather late for Arthur had gone off to Chapman & Hall – there was Evelyn sitting at a writing-desk that was in a kind of recess in the dining-room. He was writing away with intense concentration, and that he was angry was obvious from the back of his neck.

We asked him what was the matter and it appeared that he was writing a letter of protest to the Editor of *The Times Literary Supplement*, since that paper had published a review of his *Rossetti* tucked away in small print among the 'Books Received' pages, in which the author was referred to as 'Miss Waugh'. This infuriated him, but it struck us as funny since anything more unlike a 'Miss Waugh' than the formidable young man, aggressive in manner and built on the lines of a light-weight fighting bull, it would be impossible to imagine.

Evelyn, however, was not to be mollified. Part of the reason for his very real annoyance lay, I think, in the fact that the effect of much of his humour sprang from a rigidly literal interpretation of what was not meant to be literally interpreted. Take the character in *Vile Bodies* who, because she wears an armlet proclaiming her to be a Spare Driver, insists on acting precisely as that when the emergency arises; take the case of the split polo sticks in *Scoop*. *The Times Literary Supplement* had called him 'Miss Waugh' and therefore the absurd misapprehension meant more to him than it would to someone with a mind less acutely concerned with such matters.

That 'Miss Waugh' business rankled, and although after a time he was willing to laugh at it, it was dutiful laughter, as it were, without humour or appreciation. He did not forgive or forget certain things easily, and this was one of them. Besides, the *Rossetti* book was a failure.

5

MADRESFIELD AND BRIDESHEAD

Lady Dorothy Lygon

IN looking back on my friendship with Evelyn down a perspective of forty-odd years, the most predominating features are his consistent, spontaneous, irreverent wit and his capacity for turning the most unlikely situations into irresistibly funny jokes which continued to be woven into our conversations and letters with an increasing richness of texture over the years. Many of them were Rabelaisian and elliptical and a few depended on an ephemeral context that now makes it difficult to explain them.

He came to stay at Madresfield the first time because he wanted to learn riding at Captain Hance's Academy at Malvern; he never became a very expert horseman, but he was totally fearless, and he and Captain Hance developed a strong admiration for each other's very different capacities. Evelyn transposed the Captain and his family to an Olympian level at which he invented lives for them which, like the gods in ancient Greece, were still linked with the mortals below; their least pronouncement was debated and scrutinised for omens and auguries. The Captain's name was scarcely mentioned without the mystic initials GBH – which stood for God Bless Him – being added to it and his health was frequently drunk. Some of our neighbours and friends joined this mythology and one or two can be recognised as minor characters in later books.

He wrote, slowly and reluctantly, a great deal of *Black Mischief* while staying with us, groaning loudly as he shut himself away in what had been the day nursery for a few hours every day; sometimes we were pressed into service as models for the line drawings with which he illustrated it, but we hindered more than we helped and had no conscience about disturbing him and dragging him away to join in whatever was going on, or even just to chat while we stitched away at an enormous (and never finished) patchwork quilt.

All this was soon after his first marriage had broken up, but he never talked about it, nor did we ever feel that he wanted to; his spirits were resilient and he seemed to live entirely in the present. Any detail of daily life amused him and was something to be embellished; I was keeping a diary remarkable only for its dullness and found the entries – until then confined to weather, dogs and horses – enlivened by statements of incest and immorality; an innocuous and amateurish water-colour of a cart-horse had a large penis painted in – it was like having Puck as a member of the household.

Various books and plays were incorporated into our daily chat – there was one book called (I think) *Forty Years in the Frozen North* in which somebody called Pitt underwent terrible hardships and privations; when his nose became frostbitten he rubbed it with snow – 'The best thing in the world, the only remedy.' We applied this palliative to a good many unsuitable things. We all knew by heart the record out of *Private Lives* with Gertrude Lawrence and Noel Coward and quoted it endlessly: 'What fools we were to ruin it all, utter utter fools. . . . Very flat, Norfolk – That's no reflection on her, unless *she* made it flatter. . . . I swear I'll never mention her again. . . .' When Evelyn and Maimie met Noel Coward in the Ritz one day, they both collapsed with school-child giggles and ran away.

Like most families, we already had nicknames – Mary was Maimie, I was Coote, dating back to nursery days, but these were not enough for Evelyn. Maimie became Blondie, I became Poll, or little Poll, and to marry me off to various unsuitable candidates was a large preoccupation. 'Would he do?' was the question automatically asked about any new figure. Evelyn himself became Boaz, or Bo, supposed to be derived from the deeper secrets of Masonic ritual. Very few others used the names, but they persisted between us up to the end. Bloggs Baldwin (who became Frisky) was a regular visitor from Astley; he and Evelyn were both in love with Teresa Jungman during much of this time, and friendship between them grew out of what they realised to be a hopeless rivalry.

One summer, my brother Hugh and Evelyn went on an expedition to Spitzbergen with Sandy Glen; they returned with some photographs of themselves with beards and wearing ten-gallon hats; we never quite discovered what they had done, though they both claimed to have had mountains named after them.

Once, when Evelyn and I were driving down to Madresfield from London, we made a detour to see Frank and Elizabeth Pakenham, then living in a village between Aylesbury and Oxford. Father Martin D'Arcy was also there and it was soon arranged that we should stay the night. Treating me with the tolerant kindness which I am sure would have been equally displayed to a backward native in some remote missionary compound, they settled me down in a corner to darn Evelyn's socks and immersed themselves in high-level Roman Catholic topics. The next morning, we had smoked haddock for breakfast and I have always remembered Frank Pakenham's utter disregard of the bones – they interfered with neither his conversation nor his mastication, both of which continued unimpeded when one would have expected Demosthenes himself to be daunted. When we continued our journey, I could not help commenting on it to Evelyn and later, in *A Handful of Dust*, he attributed it to Reggie St Cloud.

But it was possible to get into Evelyn's bad books, and I did this once by being late when he had asked me out to dinner; he took great umbrage and our meal was eaten to an accompaniment of icy and stilted conversation; I think it must have been three years before he really forgave me.

His marriage to Laura Herbert brought him all the happiness and security one could have wished for him; their wedding was delayed by getting the necessary dispensations from his first marriage, but in the end all went well and they spent their honeymoon in Italy. He sent me a postcard – a photograph of them standing arm-in-arm on a marble pavement with huge ornate bronze doors set in a marble façade behind them:

Darling Poll,

So it is very decent to be married, very decent indeed. We are staying at a great house called Altachiara – translate that into English and you will laugh. We were very sorry about your great illness at the time of our wedding and all the more profoundly moved and touched at your appearance there. We went to Rome and saw a great deal of porphyry.* God it was pretty. Then to Assisi and then to Firenze, where we saw a great football-match v. bad taste in fancy costume. We will come back in June and hope and pray that you will stay with us. Meanwhile please write one of your long famous and libellous letters. All love Bo. Villa Altachiara, Porto Fino Mare, WOPLAND.

When the war began, Evelyn did all he could to enlist; he first joined the Marines but later transferred to SOE under Bob Laycock, one of his personal heroes. I had joined the WAAFS and one of the few letters of his which have survived a nomadic life of seventeen years dates from this time.

SS Brigade HQ,
Ardrossan,
Ayrshire.

17 May 42.

Darling Coote,

It was very nice indeed to hear from you. Can't you get posted to Ayrshire, which is full of Waafs; I live in a nice black market hotel where I have grape-fruit and large dishes of eggs daily, far from the wicked Lord Woolton.

Chucker Laycock has proved most unchucking and I am back with him and Philip Dunne and other old chums. I have been expelled from the Marines and am becoming a horse soldier like Captain Hance GBH.

---

* Much admired by my father, Lord Beauchamp, known behind his back to all of us as Boom.

On 25 May I go to Harrow for a week for a course to improve my weak intelligence. Could we not meet in London that week? and drink some utility port together.

Blondie, ever prone to bad company, seems to have fallen in with a very undesirable set of foreigners. I got her away to dinner alone once and she was heavenly, like her old self. It seems she suffers from the delusion that she is a Queen. It is quite common (see Alice in Wonderland).

You are in the country of Mrs Bendir and the Hell Fire Club.*

Could you not get into Combined Operations. Then we could write one another official letters full of deep double meanings.

All love

Bo.

For the last two years of the war, I was posted abroad; most of this time I was in Italy, in the small Apulian town of San Severo, below the mountains of the Gargano peninsula. Evelyn was going in and out of Yugoslavia, based at Bari further south, and once, when flying in to Yugoslavia with Randoph Churchill and Philip Jordan, their aeroplane crashed and caught fire. They were not badly hurt and were brought out to a Bari hospital; Evelyn sent me a telegram and I went down to see them. Randolph, complaining of water on the knee, was creating a fine fuss; Evelyn's hands were burned so that he could not hold a pen and I wrote to Laura for him. It was in the course of this visit that he talked about his next book: 'It's all about a family whose father lives abroad, as it might be Boom – but it's not Boom – and a younger son: people will say he's like Hughie,† but you'll see he's not really Hughie – and there's a house as it might be Mad, but it isn't really Mad.'

He talked on for some time in this vein, at pains to emphasise that, although he had chosen a situation which might be compared to ours at one time, he was going to treat it in a very different way – he had taken the bare bones, the skeleton, and intended covering it with muscles creating tensions, quite different from those which had influenced us – the Roman Catholic element, so powerful for him, and an integral part of the story, never affected us, and the Marchmains' matrimonial problems can in no way be equated with those which beset my parents. My father was already living abroad when Evelyn first came to Madresfield; Maimie later took Evelyn to stay with my father when he rented Gerald Berners' house in Rome. I do not think

---

* I was at Medmenham.

† He died in 1936.

he ever met my mother, but he could not have created a character more unlike hers than Lady Marchmain's. There is no resemblance between the landscape and architecture of Brideshead – set in a stone-wall country – and Madresfield, except for one detail – the art-nouveau decoration of the chapel. Madresfield is a moated house of red brick, of mainly Victorian architecture superimposed on an earlier base, while Brideshead is an epitome in stone of the Palladian style he loved so much.

Any two writers, given an identical situation, would be very un-likely to develop it in the same way; Margaret Kennedy, in *The Outlaws on Parnassus*, points out that *Old Mortality* and *A Passage to India* are really about the same situation, yet the characters and treatment are so different that one would not ordinarily relate them to each other.

I think that Evelyn conceived *Brideshead* in a mood of violent nostalgia for what he thought was a vanished past; he put into it all he most regretted and missed in pre-war life. It was much more to him than *reportage* on individuals; his characters are composite, in that they reflect here and there facets of widely dissociated people, but they were played upon and transmuted by his imagination and his considerable powers of invention. Perhaps on the surface it is flattering to a novelist when people assert that they know who his characters 'really are', even if they have little or no acquaintance with the supposed originals; it shows he has succeeded in creating entirely credible people in plausible situations; but a novelist is not a reporter and it is possible that he would in his heart of hearts prefer not to be classified as one and would rather be credited with some creative ability. I think that the resemblance between my family and the Marchmains has been much exaggerated; when I first read it, it did not seem to me he had used us as characters, nor do I think so now; he had used a situation, not the people involved in it.

When his burns had healed, he went to Rome on leave before going back to Yugoslavia and I was there as well for a day or two. Three letters he wrote me from Yugoslavia in the winter of 1944–5 have survived:

'M' Military Mission
CMF
14 Oct. [1944]

Dearest Coote,
How very businesslike of you to repay the Roman loan so promptly. Thank

you very much. I got a signal from our headquarters simply saying that they were holding 5000 lire for me without explaining where they came from. I thought it was the government's compensation for the loss of my luggage in the fire which I had assessed at 50,000 lire and felt very hard done by until Freddy Birkenhead arrived yesterday with your letter.

Freddy's arrival was as unexpected as if it had never been proposed. Randolph and I had despaired of him. It was also most opportune as I was beginning to have qualms about a winter tête-à-tête with Randolph. He also brought me 100 cigars from London so I am able to smoke again after weeks of trying to acquire the cigarette habit and failing.

We were very dismal a fortnight ago for it rained night and day for a week and local inhabitants said that it would continue to rain until the snow came, but now it is delicious autumn sunlight and the beech woods turning colour [*sic*]. It is really a very agreeable place to be. The good things are (a) walnuts (b) eggs (c) two kinds of natural mineral water (d) absence of traffic. The bad things are (a) the BBC (b) Rakia, a spirit with an all-pervading stench part sewage part stickfast paste (c) the local party bosses. Also this is not a wine growing district. I came abroad primarily because of the shortage of wine in England. I think I shall apply for a transfer to a grape country soon.

The landscape is like Surrey, neither better nor worse, but with more modest architecture.

I have had a letter from Laura written in August overflowing with gratitude to you for your letters during my great illness. She says 'I always thought her the nicest of all your friends.' Hear hear.

I think I may have to go to Bari for a few days in a week or two. If I do I will try and let you know in the hope of our meeting. Write again.

Love from Bo.

No address but presumably
Dubrovnik 25 Dec. [1944]

Dearest Poll,

There seems a hoodoo – voodoo? – about our correspondence. First Laura's letter astray, then mine, now a parcel from you. I got a telephone message the day after you left Bari to collect a parcel from the AOC. I went there and no one admitted sending the message. No one had the parcel. They all hunted high and low in well simulated concern but there was not a trace of it. I take it to have been the Trollopes. Oh dear. Is it worth while your enquiring your end?

I have had a very pleasant Christmas in unbroken solitude, which next to Laura's company and that of the few friends I can count on the toes of one foot, is what I should have chosen. The Pearl of the Adriatic is not improved by having all its renaissance façades daubed with communist slogans in red paint but it is still a handsome little town. I have a small unheated house in the slums and a fine cook, several servants of different nationalities, unlimited quantities of tolerable wine, no superior officer nearer than Belgrade, so it is what you might call 'clover' or even 'easy street', but I do not think it will last long, when I shall be consoled by the home [hope?] of seeing you again. I am afraid I felt far from well when we last met. You will think I am an invalid, but it is not always so.

Christmas makes me think a lot about Malvern–Mr H and the Capt and the handsome presents Blondie made us give them, and Jessel's boy's foie gras and the time we went up to the top of the noble line after dinner and someone gave the late Maj. Duggan* a push and he could not stop running until he reached the gates of St James Girls School and you and me and Hamish† popping into Lord Beauchamp's Home for Clergymen. Well well never again.

It seems hopeless our attempting to write to one another, but if this letter gets through, do try and send one back. It would be a treat to me.

Love from Evelyn

Capt. E Waugh
37 M Mission
CMF
8 Jan 1945

Dearest Poll,

The parcel of Trollopes has appeared as mysteriously as it vanished. Thank you so much. I will read them and return them.

They are particularly welcome here where I live in solitude in a slum with plenty of wine but no literary nor indeed literate company.

There is a terrible thunderstorm raging with the alarming result that my telephone spits blue fire. I dare not answer it when it rings for fear of electrocution; this cuts down work nicely.

Yesterday was the Orthodox Christmas. We were asked to tea at 3 pm by the local military. One never knows what form social events will take in this country. Last time I was asked to dinner there was no dinner but a series of patriotic plays which lasted until 4.20 am. The tea party began with our all being sat at table (without any greeting from the host) and given Green Chartreuse and ham sandwiches, then tea and cakes, then Cherry Brandy and cigarettes, then two patriotic speeches; it seemed reasonable to expect that the party was over – I was just scraping back my chair when cold mutton and red wine appeared. When I left at 6.30 the party was still in progress.

I don't know when I shall get back to Italy. When I do, it will be suddenly. But I will let you know.

Best love
BO.

* Hubert Duggan, brother of Alfred, the novelist.
† Hamish St Clair Erskine.

I cannot now remember if Evelyn and I succeeded in meeting in Italy again. I was on leave in Venice on VE day, which was celebrated with fireworks; we were shipped home from Naples at the end of the summer, and in 1946 I was demobilised. I have found a postcard from Evelyn at Stinchcombe postmarked 9 August 1946 and addressed to London:

Alas I leave London as you arrive. It is very unfashionable of you to go there in August. You will not find what you want under £10,000 nowadays unless you go to Invernesshire. There is nothing here except a large, sad, olde-worlde house with a fine barn and 30 acres of steep hillside and beechwood. I don't think it would suit you. Sad about little Blondy's 48 bots pop. Sad sad about Dr Mackie XXXX

Doctor Mackie had been our family doctor at Madresfield; once, when Evelyn had been in bed with flu, his prescription was: get the girls to give you a dozen oysters and a pint of fizz. This we did and the cure was instantaneous.

6

THE RELIGION OF EVELYN WAUGH

Father Martin D'Arcy SJ

BARON

Friedrich von Hügel, after praising the qualities of a certain priest, ended up, 'and certainly not a saint'. I do not think that anyone thought of Evelyn Waugh as a saint, but many were impressed by his resolute and apparently sincere religious faith. It was not always easy for them to see how this faith could be reconciled with what they knew or heard of his sometimes outrageous behaviour and savage tongue. One could, I suppose, find parallels in an Alexander Pope or a Dean Swift. Pope's virulence can partly be explained by his tiny and twisted body and bad health, and Swift was for long near to insanity. Evelyn, despite years of insomnia, was never, except for one phase in his life described in *The Ordeal of Gilbert Pinfold*, out of his mind. Medical science may some day be able to give an adequate explanation of our emotional inconsistencies and the Jekyll and Hyde syndrome. In the meantime, I think that only Laura, his wife, could throw a bright light on the complexities of his character. To an outsider at times he seemed intolerant, even to her, and peremptory to his children, but she and they saw through his weaknesses, smiled at his tantrums and were devoted to him. Mrs Frances Donaldson, in her perceptive work *Evelyn Waugh*, *Portrait of a Country Neighbour*, noticed this. She observed also that he strongly resisted any attempts to impose behaviour on him, whether virtuous or vicious. 'If he was accused of some quality usually regarded as contemptible . . . he studied it, polished up his performance, and, treating it as both normal and admirable, made it his own.' Such baffling habits make judgment on him no better than guess-work.

What is easier and more to the point is to assess the importance and influence of religion on his life. Heredity played a small and not very significant part in developing his interest in religion. He tells us in his autobiography *A Little Learning*, that 'most of my father's family were pious, some extravagantly so. I have theological and ecclesiastical interests.' He tells us also that one of his grandfathers was both malicious and generous. Being inclined to both malice and generosity himself, these two qualities do seem to have been passed on to him. But about these ancestral beliefs he writes in his diary at school in June 1921: 'In the last few weeks I have ceased to be a Christian. I have realised for the last two terms at least I have been an atheist in all except the courage to admit it myself.' This was written while at school at Lancing, a school with an Anglican tradition. This 'atheism' of his was, oddly enough, due partly to an anti-religious book called *Loose Ends*, written by Arnold Lunn, who in time to come would become a Catholic and a most argumentative one. Both he and Evelyn in later years would rest their religious views on reason and argument, though each in his own way. Even more indirectly subversive was J. F. Roxburgh who came as a master to Lancing in Evelyn's last years there. Roxburgh was greatly admired for he had 'a panache of the kind to which adolescents were specially susceptible'. He turned religious assumptions into open questions, the problems he raised about the possibility of personal survival after death could easily have given the *coup de grâce* to Evelyn's faith without hope of recovery. What reason had taken away, reason had to bring back, and later it did so.

For a time, scepticism triumphed and had a good innings at Oxford where to be a 'doubting Thomas' was fashionable at the time. He summed up his days at Oxford as '*Et in Arcadia Ego*'. One of the conditions for holding the scholarship which he won at Hertford College was membership in the Church of England. Despite this clause, he 'never attended chapel'. His opinion of clergy and their like is shown in a side-remark, which is typical of his mocking genius. In his undergraduate days at Oxford, 'bicycles and clergymen abounded, and clergymen were, with the cattle coming to market, the only hazards of traffic'. How low to the satirist religion could sink is shown in the list given in *Vile Bodies* of 'Father Rothschild S.J. and Mrs Melrose Ape together with her troop of angels, Charity, Fortitude, Chastity and Creative Endeavour' (incidentally, there was no priest in Oxford at that time who remotely resembled Father Rothschild).

What happened before he came to Farm Street to be received into the Catholic Church is easily told, but why he so acted has puzzled many of his critics and some of his friends. It has even been said that his religious faith was a pose. Nothing could be further from the truth. His close friends Gwen Plunket-Greene and her daughter helped to make him act, but they did not make up his mind for him. Gwen Plunket-Greene was the niece of Friedrich von Hügel and the recipient of many letters from him, which were afterwards published. In *A Little Learning*, Evelyn's friendship with them is summed up in these words: 'I had fallen in love with an entire family and . . . had focussed the sentiment upon the only appropriate member, an eighteen year old daughter. . . . In less than a year our relationship became one of intimate friendship.' They both had become Catholics, but Gwen's bent was mystical, and not at all Evelyn's fancy, and Olivia had a peculiar and inimitable cast of faith of her own. Evelyn was never a borrower and had almost too set a mind to accept advice. No one could have made up that mind of his for him no more than anyone could have been co-author of his novels. Gwen and Olivia served like a Greek chorus to sympathise with and echo his *cris de cœur*.

His undergraduate life did not push him positively towards any religious belief. At its best it was Arcadian, at its worst a time of protracted frivolity. Most of his friends were more boisterous than religious, though some of them, such as Harold Acton and Douglas Woodruff, were Catholics, and Christopher Hollis, Lord Wicklow and Lord Longford were on their way to the Catholic Church. There is no evidence, however, of their having helped to rebuild his religious beliefs. Intelligent sceptics at Oxford, like Roxburgh at Lancing, and his own reading, probably deepened his disbelief even as Winwood Reade, Gibbon and Lecky turned Winston Churchill into an agnostic when a young man, as he records in *My Early Life*. Churchill goes on to tell that his lived experience served to counteract the propaganda of these writers, that and the saying of Pascal that *'le cœur a ses raisons que la raison ne connait pas'*. Evelyn never liked the heart to sidetrack reason or serve as a substitute. On the other hand, the heart's desire, the cry of the innermost self, could ally itself to reason and set him on the quest for a Holy Grail (it was not without unconscious or conscious anticipation that Evelyn Waugh's first book was on the Pre-Raphaelite Rossetti). It is this special kind of combination of a sick self, bored with and feeding on emptiness, and a hard brain, which prevented him from being taken in by the popular idols.

The steps which brought him to his embracing the Catholic faith are visible in the themes of his novels. The character of the innocent man – or half-innocent because he has no positive virtues – thrown to the wolves appears in Paul Pennyfeather of *Decline and Fall*, Adam Symes in *Vile Bodies* and Tony Last in *A Handful of Dust*. The heroes' complacent ignorance of the 'satanic mills' in which they live leads to the appalling fates they have to suffer. The ultimate cry is that of Poppet Green: 'Where is my gas mask? I'm going to be killed! I shall go mad if I don't find my gas mask' (*Put Out More Flags*). All these wordlings, whether innocent or guilty are doomed, doomed to suffer an equivalent of Hell in this life. In *The Loved One*, he sees the gulf between the wordly attitude to death in the whispering glades of

Forest Lawn and the dignity with which Christianity surrounds it.

This is Evelyn Waugh's judgment on the world in which he had been living: the 'Locust Years' as he called them, in which he had found nothing positive or creative. The alternative in his eyes was a profession in which he could find a meaning for his own life as well as a stimulus. It would give him also a vision which could satisfy his mind and heart. Such a spectacle and a reality for nineteen centuries lay before him in the Catholic Creed. When asked to contribute to a book called *The Road to Damascus* and to give the reason why he turned to religion and the Catholic version of it, he gave a short but comprehensive survey. He told how as a small boy he alarmed his parents by saying that he intended to become a clergyman. 'The appeal then was part hereditary part aesthetic.' The Church of England was caparisoned in the vestments of the ancient Catholic faith in England, and glorious 'with its medieval cathedrals and churches, the rich ceremonies that surround the Monarch, the historic titles of Canterbury and York, the social organisation of the country parishes, the traditional culture of Oxford and Cambridge, the liturgy composed in the heyday of English prose style . . .'. The first ten years of his grown-up life proved to him that life in England or any-where else was 'unintelligible and unendurable without God'. Once he had arrived at this conclusion, he turned inevitably to the Catholic Church. England had been Catholic for nine hundred years, 'the Catholic structure still lies lightly buried beneath every phase of English life; history, topography, law, archaeology, . . . and foreign travel anywhere reveals the local, temporary charcter of the heresies and schisms and the universal, eternal character of the Church'. 'If the Christian Revelation was true, then the Church was the Society founded by Christ and all other bodies were only good in so far as they had salvaged something from the wrecks of the Greek schism and the Reformation.' The same kind of criticism and appreciation appears in *The Holy Places* after his visit to Palestine.

Everything about the new religion was capable of interpretation, could be refined or diminished, and everything except the unreasonable assertion that God became man and died on the Cross; not a myth or an allegory; true God, truly incarnate, tortured to death at a particular geographical place, as a matter of plain historical fact. This was the stumbling block in Carthage, Alexandria, Ephesus and Athens, and at this all the talents of the time went to work to reduce, hide or eliminate.

(*The Holy Places*, p 12)

Converts to the Catholic Church can vary greatly in explaining why they are drawn to join it. The text of Simon Peter's answer to Christ in St John's Gospel (chapter VI) covers most, if not all, cases: 'To whom shall we go? for Thou hast the words of eternal life.' Few, however, can have been so matter of fact as Evelyn Waugh. As he said himself: 'On firm intellectual conviction but with little emotion I was admitted into the Church.' All converts have to listen while the teaching of the Church is explained to them – first to make sure that they do in fact know the essentials of the faith and secondly to save future misunderstandings, for it can easily happen that mere likings or impressions, which fade, may have hidden disagreements with undiscovered doctrines. Another writer came to me at the same time as Evelyn Waugh and tested what was being told him by how far it corresponded with his experience. With such a criterion, it was no wonder that he did not persevere. Evelyn, on the other hand, never spoke of experience or feelings. He had come to learn and understand what he believed to be God's revelation, and this made talking with him an interesting discussion based primarily on reason. I have never myself met a convert who so strongly based his assents on truth. It was a special pleasure to make contact with so able a brain. Nor, though he writes about 'little emotion', was his conversion so very matter of fact, because it proved to be an illumination and an in-spiration. Hard, clear thinking had with the help of grace given him the answer for which he had been searching, and one can see its effect in his subsequent writings.

In them, punishment still fits the crime or rather the half-inno-cents who meet their grim fates in a 'faithless world'. But now a contrasting world has appeared over the horizon, and the worst can be remedied, though in strange ways. Sebastian in *Brideshead Revisited* comes near to damnation as a dipsomaniac in his weak-willed state, but he is given a strange respite in the humblest of offices. Julia Flyte tries to defy her faith, but a quotation from G. K. Chesterton's Father Brown shows that she is not lost: 'I caught him with an unseen hook and an invisible line which is long enough to let him wander to the ends of the world and still be brought back with a twitch upon the thread.' The same note is struck when Charles Ryder, now a convert, says, looking back on his past: 'something quite remote has come out of the fierce little human tragedy in which I played; something none of us thought about at the time ...'. Here a very personal view of Providence is beginning to appear. It is more fully

Artist

DISTINGUISHED AUTHOR SHOWS CONTEMPT FOR THE PUBLIC.

145, North End Road,
Hampstead, N.W.3.

Caricature by the author of his brother c 1919.

Woodcuts by Evelyn Waugh, with characteristic fauns and satyrs and unhappy urban man.

For Harold from Evelyn 1925

Evelyn Waugh was commissioned to design several book-jackets, including Circular Saws *by Humbert Wolfe.*

Three Christmas Cards, for 1923,
1927 and 1929, designed for selected friends.

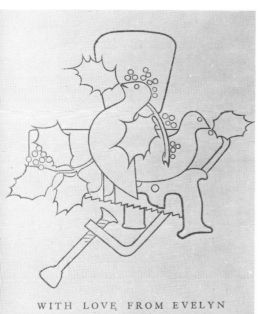

WITH LOVE FROM EVELYN

CHRISTMAS 1927.

BE A SUCCESSFUL ARTIST
There is Joy and Profit in Creative Art.

With best wishes from Evelyn Waugh. Christmas 1929

Three among the several bookplates he drew.

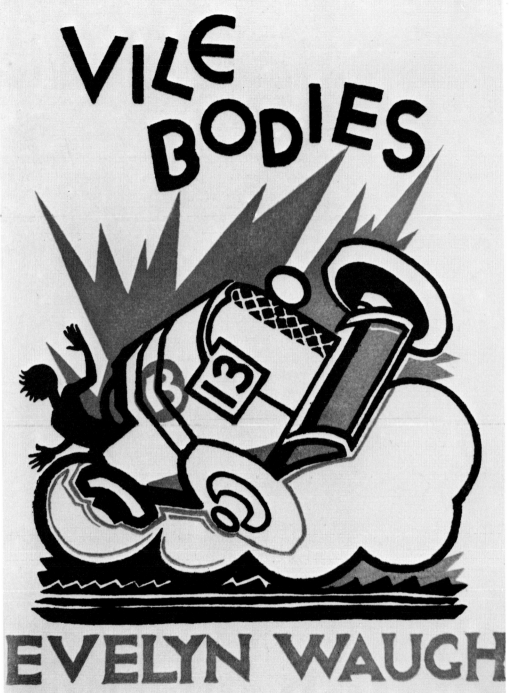

LOVE
AMONG
THE RUINS

A. CANOVA ET E. WAUGH FECERUNT

expressed in *Helena* and to this I must return. In his last work, the trilogy on the last world war, the hero Guy Crouchback, a Catholic of an old stock, moves sadly through the pages, stripped of all the ideals which he had associated with his faith. They have proved to be illusions; all the banners he had waved, love of tradition, of country, aristocracy, love itself, by now have drooped to the ground. His faith remains, but it is accompanied with no leaping of the heart.

After his conversion, Waugh could hope for a recrudescence of hope and even gaiety. He did find in his family life and in his relations with close friends, who were mostly Catholics or like-minded, a peace and a joy. His life of St Edmund Campion was in a way a thank-offering and limned the contrast between the 'whole dark pile of human mockeries' and the inner joy of the martyred Englishman, between Babylon and the drawbridge into the Heavenly City. At the end of a travel book called *Labels*, written before 1930, he wrote: 'For fortune is the least capricious of deities and arranges things on the just and rigid system that no one shall be happy for very long.' In *Edmund Campion*, he begins with the scene of Queen Elizabeth dying! 'She sat on the floor . . . sleepless and silent, oblivious to the coming and going of her councillors and attendants.' Earlier, she told Lady Scrope that 'she . . . had seen a hideous vision of her own body, exceeding lean and fearful in a light of fire'. At the end of his life, the saint Campion is unable to raise his hand to signify his innocence because of the racking he had suffered, and then dies triumphantly on the gallows. In 1952, in *The Holy Places*, Evelyn writes of having attended Mass at 4.30 in the Sepulchre in Jerusalem and goes on:

One has been in the core of one's religion. It is all there, with its human faults and its superhuman triumphs, and one fully realises, perhaps for the first time that Christianity did not strike its first root at Rome or Canterbury or Geneva or Maynooth but here in the Levant where everything is inextricably mixed and nothing is assimilated. . . . But our hope must always be for unity, and as long as the Church of the Sepulchre remains a single building, however subdivided, it forms a memorial to that essential hope.

In so writing of the 'core of one's religion', Evelyn reveals the questing nature of his mind, what the Catholic faith meant to him, and what he would have present in his thoughts for the rest of his life: '*Accedit ad cor altum*' (Psalm 63) – which incorrectly but happily has been translated: 'Man shall come to a deep heart; and God shall be exalted.' His quest was governed by a needling mind with an unflinching eye which, I think, was never completely taken in by what he met in the world in which he lived. Like Swift, he could recognise evil unerringly and his mind looked for a truth which could make life meaningful. Some, as I have said, have doubted this and maintained that his religion either was a pose – because it emphasised his singularity, or could serve to baffle or annoy. His writings, however, show what nonsense this is, and also his behaviour.

A single example may suffice. When he decided to become a Catholic, he took for granted that his act would extinguish any hope of marrying again, for the Catholic Church does not accept divorce. He had divorced his first wife, but he still longed to have a wife and a family. There was therefore a serious sacrifice in choosing to be a Catholic. It was only by a piece of luck that he discovered that his first marriage might be invalid in the eyes of the Church; by luck, I say, because a friend with legal and canonical knowledge, having heard of the circumstances of his first marriage, strongly advised him to bring his case before an ecclesiastical court. This he did and apparently the case was straightforward, so that the court quickly decided on the nullity of his first marriage. The documents then had to be sent to Rome to receive confirmation, and the ecclesiastic who was president of the court told us that these papers had been sent to Rome and that he was expecting their return after a short time. Time passed, however, and nothing happened. Now, the ecclesiastic was well-known for leaving things undone and fancying that he had done them, and to my consternation, as the weeks and months passed, the vice-president of the court discovered that the papers had never been sent. As the ecclesiastic kept on assuring us that they had been sent, we were in a quandary for it might have been fatal to imply that he was lying. Evelyn had been so assured of the nullity that he was looking forward to marrying again and I was naturally worried what might be the effect of all this on his newfound faith. He realised my fears and wrote me a letter, which seems to have been lost, to the effect that I need not worry about his faith as no amount of bungling or knavery in Church circles would weaken it. By good fortune, at this moment a new Head of the diocese was appointed. He changed the personnel of the ecclesiastical court, the papers were sent to Rome and quickly returned confirming the decree of nullity.

He was received into the Roman Catholic Church at Farm Street on 29 September 1930. Free now to marry, he became engaged to Laura Herbert, the daughter of Aubrey and Mary Herbert of Pixton Park,

Somerset, and in family life and among his friends he showed himself less grouchy and farouche than before. Nevertheless, he continued to make enemies and to be unpredictable in his meeting with others.

No one, I think, can hope to diagnose another's character, and I am concerned with it only in its relation to his faith. While giving a chapter in his autobiography to his antecedents, he expresses little belief in their power to explain personality. Each person suffers his own fate. *'Quisque suos patitur manes.'* He uses the image of a card-hand dealt in a poker game, in which the value of the hand 'depends on the combined relationship of the components, not on the sum of its numerals'. All who met him or knew him became aware of moods – the rapid passing from gaiety to icy depression. This depression could be felt almost physically. Then, in some moods, he could be not only prickly but savage – *'nemo me impune lacessit'* – and he would be aggressive and biting. There lay behind these varying moods a spirit of revolt, in the sense that everything in his experience, living beings and things revolted him: hence his Swiftian satire, his imagination playing on the world and its creatures and making them fantastically foolish, monstrous and macabre. In his faith lay the only source of joy and hope. Insomnia in his later life increased his despondency. One of the most noticeable traits grew with this sleeplessness or *taedium vitae,* a boredom which was almost constant. Frances Donaldson tells that 'twice a week he spent the afternoon in the cinema in Dursley, irrespective I think of programme' – this to get away from boredom and himself.

In *The Ordeal of Gilbert Pinfold,* we come the nearest possible to knowing what he thought of himself. Mr Pinfold is a half-amused self-portrait: a man who 'looked at the world *sub specie aeternitatis* and he found it flat as a map' except when he was annoyed. When he was annoyed by an impertinent stranger or a fault in syntax or a bad bottle of wine, 'his mind like a cinema camera tracked furiously forward to confront the offending object close-up with glaring lens'. Mr Pinfold compares himself to a drill sergeant, his eyes 'bulging with wrath that was half-facetious and with half-simulated incredulity'. All who knew Evelyn Waugh will recognise the verisimilitude of this description. Close to the knuckle also is the following: 'The part for which he cast himself was a combination of eccentric don and testy colonel and he acted it strenuously, before his children at Lychpole and his cronies in London, until it came to dominate his whole outward personality. . . . He offered the world a front of pomposity mitigated by indiscretion that was as hard, bright and anti-quated as a cuirass.' Only the word 'pomposity' is unsuited and unfair. For Mr Pinfold, 'the tiny kindling of charity which came to him through his religion, sufficed only to temper his disgust and change it to boredom'.

Where this portrait fails is in its concealment of the author's better qualities and the momentum of his faith. It would seem too that he did not realise fully how splenetic or atrabilious his conduct could appear to some who met him. In *A Little Learning*, there is an admission of misanthropy and despair. Life kept on falling empty, and it was this emptiness for which he compensated by savaging even his friends. But religious faith did profit him by setting his mind at rest, giving it a rectitude and a new and prolonged affection for family and friends. He bolstered this new life attitude by assuming rôles, casting himself as an eccentric don or testy colonel or Victorian country-gentleman even to the carrying of an ear-trumpet, acting a part, especially when joking made it difficult for others to distinguish between jesting and reality, caricaturing and hatred, satire and uncharity. He disliked the Dean of Hertford College (and the dislike was mutual) and accordingly he regularly gave the name of the Dean to one of the worst of the characters in the first novels. Was this malignancy or dislike sublimated into farce?

Some of his libellous remarks in conversation or letter raise the same problem, and I like to think that he meant them more in fun than in full earnest; so too with his abrupt and hard sayings. I remember him saying one evening to Sir Edwin Lutyens, who liked to play possum when conversation ran onto religion: 'Ned, you had better hurry up to be an R.C. or else when you die you will begin to burn.' Lutyens was half amused but also half upset by this remark. On other occasions, listeners to him could be disconcerted by his intran-sigence on matters of religious faith and his carelessness in offending. It may be that he had a real missionary zeal and spoke and acted with the doctrine of the 'One ark of salvation' in mind. When his friend Hubert Duggan, a fallen-away Catholic, was dying, he took great trouble to have a priest near him before he died. Such acts suggest that some of his unwelcome remarks were more akin to cautionary tales than jokes or slaps in the face.

He remained unchanged by success, and the more he had, the more he gave away for deserving causes and cases which he could help. The Catholic Chaplaincy of Manchester University was given a yearly grant, and Campion Hall, Oxford, benefited by many gifts, including the royalties from at least one of the Penguin editions of his novels. One heard by accident of many donations to those in need and causes which he judged Christian. Though thought to be unforgiving, he forgave the person who had injured him most and proved to be a loyal friend despite provocation. He found true happiness among old friends, the Plunket-Greenes, the Asquiths and Mgr Ronald Knox. One incident of his kindness which few know about, is revealed by Frances Donaldson. When Mgr Knox had been operated on for cancer and in vain, his friends hoped that he might benefit by moving for a while to Torquay. They themselves were not free to accompany him, so Evelyn took him and kept him company at a hotel and watched over him for several weeks, during part of the time all by himself. All knew of his extraordinary courage, but few knew how capable he was of unselfishness.

One black mark against him in the view of many was his snobbery. He cared so little about such kinds of criticism that he may have simulated it just to annoy. Snobbery is one of those pejorative words bandied about but having many senses. Undoubtedly, Evelyn liked the company of those with traditional manners and loyalties, especially those who could share his tastes and outlook. Harold Acton in his *More Memoirs of an Aesthete* writes that 'he preferred the society of his Oxford cronies whose foibles continued to amuse him'. His personal privacy was sacrosanct and he made no effort to court popularity with strangers – I might add, no matter who they were. His wife's family had a long and distinguished history, but far from courting he could be uncivil to them. His remarks and letters to Randolph Churchill were far from sycophantic. The truth is that he had a nostalgia, as a critic has said, for a style of living of the past, for an aristocratic ideal justified by religion not by genealogy. This was due to a lively, even romantic sense of history, which comes out in his life of *Edmund Campion* and *The Holy Places*.

One of the reasons which drew him to the Catholic Church was its ever ancient and ever fresh character. He quoted with relish the words of Campion at the end of his trial in Westminster Hall: 'In condemning us you condemn all your own ancestors, all the ancient priests, bishops and kings, all that was once the glory of England, the island of saints and the most devoted child of the See of Peter.' Ideals such as this served as a cloth-of-gold to his faith, and to his dismay, as the years passed, he saw the practice of these ideals die out. In *The*

Holy Places, he called his love of country in his youth a 'first, flushed calf love'. In 1952 he wrote: 'one element certainly is dead for ever – the pride of country'. Pride, too in aristocracy and tradition, has gone in the theme of *Brideshead Revisited*; and in the war trilogy, we find the melancholy epitaph on the Halberdiers and those whom he had honoured in his youth. The last title is significant – *Unconditional Surrender*. The pilgrim's faith remained, but even that was dimmed for a while, before he died, by the novelties and tasteless vulgarities, as he regarded them, introduced into the Church's liturgy after Vatican II.

Fortunately, his strong reasoning powers were not eclipsed by his forebodings and melancholy, and he had an abiding conviction to fall back upon. This roughly was based on what he believed to be a notable characteristic of Divine Providence, and it became the key to his religious philosophy. He exemplified the nature of this belief in the novel *Helena*. In his Introduction to *The Holy Places*, we are told that at the age of thirty-two, he began to plan a series of books about 'great and strange Britons' who had an association with the Holy Places: 'Helena above all first began a ferment in my imagination which lasted for fifteen years.' The novel *Helena* was the result. Though perhaps his least successful work, it was his favourite because it expressed his deeply-felt religious confidence in the divine guidance of individuals' lives. Helena, he tells us, had no 'particular suffering that we know of, neither physical, spiritual or mental. She led a normal life except that she lived in an age when one had to choose between flight or brutal punishment.' Her history suggests that she accepted God's will in first making her an Empress, and later a discarded one, so that she might live on as a kindly old lady. 'She might claim, like that other, less prudent queen: "in my end is my beginning". But for her final, triumphant journey she would have no fame.' Yet in God's purposes she had still something to do – something unforeseen – the finding of the Cross. At a crisis of Christendom, with her son Constantine not yet baptised and 'fuddled perhaps by dreams of Alexander', God sent from retirement 'a lonely, resolute old woman with a single, concrete practical task clear before her: to turn the eyes of the world back to the planks of wood on which their Salvation hung'. In reading her history, despite all that might be legendary in it, Evelyn felt that he had been given an insight, though a distant one, into God's dealing with human souls. God 'wants a different thing from each of us, laborious or easy, conspicuous or quite private, but something which only we can do and for which we were created'.

To those of us who knew of this strong conviction of his, the manner of his sudden death seemed to be almost foreseen and to be a seal upon his work and religious hope. On the eve of Easter, April 1966, a priest came to see him and his wife Laura at their home, Combe Florey. Knowing of a wayside Catholic chapel nearby, where Mass could be said, they asked him to stop the night and celebrate Easter by saying Mass at this chapel. He agreed, and so on Easter morning all the family who were at home went to Mass and to Communion together. After returning home, Evelyn left the room and fell dead. His life had reached its consummation like that of St Helena.

7

LUSH PLACES

Eric Newby

HIS first travel book, *Labels*, was published in 1930, two years after *Decline and Fall*. It is the journal of a journey in the Mediterranean in 1929. He makes England sound like hell that February: 'People shrank, in those days, from the icy contact of a cocktail glass, like the Duchess of Malfi from the dead hand. . . .'

He had planned to go to Russia but did not do so; some trouble with visas. Instead, he flew in an airliner to Le Bourget from Croydon, to start the travels from which he derived the least material for his subsequent novels. As he himself wrote, 'all the places visited are already fully labelled', and his reason for persisting in spite of this seems positively ponderous: 'The interest I have found in preparing this book, which I hope may be shared by some of its readers, was that of investigating with a mind as open as the English system of pseudo-education allows, the basis for the reputations these places have acquired.'

In Paris, he stayed at the Crillon for one night, where he was charged 140 francs for a single room, subsequently at one with some-one's false teeth under the pillow, which cost 18. He makes the night-clubs sound even more tedious than they are today, except the Negro place, Brick-Tops. He intensely disliked Lalique glass (although later he allows Charles Ryder to have some in his rooms in Oxford in *Brideshead Revisited*), Foujita and Marie Laurencin among the painters and a work executed in white wire, *Tête: dessin dans l'espace*, by Cocteau.

At Monte Carlo, he joined the *Stella Polaris*, a six-thousand-ton Norwegian luxury motor yacht, for a Mediterranean cruise. The other passengers were mostly well-off English people. The ship sailed, but nothing can really save the account of his subsequent voyages from the banality that anyone who has ever attempted a factual account of a pleasure cruise knows to be inevitable. His companions were a couple called Geoffrey and Julia, though Julia was actually Evelyn, the wife whom he had recently married. He saw Messina, not yet rebuilt after the earthquake, played dreadful deck-games and even became a member of the Games Committee, visited the Holy Land, much as it is today apart from a preponderance of Arabs, ate rissoles in a German hotel in Nazareth and disliked the wine.

In Cairo, still with Geoffrey (Julia had pneumonia) he stayed at Mena House, visited some pyramids on various sorts of animals, was unimpressed by the sphinx, attended a bogus native dance in a tomb, was impressed by the treasures of Tutankhamun but was bored by the mosques and the geometric convolutions of Arab art.

In the Cyclades, he saw a volcanic island steaming, newly-risen from the sea and, passing through the Sea of Marmora, he arrived in time for a prospect of Santa Sophia with a great splash of setting sun illuminating its domes. Turkish art he considered even more degraded than Arabic – the tiles of the Blue Mosque were 'Reckitt's Blue'; the Serai reminded him of Earl's Court Exhibition. Across the Golden Horn, at the British Embassy in Pera which had not yet been transferred to the new capital, Ankara, he met Sacheverell and Osbert Sitwell, there on a visit.

In Athens, he stayed with a friend called Alastair (Graham), the first name of one of the characters who is to persist as long as any in his novels. This is a different sort of Alastair however, with a house filled with ikons and singing birds, who gives him champagne with a piece of sugar in it which has been soaked in angostura and rolled in red pepper as a restorative after a ship-board ball. The other Alastair would have given him Black Velvet.

With Alastair and Mark (Ogilvie-Grant) he saw, at a distance, the Acropolis, the colour of which reminded him of the milder parts of a Stilton which has had port poured into it; saw the mosaics at Daphne which his friend Robert Byron had written about, thereby absolving him from attempting to do so. Later, they went to a nightclub at which there was no cabaret because a German had so severely bitten the girls' legs the previous night that they were unable to perform.

Venice he was disinclined to write about and did not until nearly twenty years later in *Brideshead Revisited*; Dubrovnik, the old city, little changed except that more people wore local costume, then Cetinje, the capital of Montenegro, where the shore-going party ate their awful lunch; Etna at sunset – 'Nothing', he wrote, 'I have seen in art or nature is more revolting.' The greatest loathing of the whole trip was reserved for Gibraltar. He compared it with Colwyn Bay, Manchester and Stratford-on-Avon, coming to the rather far-fetched conclusion that it most resembled Shoreham in Sussex, deprived of its churches, plus Aldershot, the whole thing being transferred to the east coast of Scotland or the coast of Wales.

In *Remote People*, published in 1931, a new enthusiasm is apparent which is absent from *Labels*. It is particularly noticeable in that part of the book which deals with the coronation of the Emperor of Abyssinia, at which he was present in the guise of newspaper correspondent, although whether he actually ever despatched any news about it is not clear. The book begins well: 'They were still dancing when, just before dawn on October 19th, 1930, the *Azay le Rideau* came into harbour at Djibouti.'

He goes ashore and we are off with him into a country in which the happenings and the people he meets are so fantastic that when, a year later, he wrote *Black Mischief*, there was scarcely any need for him to invent anything at all. Abyssinia was like some huge quarry with the stone already hewn in it in which, like a sculptor, he could find everything he needed.

No catalogue of events [he wrote about the coronation] can convey any real idea of these astounding days, of an atmosphere utterly unique, elusive, unforgettable. If in the foregoing pages I have seemed to give undue emphasis to the irregularity of the proceedings, to their unpunctuality, and their occasional failure, it is because this was an essential part of their character and charm. In Addis Ababa everything was haphazard and incongruous; one learned always to expect the unusual and yet was always surprised.

He did not have to wait until he reached the mountain capital or even Abyssinia itself for the unusual or surprising to happen. Almost immediately upon his landing at Djibouti, the houses in that decrepit place began to collapse before his eyes, as if they had been waiting for some chronicler to arrive and record the event.

. . . while we looked they actually did begin to fall. Great flakes of stucco crumbled from the front; a brick or two toppling from the coping, splashed into the mud below. Some scared Indian clerks scampered into the open, a Greek in shirt-sleeves appeared from the house opposite, a group of half-naked natives rose from their haunches and, still scouring their teeth with sticks of wood, gazed apprehensively about them. It had been an earthquake which, in the sensible motion of the cab, had escaped our notice.

In spite of his claiming, in a preface to a new edition of *Black Mischief* published in 1962, that the setting for it was not Abyssinia, it is difficult to accept what he says. Almost everything and everyone in *Black Mischief* are in *Remote People*, under different names. Only the penurious, decayed Arab gentry chewing *khat* and bemoaning the past, and the old wooden houses which they inhabited, are of a later stage in the journey: the houses, 'With fine doorways of carved wood and massive doors studded with brass bosses', he saw in Zanzibar – the Arab gentry themselves had long-since become strangers to their own houses which by then had become counting houses filled with Indian clerks. The Arabs themselves he met in a club in Crater at Aden. There were no Arabs in Djibouti, or if there were any, he does not mention them.

In both books there is the same dreadful train journey from the coast to the capital through dessicated, thorny, stony, ant-ridden country in the midst of which, assembled at a halt, semi-savage, white-clothed, bearded, barefooted members of the army, each company with its chief wearing a lion's mane headdress, stand watching the train go by loaded with guests. In the capital there is an English girl in a riding-habit (Irene Ravensdale, whom he knows) who is not eaten, as Prudence is finally in *Black Mischief* but, almost equally improbably, appears in the middle of the ceremonies in a taxi 'surrounded by a band of mounted musicians playing six-foot pipes and banging saddle drums', caught up in a royal procession; and there is the Emperor himself, Haile Selassie, a far more extravagant and incredible figure than Seth ever was in *Black Mischief*: ' . . . passing in a great, red car surrounded by cantering lancers. A page sits behind holding over his head an umbrella of crimson silk embroidered with sequins and gold tassels. A guard sits in front nursing a machine gun under a plush shawl; the chauffeur is a European wearing powder-blue livery and the Star of Ethiopia.'

And, as in *Black Mischief*, there is even a dispossessed claimant to the throne, Lej Yasu, who, like Achon in the novel, has been kept in captivity for years and has long since become unfit for public exhibition; and there are banquets, though not cannibalistic, from which the chiefs stagger, bloated and greasy from gnawing great gobbets of meat, unsteady from over-indulgence in the local liquor, *tedj*. Just as in Seth's capital, Debra Dowa, in Addis Ababa executions were carried out in the same, rather off-hand manner though they had recently ceased to be performed in public and, in cases of homicide, were now carried out behind closed doors by the bereaved. At Addis Ababa, there was even a British Legation at the end of what had been until recently a road every bit as appalling as the one which led to the Legation outside Debra Dowa with a staff which, while certainly not as unhelpful to British nationals as that in the fictional state of Azania, can scarcely be said to have been chosen for service in Abyssinia by reason of their previous experience – the Minister was a Chinese scholar, recently arrived from Shanghai, the Secretary had come from Constantinople, the Consul from Fez – none of them knew any of the local language, Amharic. These and some other, newly-arrived officials, plus a number of uncles and aunts and cousins who 'have come out from England to see the fun', then proceeded to lose the Duke of Gloucester's luggage.

It is a pity that the Duke fails to make an appearance in *Black Mischief*; but then neither does a whole host of characters – the Duke's German cook whose skirt becomes displaced in the royal presence showing her to be wearing red flannel drawers, the Italian Prince Udine (who gives the Emperor an aeroplane), the German delegation which gives him a picture of Field-Marshal von Hindenburg, a British Marine band and a Belgian colonel on a horse who attempts to stop the band taking part in the ceremonies, to name only a few. There are two hatchet-mouthed women, exact facsimiles of Dame Mildred Porch and Miss Sarah Tin, wearing solar topis. The only difference between fact and fiction is that instead of working for the abolition of Cruelty to Animals they are exclusively concerned, and equally hopelessly, in Abyssinia with the abolition of Vice.

At Harar, Waugh passes some days in a terrible hotel run by a Mr Bergebedgian, an Armenian who 'sold great quantities of a colourless and highly inflammatory spirit distilled by a fellow countryman of his and labelled, capriciously, "Very Olde Scotts Whiskey", "Fine Champayne" and "Hollands Gin" '.

In *Black Mischief*, Mr Bergebedgian appears as the more repellent Mr Krikor Youkoumian, and Basil Seal who is, himself, what Waugh might have been, if his parents had been better off, helps Mr Youkoumian to make and bottle the champagne for the great Victory Ball at which the Earl of Ngumo, 'one of the backwoods peers, feudal overlord of some 500 square miles of impenetrable highland territory', makes such an impressive debut:

> . . . on his head a lion's mane busby; on his shoulders a shapeless fur mantle; a red satin skirt, brass bangles and a necklace of lion's teeth; a long, ornamental sword hung at his side; two bandoliers of brass cartridges circled his great girth; he had small blood-shot eyes and a tousle of black wool over his cheeks and chin. Behind him stood six unsteady slaves carrying antiquated rifles.

This astonishing figure is not a product of the imagination. The description is based partly on the appearance of the leaders of the Abyssinian Army but perhaps more particularly on that of its commander-in-chief, Moulungetta: 'a mountain of a man with a grey beard and bloodshot eyes; in full dress uniform with scarlet-and-gold cloak and lion's mane busby, he looked hardly human'.

All that is really wanting in the Abyssinian chapters of *Remote People* to convert it into a Waugh novel is some dialogue. It is rare for any of the characters to be invested with the power of speech. An exception is made in the case of a tiresome American professor, an alleged authority on Coptic ritual, who has already extensively misinterpreted the coronation Mass and with whom Waugh sets off to visit the monastery of Debra Lebanos which, in *Black Mischief*, becomes the monastery of St Mark the Evangelist, from which the completely ga-ga Achon is taken for his coronation after forty years of incarceration, in the course of which, at the moment at which the crown is placed on his head, he expires. The Professor is so dreadful and so skilfully evoked that it is a wonder and a pity that he never appears in any subsequent book.

It is after attending a Coptic Mass at Debra Lebanos, or rather acting as a bystander, as it largely takes place behind closed doors, that Waugh makes one of the few observations in *Remote People* that one feels he means to be taken seriously:

I had sometimes thought it an odd thing that Western Christianity, alone of all the religions of the world, exposed its mysteries to every observer. .... At Debra Lebanos I suddenly saw the classical basilica and open altar as a great positive achievement, a triumph of light over darkness consciously accomplished, and I saw theology as the science of simplification by which nebulous and elusive ideas are made intelligible and exact. And I began to see how these obscure sanctuaries had grown, with the clarity of the Western reason, into the great open altars of Catholic Europe, where Mass is said in a flood of light, high in the sight of all, while tourists can clatter round with their Baedekers, incurious of the mystery.

From Abyssinia he went to Aden, paid a visit to the Sultanate of Lahej, of which he leaves an interesting account, and attended a meeting of the Aden troop of Boy Scouts, some of whom were Jews, some Arabs, at which fire-lighting tests, assisted in some instances by the furtive use of paraffin to encourage combustion, and examinations in the Scout Law, were being conducted by the British Scoutmaster.

'Very good, Abdul. Now tell me what does "thrifty" mean?'
'Trifty min?'
'Yes, what do you mean, when you say a scout is thrifty?'
'I min scoot hass no money.'
'What does "clean" mean?'
'Clin min?'
'You said just now a scout is clean in thought, word and deed.'
'Yiss, scoot is clin.'
'Well, what do you mean by that?'

'I mean tought, worden deed.'
'All right Abdul, that'll do.'
'Pass, Sahib?'
'Yes, yes.'

An enormous smile broke across his small face, and away he went capering across the parade ground, kicking up dust over fire-makers and laughing with pleasure.

'Of course, it isn't quite like dealing with English boys', said the scoutmaster again.

From Zanzibar, which he found excruciatingly uncomfortable because of the heat and the humidity, Waugh went to Mombasa and then to Nairobi for Race Week, and from there to the Kenya Highlands where he stayed in various settlers' houses, some rather grand, others less so. One of the former sort, at Eldoret, was the most English he had yet seen – 'old silver, family portraits, chintz-frilled dressing tables'.

Of all this Kenyan scene, he writes far more effectively in *Men at Arms* than in *Remote People*, when he makes Guy Crouchback and Virginia recall their life in Kenya together on what is to be a disastrous evening at Claridge's.

The group of bungalows that constituted their home, timber-built, round stone chimneys and open English hearths, furnished with wedding presents and good old pieces of furniture from the lumber rooms at Broome. . . . Evening bathes in the Lake, dinner parties in pyjamas with their neighbours. Race Week in Nairobi, all the flagrant forgotten scandals of the Muthaiga Club, fights, adultery, arson, bankruptcies, card-sharping, insanity, suicides, even duels – the whole Restoration scene enacted by farmers, eight thousand feet above the steaming seaboard.

At Tabora, in Tanganyka, he stayed at yet another terrible hotel, and then crossed Lake Tanganyka in a storm, took train to Kabalo and then travelled up the Lualaba (Congo) with a mad ship's captain who insisted that he was secreting a motor cycle in his cabin. Eventually, he reached Elizabethville and, finally, Capetown which he disliked intensely – it is interesting to compare his subsequent, almost ecstatic description of it in *Officers and Gentlemen* when X Commando is given shore leave there in 1941. At Capetown, he took a third-class berth, which he shared with two others, in a ship which was sailing to Southampton. It cost £20. By the time he reached England, he had been travelling for about five months. The total cost of his journey 'including a good many purchases of tropical clothes, local painting, carving, etc. and consistent losses at all games of skill and chance came to a little short of £500'.

As he himself would have been the first to admit, apart from the discomfort occasioned by excesses of heat or cold, food and drink or the lack or badness of them, boredom and the fact that such things as coronations tended to go on far too long, which are just a few of the crosses which anyone who is rash enough to travel has to bear whether they want to or not, the discomforts which he endured in the course of his first African journey and the subsequent one during the Abyssinian war seem only a degree or so more arduous than those he suffered during his trip round the Mediterranean. On none of them was he ever very far removed from other Europeans or an hotel, however bad.

But the journey he made in South America in 1932, of which he wrote in *Ninety-Two Days*, is sterner stuff. That year he travelled far from the haunts of Europeans and his compatriots, and much more in the manner of a Victorian explorer: with guides who were at the best unpredictable, through country in which there was a considerable degree of danger. From Georgetown in British Guiana, he travelled first by train, then by steamer to New Amsterdam, then through bush and tropical forest to Kurupukari on the Essequibo river, all the time in company with a District Commissioner who is nothing like the usual colonial figure of the imagination but a harassed, emaciated man, part Indian, part Creole.

From this remote place, after a series of scarcely believable misadventures, he set off for the savannah with an extraordinary little band of followers, all more or less coloured: a charming, middle-aged Negro man called Yetto, Sinclair, an odious, but invaluable youth, and Jagger, a spectral figure, who gets left by the wayside *en route* and about whose survival Waugh speculates mildly.

Out on the burnt savannah, under the huge sun among the sandpaper trees which give no shade (where the staple food of those mad enough to live there is *farine* and *tasso*, the former resembling coarse sawdust, the second, a sun-dried, salted meat), they eventually reach a ranch, a collection of huts inhabited by a Mr Christie, a Negro and a religious maniac who on Sunday preaches to the local Indians for hours on end. Mr Christie is the original of Mr Todd, the terrifying lunatic in *A Handful of Dust* who makes the hero, an involuntary and unwilling guest in his house, read Dickens to him for the rest of his life, which, with the possible exception of the moment in *Black Mischief* at which Basil Seal discovers that he has assisted at a cannibal feast in which his girl friend was the *pièce de résistance*, and certain passages in *The Loved One*, is the most macabre incident in any of his novels.

Eventually the party, tormented by cabiri flies, arrives at St Ignatius, a Jesuit settlement on the Guianyan bank of the Ireng river, and after staying there for some days with the priest and sending the rest of the party back to where they came from, he sets off with a guide furnished by the priest for Boa Vista on the Rio Branca in Brazilian territory, a place which he has been led to believe is one of some consequence.

His expectation is not fulfilled. Boa Vista turns out to be a place of no consequence at all and one in which the greater part of the male population appear to have homicidal tendencies and are deterred from more frequent indulgence in their proclivities only by the apathy brought on by semi-starvation. 'Closer investigation', he wrote, 'did nothing to restore it [his expectation of the place]. There was the broad main street up which he had come; two parallel, less important streets and four or five more laid at right angles to them. At a quarter of a mile in every direction they petered out into straggling footpaths.' He has more than ample time for a description of the place and its inhabitants while waiting, marooned in a Benedictine Priory whose occupants have gone to pieces, for a boat to take him down to Manaos at the confluence of the Rio Negro with the Amazon. It never comes and he eventually escapes by returning to British Guiana.

Apart from the chapters in *A Handful of Dust* which have the setting in South America, the only other passages in his novels which make mention of it, and of Mexico (of which he wrote in *Robbery Under Law*, a book which, once published, he did not wish to keep in print), are two short but memorable passages totalling not more than twenty lines, in *Brideshead Revisited*.

In 1935, he went as a newspaper correspondent to cover the Abyssinian war and when he returned from it wrote *Waugh in Abyssinia*, a title which he says was not of his choosing. The novel which was based on it, *Scoop*, appeared three years later. No one can accuse him of squandering material from his Abyssinian journeys. Two visits gave him enough material for four books and it is a credit to his skill that although the backgrounds are almost identical in both novels, the books are quite easily kept separate in the reader's mind, although anyone who has read all four books will find it almost impossible to distinguish the real hotel keepers and café proprietors from the fictional ones and remember in which books they appear

– Mr Bollolakos, Mr Bergebedgian, Mr Youkoumian (the most memorable), Mr Kakophilos, Mr Carassellos who runs an awful, newly-arisen hotel at Harar on Waugh's second 'real' visit, Mr Popotakis who owns a ping-pong saloon in *Scoop*. All have a number of things in common – they are all either Greek or Armenian, their hotels and the food and drink they serve in them are terrible and over all their various properties there hangs the grave-smell of defective drainage.

Just as in his later creation, William Boot in *Scoop*, author of *Lush Places* 'a countryman's notes', is caught up in a vast Beaverbrookian misunderstanding, buying humidors, portable operating tables and cleft sticks at Fortnum's (or was it the Army and Navy?), so Waugh himself prepared to go to the wars that summer: ' . . . there was a heatwave. I trod miasmic pavements between cartographers and consulates.'

Eventually, he assembled a vast amount of gear which was stacked in the vestibule of his club:

There are few pleasures [he wrote] more complete or to me more rare, than that of shopping extravagantly at someone else's expense. I thought I had treated myself with reasonable generosity until I saw the luggage of my professional competitors – their rifles and telescopes and ant-proof trunks, medicine chests, gas-masks, pack saddles and vast wardrobes of costume suitable for every climatic emergency.

These men are the harbingers not only of William Boot but of Apthorpe in *Men at Arms*, surrounded by his brass-bound chests, shapeless canvas sacks and buffalo hide bags, seated on *Connolly's Chemical Closet*.

At Port Said, a Mr W. F. Rickett joined the ship – it eventually transpired that he was engaged in negotiating an immense oil concession with the Abyssinians. From time to time, he received long cables in cypher, one of which he pocketed nonchalantly, remarking, 'From my huntsman. He says the prospects for cubbin' are excellent . . . .' It needs little imagination on the reader's part to accept the transformation of Mr Rickett into the mysterious Mr Baldwin of *Scoop* who has a valet called Cuthbert – 'He never left my side, so I recommended him for the V.C.'; a pack of hounds in the Midlands – 'We march with the Fernie'; and a vineyard – 'On the opposite side of the hill to Chateau Mouton-Rothschild where in my opinion the soil is rather less delicate than mine.' I like to think that

Waugh would have been not only surprised but pleased if he had known that after the war Rickett's son did just what he himself would have like to have done during it, went into the Guards, having won the Sword of Honour at Sandhurst.

When he arrived in Addis Ababa, Waugh found that a new and awful hotel had arisen, Kakophilos's. Instead of staying there, he went with Rickett, who had found the suite he had ordered by cable in the principal hotel non-existent, to stay at the *Deutsches Haus*, which in *Scoop* becomes the Pension Dressler, of which it is almost a facsimile, except that the real proprietress is a little more *gemütlich* – there is a free-ranging pig in both places, although the real one ends up as *wurst* – and a terrifying gander. The *Deutsches Haus* is sited near the tannery which is managed by a Russian prince who previously ran a brothel in the city without much success. (In *Black Mischief*, he runs the night club.)

It would be difficult to make the representatives of the Press in *Scoop* more unpleasant than they were in reality, or the head of the Press Bureau, who is successful in both fact and fiction in preventing the correspondents from going anywhere or seeing or hearing anything of interest, although just as William Boot gets his exclusive story so does Evelyn Waugh when he receives from a spy information on the fate of the French Consul and the news that twelve Roman Catholics 'and four Maltese Popes', have been sewn in skins and burned alive. The only thing that is completely different this time is the composition of the ruling House in the novel. In *Scoop* they are the Jacksons, a long-established and infinitely ramifying bourgeois family of darkies. One would have to travel to the other side of the continent to find anything remotely similar.

Waugh in Abyssinia was followed, after a gap of twenty-five years, by *A Tourist in Africa*, the last of his travel books, although in the novels there is evidence of extensive travel both before and after the war. In September 1939, the trumpets had sounded a martial call to the English – and the Welsh. (The bagpipes performed a similar though more dissonant function for the Scots and Irish.) It was a muted rather than clarion call, not intended to be heard or answered by men of the age or physical condition of Evelyn Waugh.

Nevertheless, he rose from his desk, gave up his preoccupation with the refugees who were swarming in the part of rural Somerset in which he lived, some of whom were remembered as the appalling Connolly children later in the war, when he wrote *Put Out More Flags*, and presented himself as a candidate for active service. 'There is a symbolic difference between fighting as a soldier and serving as a civilian', he wrote at the time. 'Even if the civilian is more valuable.' In that long winter, during which the gelid antagonists peered out at one another from their respective casemates in the spirit of live and let live, more people were employed in keeping men such as Waugh out of the armed forces than were engaged on active service, and for a time they were extremely successful in keeping him out too.

At first, his hopes centred on a commission in the Irish Guards, later he gained one with the Welsh Guards and he was in fact interviewed at their depot by two genial officers, though unlike Basil Seal in his disastrous interview with a Lieutenant-Colonel of the Bombadiers – 'If I had to join the Foot Guards, I'd soonest join yours. You aren't as stuffy as the Grenadiers and you haven't got any of those bogus regional connections like the Scots and Irish and Welsh' – he was put on a list by them as someone likely to be accepted when the time came.

But although he was on all sorts of lists, including Ian Fleming's 'secret list' at the Admiralty, and Ian Hay's at the War Office in which he took to haunting the dreary offices of majors who endlessly drank tea out of mugs, everything came to nothing as it invariably continued to do in this, for him, most unsatisfactory of wars, and he would return to the St James's Club to recruit his spirits with food and drink – '$\frac{1}{2}$ a dozen oysters, $\frac{1}{2}$ a grouse, a whole partridge and a peach, $\frac{1}{2}$ a bottle of white wine, $\frac{1}{2}$ a bottle of Pontet-Canet, 1924' being noted in his journal as a typical repast.

Finally, with the help of Brendan Bracken, a 1939 whizz-kid, he was accepted into the Royal Marines (the Halberdiers of the military trilogy) and spent the rest of that sub-zero winter training in Kent in what was perhaps the happiest time he was to know as a soldier. So his war begins as does that of his principal military creation (with the exception of Apthorpe who is immortal), Guy Crouchback, who is a sort of *doppelgänger*, not precisely a twin, however. Guy is by nature retiring but eminently clubbable (always very popular at Bellamy's Club), not given to controversy, unlike Evelyn who conducted a preposterous 'most secret' correspondence with a senior officer of the Special Service Brigade – actually 'Shimi' Lord Lovat, who emerges as equally tiresome. At times, it is as if Apthorpe were inhabiting the body of Evelyn Waugh. Guy is never rude, particularly to senior officers, accepting without demur the injustices which are so much a part of military life, good at military administration and, though he suffers an equally ludicrous series of almost identical physical mishaps (both damage limbs parachuting out of aeroplanes) not quite so preternaturally decrepit.

What they share is physical courage. 'I've always known you were as brave as a lion', Virginia, Guy's ex-wife, says and in Crete Evelyn records with remarkable detachment the collapse of the Commonwealth army in his *Memorandum on Layforce*, an extended *aide-memoire* which he wrote at the time, large parts of which are incorporated in *Officers and Gentlemen*. It is instructive to compare his dry comments on the abject behaviour of so many amateur and professional soldiers, many of them still living, with their own personal assessment of their careers and abilities in *Who's Who*.

Almost all the characters, good and bad, brave and craven, probable and improbable, who appear in the war novels are present in his journals under their real names, most of them protected by the laws of libel. Ritchie-Hook, the much-mutilated officer who is finally killed outside a blockhouse in Croatia, where Waugh's own war might be said to have come to an end, had a real life equivalent, a brigadier who used to booby trap the bedroom door against his wife returning from comforting their child in the middle of the night; Ludovic, the sinister Corporal-Major who kept a diary about his officers in Hookforce, had a likeness in a sergeant in Layforce, the commando force under the command of Colonel, later Major-General Sir Robert Laycock (the Tommy Blackhouse of the novels), one of the few soldiers – together with Wavell – whom Evelyn unconditionally admired. Almost too real was the awful Lord Kilbannock, the ex-journalist who forces Guy to second an even more awful Air Vice-Marshal's election to Bellamy's; so was the savant who forced the soldiers to live on seaweed, and so were Eddie and Bertie, two large amiable Guards officers, one of whom chased an ostrich round the Capetown Zoo. Real too were most of the members of the fictional Military Mission to Yugoslavia, in the course of his attachment to which Evelyn really did become involved in the improbable-sounding attempt to save the Jews, recorded in *Unconditional Surrender*, which he pursued to the exclusion of almost all other work. One of the few characters missing, so far as one can see, from the 'real' military world of his journals is Apthorpe.

If the height of Waugh's attachment to the military life was when he first joined the Marines, then the descent into the abyss of disenchantment could be said to begin with what can only be considered in the light of what happened to him subsequently to be his mistaken transfer into the Royal Horse Guards; the time of his greatest misfortune when, with other unwanted officers, he was left to rot at Windsor where there was nothing for them to do but scour the houses of acquaintances in the surrounding country for whisky to drink.

8

RECOLLECTIONS

Penelope Chetwode

THE first time I ever heard Evelyn's name mentioned was when I was a débutante in 1928 and my mother was discussing a very *risqué* book with my brother Roger at the far end of our drawing-room in Alma Tadema's old house in Grove End Road. The book was called *Decline and Fall*, and when I approached them to enquire about it they shut up like clams.

I met the author four years later when I was engaged to John Betjeman and he took me to stay with his great friends Christine and Edward Longford at Pakenham Hall in County Westmeath. To begin with, we were the only visitors, and I asked Edward if there were any horses to ride. He said that he feared there were none, but when I went down to the farm that afternoon I found two: a fourteen-hand bay pony and a fifteen-hand bay cob. I imagine the bailiff was doing a bit of horse-dealing on the side, and when I asked him if I could ride the larger of the two animals, the answer was in the affirmative but I was warned that he was only a three-year-old and a 'bit wild'. Accordingly, I returned the next morning in jodhpurs and was surprised to see three farm hands standing at the ready with ash plants in their hands. The horse was led out and I was given a quick leg-up, whereupon he ran back and was set upon with the sticks and flew out of the yard only to start napping again a little way down the lane. The farm boys chased him, and the whole performance was repeated several times. The three-year-old was virtually un-broken, had never been mouthed or lunged, and was positively dangerous to ride in its present state. So I asked for the pony which was a good deal older and a reasonably good hack and I enjoyed myself exploring the park on him and riding round the great lake while Edward and John Betjeman spent the morning – as always – singing hymns to our host's extraordinary accompaniment which consisted of thumping his hands down on the piano to produce a series of unrelieved discords.

Then Evelyn arrived to stay. While at Madresfield, he had recently been on an equitation course with the Lygon girls at Captain Hance's then famous establishment nearby. He immediately asked if he could ride, as I had done on arrival, and Edward said that he was welcome to try the horses I had discovered on the home farm. I soon told him the truth about them and said that we had better take it in turns to ride the pony, but with the courage of ignorance he insisted that we should go out together, being confident that he would be able to manage the unmanageable bay cob.

The next morning, we walked down to the farmyard, where everything happened as I had predicted: the green horse napped and napped but Evelyn stuck determinedly to the saddle and was eventually carried right out of the yard down the grass track to Lake Deravara at a fast and furious gallop. The cob then reared right up under an oak tree and deposited Evelyn on a high branch, on which I saw him perched when I cantered up a few minutes later. I dismounted so that he was able to hang by his arms – as opposed to the hair of his head like Absalom – and just reach the saddle with the tips of his toes and gradually let himself down into it with the aid of other branches. Much later, Evelyn said how grateful he was to me for not making a funny story out of this incident, but I have no compunction about telling it now as I think it shows considerable physical courage on his part in having stuck to the saddle as long as he did. He was a novice and did not realise that the poor brute he was trying to control was quite unrideable even by an expert.

John Betjeman and I were married in the late summer of 1933, and early in 1934 we went to live at Garrards Farm, Uffington, which we rented for £36 a year. Evelyn frequently came to stay and during the summer of that year I motored him over to Lyford Grange, which he was anxious to see in connexion with the life of St Edmund Campion which he was then writing. At that time it belonged to Douglas and Mea Woodruff but was let to a local farmer and occupied by two farm workers and their families, and the interior was a bit depressing. Much later, the Woodruffs sold it to two Catholic converts, Miss Morrell and Miss Whiting, who had it brilliantly restored by Lewis Stafford Northcote; during the course of the alterations, a sixteenth-century Agnus Dei came to light and was presented to the Jesuits of Campion Hall. Personally, I think that Evelyn's description of Campion's last Mass and sermon at Lyford, followed by his being squashed into a hiding-hole with two other priests and his final discovery and arrest, is among the most agonisingly dramatic passages in all his writings.

After one of Evelyn's visits to Uffington, he sent me a copy of *Black Mischief* instead of a bread-and-butter letter. This has remained my favourite of all his books and although I had already read it at the time, I was delighted to get a copy from the author until I opened it and found it consisted entirely of blank pages. I realised that it was sent to commemorate a row we had had, and subsequently used it as a visitors' book.

When, in 1937, Evelyn married Laura Herbert, the ethereal pre-Raphaelite girl of his dreams, they bought Piers Court, at Stinchcombe in Gloucestershire, familiarly known to their friends as 'Stinkers'. Here he was able to indulge his taste for Victorian furniture, pictures and garden statuary, one of his most treasured pieces being an elaborate William Burges washstand given to him by John Betjeman. In a subtle way, I think he achieved the effect he desired, which was to give the impression of a country house lived in by the same family for several generations.

Generosity to both his friends and the Church – all the royalties from his book on Campion went to Campion Hall – was one of Evelyn's most endearing characteristics but he had a horror of getting involved in conventional good works and he told me that his parish priest at Stinchcombe once came and asked him if he and Laura would have a fête at Piers Court in aid of the church heating.

'How much will it cost to instal?' he asked.

'The estimate is £300.'

'Then here's a cheque.' And he sat down and wrote it there and then, and the fête was never held.

Soon after the war, the Waughs moved to Combe Florey, not far from Pixton where Laura was brought up. Their new house stood on a hill surrounded by rolling parkland with large walled kitchen-gardens to the west, in which Laura was able to indulge her inherited passion for farming and gardening. I remember Evelyn complaining a lot about the food when I went to stay there, which was of the nursery variety with liberal supplies of mashed potato. But Laura was by nature a farmer, not a cook, and took a lot of trouble over the correct feeding of her Jersey herd. In the summer of 1950, Evelyn wrote to me: 'Laura has built an all-electric bungalow for her cows. She is £6,420 overdrawn . . . I have spent £10,000 and not put any aside for taxation so it looks like prison pretty soon, where I am told one has the wireless playing ceaselessly night and day.'

Some of my Anglican friends maintain that Evelyn was largely responsible for my conversion to Rome. This is completely untrue as he never tried to convert me. In my case, it was a long slow process covering twenty years and started at Assisi in 1927, several years before I met Evelyn for the first time. However, when I let him know that I was under instruction with the Dominicans in Oxford, he was naturally delighted (though he would have preferred the Jesuits as he thought, or pretended to think that all Dominicans were Communists) and wrote me a series of encouraging letters. In India, I had been attracted to the Parsi religion and called my first horse out there – a delightful dark bay country-bred – Zoroaster. No one commented on this until his name appeared in a list of prize-winners at the Delhi Horse Show whereupon a devout Parsi quite justifiably wrote and complained to my father saying: 'How would you like it Sir if I called my horse Jesus Christ?' The dualism of the ancient Persian faith had always seemed to me very logical: that Ahura Mazda had created good creatures and Ahriman unpleasant ones. I had felt this very forcibly when contemplating the crocodile which had always seemed to me the personification of evil, even more than the snake. When I confided this to Evelyn he wrote back: 'You must fly dualism like the plague – it is at the root of almost all heresy. . . . The crocodile serves man in many ways – his hide for note-cases, bags, and dago shoes, his name to enrich our literature with metaphor, "crocodile tears", "as warm and friendly as an alligator pool" etc. Most especially he is a type and sign for us of our own unredeemed nature.'

I was received into the Roman Catholic Church in March 1948, and a little over a year later I was confirmed – along with a number of other adult converts – in the chapel of Blackfriars, Oxford. Nobody told me that it is usual for each candidate to have only one sponsor, and I somehow had it firmly fixed in my head that I, being female, should have two women sponsors and one man. I therefore asked Agnes Eyston, Elizabeth Pakenham and Evelyn. Elizabeth was unable to come, and Agnes and I arrived just as the ceremony was beginning, my Ford van having broken down on the way so that we had had to thumb a lift from a Birmingham business man in a Rolls who remarked: 'The trouble with you girls today is that you're too lazy to walk.'

Arrived at Blackfriars, we found Evelyn waiting impatiently at the back of the chapel, talking to Maurice Bowra who had come to see me confirmed. We hurried into a pew, I sitting between my male and female sponsors, when a lady in the pew behind leaned forward and said to Evelyn in a loud whisper that he ought to be on the other side of the chapel as this side was reserved for women candidates and their sponsors. Evelyn was furious and told her in no uncertain terms to mind her own business and when the time came for me to go up for the laying on of hands, Evelyn, undeterred, marched up with me and put his right hand on my left shoulder while Agnes stood on my right.

Sometime during the late Fifties, Evelyn and I and Christopher Sykes found ourselves together at the Grail in Sloane Street where Ronnie Knox was giving two lectures 'On Englishing the Bible', one in the morning and one in the afternoon. In between, Evelyn took him to lunch at White's. Ronnie was not a good extemporary lecturer, he simply wrote a beautiful essay and read it aloud, sitting down except when in the pulpit. The room was hot, he had doubtless had some excellent claret at White's and most naturally he dropped off for a couple of seconds over his afternoon paper: he nodded, then looked up startled and continued to read from the typescript on the table before him. We have all of us fallen asleep at lectures, especially when attending one after lunch, but it must be a fairly rare experience to be present at a lecture at which the lecturer himself falls asleep. As we were all trooping out afterwards Ronnie said to Evelyn:

'Did I go to sleep in that lecture?'

'Yes.'

'How long for?'

'Twenty minutes.'

9

'JUDGE AND JURY MUST DECIDE'

Douglas Woodruff

CONSERVATIVES were thin

on the ground in the Oxford Union in 1921, as the Coalition Government, with its huge Conservative majority and its Radical Prime Minister whom the majority did not trust, especially over the issue of Ireland, moved into its last year. The Union was full of Asquithian Liberals ranged against the Coalition, and so when word went round that Alec Waugh's younger brother had appeared at Hertford a strong Tory, I remember as President putting him down to be a speaker 'on the paper' for the Conservative side of a motion as E. A. St J. Waugh of Hertford. However, he did not persevere with any Union ambitions he may have had to become a speaker. Nor for that matter did he persevere as a scholar, and, as he tells us in the only volume he completed of his autobiography, his time at Oxford ended very unsatisfactorily, leaving behind a hazy memory of highly enjoyable social evenings in mushroom clubs and strange little pubs like the Nag's Head on the Canal in Station Road. So we were not in the least prepared for his sudden immense success as a comic novelist in 1929, when one would meet him at the luncheon parties of society hostesses, arriving in a large limousine and offering to take any of the guests anywhere they wished, saying 'I have a large car at my disposal because I am *nouveau riche.*'

It was only some two years later, after he had been received into the Church by Father Martin D'Arcy, our mutual friend, that I began to know him well, staying with him at the cottage he had taken near Salisbury from the painter Henry Lamb. His short-lived first marriage had broken up while he was following *Decline and Fall* with *Vile Bodies*, and beginning to show the world that his first book had been no isolated firework, but was the announcement of an extraordinarily rich and unfolding talent. An acute observer might have deduced from his first serious book, a study of Rossetti, how deep were the springs of romanticism in him. I believe that when he became a Catholic, he was quite prepared to take the consequences against his being able to marry again while his first wife lived. He had been educated at a High Anglican school, but in his revulsion against the moral laxity and crumbling standards of the Twenties, he did not feel any attraction towards the Church of his upbringing, because of the lack of steel in its structure; part of what appealed to him in Rome was that the Roman Church was a religion of authority. He was told that he might and should apply for an annulment of his first marriage on the ground that plainly one, and possibly both, of

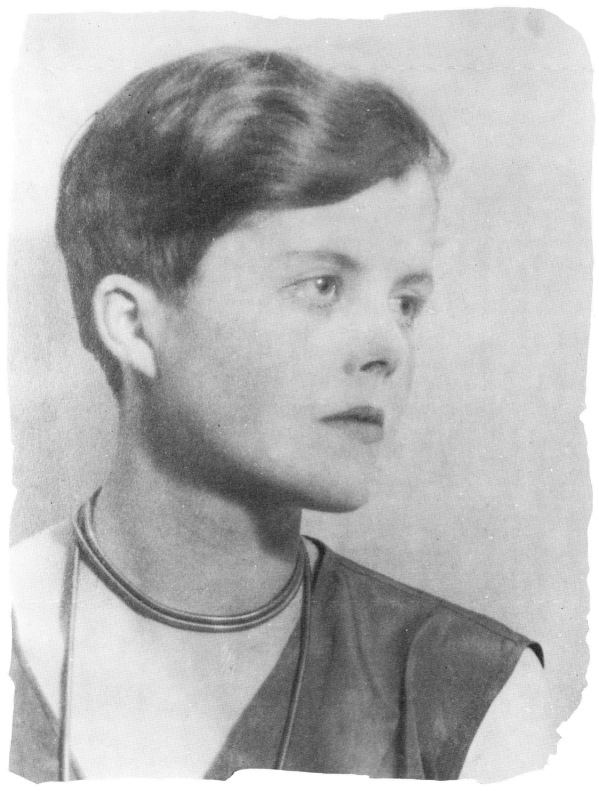

Hon Evelyn Gardner, his first wife, and a niece of Lord Carnarvon, the discoverer of Tutankhamun's tomb.

Canonbury Square

*Sitting-room of the Waughs' house in Canonbury
Square, Islington.*

No. 607.

Metropolitan Police.

_E_ ——— Division.

Bow St ——— Station.

Take Notice, that you _Evelyn Waugh_

are bound in the sum of _£2 · 0 · 0 (Two)_ Pounds to

appear at the _Bow St_ ——— Police Court, situated at

Covent Garden ——— at _10_

o'clock _A_ M., on the _7th_ day of _April_

192 _5_, to answer the charge of* _Drunk & Incapable_

and unless you then appear there, further proceedings will be taken.

Dated this _7th_ day of _April_

One Thousand Nine Hundred and _25_

T. Atmore Insp

Officer on Duty.

* Being found drunk in a public street, or being guilty, while drunk, of disorderly behaviour in a street, or whatever the charge may be.

50000-12-22-M.P. c5

An incident later transferred to Brideshead Revisited.

Villefranche has been full of those who write for publication, and here are the Hon. Patrick Balfour, Lord Kinross' eldest son and heir, and Mr. Evelyn Waugh, the well-known young novelist, seeking a bit of inspiration diluted with ozone. The Hon. Patrick Balfour is a diligent paragraphist and first-nighter

Taken from The Tatler c. *1930.*

With Patrick Balfour (later Lord Kinross) at the wedding of Alec Waugh. Inscribed on the back with:

Happy Augury of Industrial Peace.

Rich and Poor Mingle at Church Door.

Vicar says, 'Equal in the Sight of God'.

Evelyn Waugh: 1932.

A house party at Madresfield recorded in The Tatler c *1934*

In this snapshot a group of the young Intelligentsia may be seen engaged in the simple pleasure of making daisy-chains. They are LADY MARY LYGON, MR. OGILVIE-GRANT, MR. ALAN PRYCE-JONES (the brilliant young author), and LADY DOROTHY LYGON (l. to r.); and MR. and MRS. JOHN MASON in the background.

At Madresfield, from left to right: Evelyn Waugh,
Hamish St Clair Erskine, Lady Dorothy Lygon,
Hubert Duggan.

*With Lady Mary Lygon (left)
and Lady Dorothy Lygon.*

*Evelyn Waugh, duly labelled by himself, at Captain
Hance's riding school.*

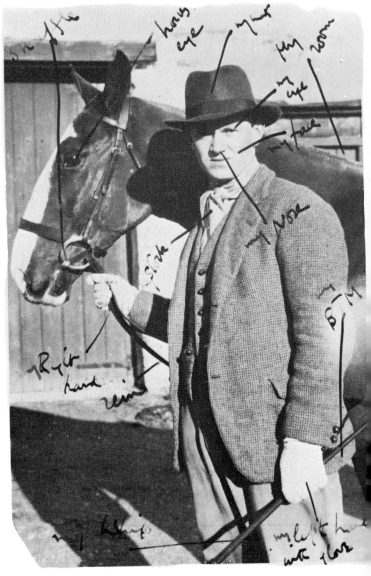

The original caption in The Tatler *runs: 'Mr Evelyn Waugh, the young novelist whose book,* Vile Bodies, *has been transformed into a successful play, was snapshotted recently as above when staying at Madresfield Court, the seat of Lord Beauchamp. He is posed beside a bust of the gluttonous Roman Emperor Vitellius – certainly a classical 'vile body'! Mr Waugh's new novel, which contains an account of a cannibalistic banquet, will soon be published.'*

With Alec Waugh on holiday at Villefranche.

Alastair Graham, the 'Hamish Lennox' of A Little Learning.

At a picture exhibition with Lord Berners and Lady Rosebery.

THE HON. NANCY FREEMAN MITFORD

'Your public, darling?' The inscription on
The Romance Reader, *a postcard sent to Nancy Mitford.*

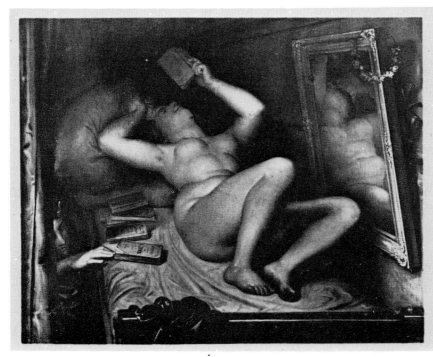

The Railway Club, Oxford, 1925.
Centre row, left to right: Lord Rosse, John Sutro,
Hugh Lygon, Harold Acton, Bryan Guinness (Lord
Moyne), Patrick Balfour, Mark Ogilvie-Grant, John
Drury-Lowe.
Rear row, left to right: Two porters, Henry Yorke
(Henry Green), Roy Harrod, Lord Weymouth (Lord
Bath), David Plunkett-Greene, Lord Stavordale,
Brian Howard.

The Railway Club on a last trip to Brighton, 1963.
Standing, left to right: Roy Harrod, Desmond Guinness,
Evelyn Waugh, Lord Boothby, John Sutro, Harold
Acton, Cyril Connolly, Henry Harrod, Giles
Fitzherbert, John Sparrow, Lord Antrim, Auberon
Waugh, Dominic Harrod.
Seated: Christopher Sykes, the chef, *Lord Bath.*

Staying at Mells: Osbert Sitwell (left) and Lord David Cecil.

The opening ceremony of Campion Hall, Oxford, 1934.
Front row, left to right: Sir Edward Lutyens, Father
D'Arcy, The Duke of Alba (Spanish Ambassador),
Sir David Lindsay (Master of Balliol), Father Ronald Knox.
Rear row, to Evelyn Waugh's left: Lady Horner,
Mrs Raymond Asquith, Mrs Aubrey Herbert.

the partners had not intended to form an indissoluble monogamous union. But he also knew that the Church authorities looked at the law of any country and it took, in fact, many years before the canonical obstacles were cleared.

Some of the delay was due to the personal weaknesses of the Westminster prelate through whose hand the application had to pass, and who was notorious for the way in which papers remained on his desk. Waugh was advised to give this prelate the best possible lunch in order to make a lasting and favourable impression, and so he invited him to the Ritz, and began with the usual preliminaries. 'Will you have oysters? caviare? smoked salmon?' To which the prelate said 'That would be very nice', and he had all three – a story not really to his discredit, for it shows how little accustomed he was to moving among the fleshpots, and that he had, indeed, spent most of his life in a seminary in which the peculiarly discouraging alternative of tea or water used to be offered at meals.

It was, I think, in 1932 that I took Evelyn to Stonyhurst for the retreat at which others who were not Old Stonyhurst boys were also welcomed. I took him by my usual method, which was the night train, changing at Crewe for Preston at about half past three, and walking about in Preston round the bandstand in the public gardens till the branch-line train to Whalley left at seven, which meant that one reached the College just in time for breakfast. He did not think this a very competent or agreeable method of travelling, though he saw that it had certain advantages in terms of a pilgrimage preparatory to a retreat. When the autobiography of the Elizabethan Jesuit, John Gerard, was read aloud in the refectory, he found full scope for his ear in detecting how far it had been modernised.

Stonyhurst is uniquely rich in manuscripts and other memorials of the centuries of persecution, and I think that this visit helped to awaken an interest which made him write as a thank-offering to Father D'Arcy, at that time Master of Campion Hall, his study of Edmund Campion, which was awarded the Hawthornden Prize for a work of marked distinction by an author under forty. I am thanked in the preface of that book for 'advice on several delicate matters of taste and discretion'. This was a private joke. I had just acquired the farmhouse in the Vale of the White Horse at which Campion had been captured, and I did not much relish seeing it described thus: 'The dissolute farmhouse now in the possession of Mr Douglas Woodruff, bears little resemblance to what it once had been.' And it is true that the most important part of a house big enough to require sixty men to surround and search it no longer exists, that what has gone includes the grander rooms and the staircase behind which Campion's hiding-place was found, and that of the moat that surrounded the whole property only two segments remain. But Evelyn saw my point, and substituted, 'The Grange still stands, shorn of its ancient grandeur, but still a place of poignant association to the Catholic visitor.' This began an interest in the English martyrs which continued and nourished an anti-ecumenical spirit which always filled him and made him very pointedly restrict the term of Christian to Catholic.

I was, in the early Thirties, still on the editorial staff of *The Times*, and in what was called the Imperial and Foreign Department, so it was not difficult for me to get him accredited to cover the coronation of the Emperor Haile Selassie as a *Times* Special Correspondent, after he told me that he was planning to go there in company with one of Lord Curzon's daughters, Irene Ravensdale. This had an important consequence, because what he wrote with his usual distinction on that occasion caused him to be approached by *The Daily Mail* the next year, to go back to Abyssinia to report, from the Italian side, the Italian invasion, and, as the coronation gave him material for *Black Mischief*, so the Abyssinian War gave him material for *Scoop*. These two hilarious works were an invaluable counter-balance to the profoundly serious book which I have always considered a masterpiece, *A Handful of Dust*, in which he said what he had to say about modern society without the religious dimension. The line he took about the Italian invasion, that it was a substitution of one imperialism for another, made him very unpopular with those who had been romanticising not only Abyssinians but, more reasonably, the League of Nations, whose future by the middle Thirties was plainly extremely parlous.

In the next year, 1936, there came the Spanish Civil War, which had a sundering effect on many literary and journalistic friendships. The supporters of what was called the Government or Republican or Loyalist side, but which was really the opposite of the western democracy of which it was pretending to be part, sought to enlist, as was easily done, the support of writers, or for that matter of actors and film stars. Evelyn was one of the small minority who stood up to be counted for the Nationalists.

But I think that he was growing increasingly tired of the way of life which London then offered to a young and successful writer, and when he married a wife who had been brought up in the country of the West of England, he bought a house in Gloucestershire near Dursley. In those years, he was busy buying, often for a very few pounds, the large 'situation' canvasses of Victorian painters, like Augustus Egg. These have since greatly appreciated, as Evelyn always believed they would. He was very far-sighted, and when after the war nearly everyone else was moving into smaller houses because of the difficulty of getting any domestic help, he moved into one much larger, some six miles from Taunton, where his eldest son has succeeded him. This again gave him scope for both pictures and books, discerningly bought, and after his death, rewardingly sold. He was particularly proud of a carpet in the bright colours of the Great Exhibition of 1851 which he had copied.

In the wartime years, we met only sporadically when he came on leave from the Marines at Deal, where the other officers of the Mess so feared his tongue and temper, according to his own account, that there were generally five places left vacant each side of him at meal-times. The first volume of his wartime trilogy, in which Guy Crouchback was the same age, thirty-six, when he began his life as a subaltern in the Halbardiers, showed the generation gap between him and the other subalterns, while the beginning of *Brideshead Revisited* shows in the character of Hooper what he found unpalatable in the younger generation of his fellow officers.

He grew restless in the Marines, and at one moment was appointed to the staff of a Major-General who, after the first evening, according to Evelyn, sent for him and told him that he could not have on his staff officers who got 'foxed', an expression which Evelyn found new but whose meaning he gathered. He replied that from his point of view there could be no question of changing the habits of a lifetime for a purely temporary appointment. Following this brief encounter, he claimed that a friend in the War Office told him that he was simultaneously on two different lists. One was that of officers available for general employment, which led to his being offered the management of a hospital in India which he asked leave to decline, but there was another list of officers unsuitable for responsible employment owing to habits of inebriety. This was no doubt mythical, because he did succeed in being further employed, though he was finally disappointed. He enjoyed military life much more after he had secured a transfer to the Commandos, and when he was a member of the Household Cavalry, he observed the greatest punctilio, being delighted that he must never be seen carrying a parcel or riding in a bus.

The transfer was made possible by his wide acquaintance in White's and Buck's with those who were organising Commandos, and he achieved his great ambition of being in action, in Crete. He sprained his foot in the first stages of parachute training which involved jumping from a moving car, and lay up for some time in the Hyde Park Hotel. I always thought that he was a very odd choice as a member of the mission to Tito. He would have been much more at home with the mission which the British Government also maintained for a time with Mihailovic and the anti-Communist Serbian forces; it was the opportunism of our policy towards the Serbs, Croats and Slovenes which he saw at such close quarters which accounts for the bitter note on which his trilogy ends, with the title *Unconditional Surrender*. I do not know the circumstances which led to his being disappointed and left out of the Normandy Invasion, but it required all his reserves of fortitude to retire to his favourite writing retreat, Chagford in Devon, to write *Brideshead Revisited* in the early months of 1944. Certainly, he retained a lasting grudge against some who had been his superiors, though not against Robert Laycock, one of the three dedicatees of *Sword of Honour*. He was not surprised at the post-war developments in Britain which were not at all to his liking.

I think that he was sorry that it became the general custom after World War II for those who had held temporary commissions to drop their military rank, in sharp contrast with the dominant custom after the First World War which filled society with majors and captains, and while he played for a time with the idea of calling himself Captain Waugh, he had to drop it after a few years, though he was sufficiently attached to it for some of his acquaintances, like Osbert Lancaster, to get in the habit of talking of him as 'the Captain'.

He found much satisfaction in his young family, and in playing the part, as he conceived it, of the affectionate but strict *paterfamilias* of nineteenth-century children's books, of the kind in which, when the father sent for his daughter to scold her, the author would write: 'she entered the presence of the august author of her being'. He said that one of the particular pleasures of being a father was when the children believed what they were told, and he would point to the golf links near Dursley and expound how it was a punishment ground or exercise yard in which poor colonels had to go round and round, hitting a ball into a distant hole, and then starting all over again before they were allowed anything to eat. But then he had very strong views against exercise, taking the line that in middle life everyone's inside is full of poisons which will lie dormant unless provoked by violent exercise and sent swirling round inside their unfortunate carrier. A little archery, with the targets not too far away, was about as far as he would go. A gentleman's residence should have grounds in which their owner might stroll sedately up and down, surveying his peacocks, of whom he approved as dignified creatures.

In 1947, I took him to Spain on an unlikely outing. The Spaniards have always felt that Protestant prejudice has given to Hugo Grotius the credit, which should really belong to the Spanish Dominican Francisco de Vittoria, of being the father of modern International Law, for Vittoria was a sixteenth-century and Grotius a seventeenth-century figure. With the rise of sovereign states and the collapse of the medieval attempts to create some sort of universal jurisdiction, there was obviously a crying need for the formulation of what we have come to call International Law, though I believe that the word 'international' itself we owe to Macaulay. Anyway, the Spaniards staged a Congress of International Lawyers for the fourth centenary of Vittoria's birth. The Congress came a little soon, two years after the end of the war in which General Franco had sent a Blue Division against the Russians, who had not unnaturally wanted the Allies to proceed against him after their victory. The Allies only went as far as withdrawing their ambassadors. But it was not altogether a propitious moment for the Spaniards to appear as champions of International Law, and they did not get as many professorial acceptances as they would have liked. So it was indicated that one did not have to be a professor of Law to be very welcome at these celebrations, and Evelyn gladly accepted an invitation for the chance of a new experience.

The result of his visit was *Scott-King's Modern Europe*, in which, with his usual deftness, by saying that the action had happened in a former portion of the Hapsburg dominions, he suggested Central Europe, being conscious that this was really rather a poor return for Spanish hospitality. He had quickly discerned one of the chronic weaknesses of commemorative celebrations, that they tend to end very abruptly when those who have been retained to look after the guests, reach the day and the hour at which their obligations cease. As official hospitality is ended, the guests may find themselves left to their own devices, and some of the professors who hoped that they had lived up to the best traditions of Spanish hospitality, which are very high, were much mortified to find the impression they had left, not making enough allowance for the novelist's skill and imagination. There was a very severe currency control in Spain at that time, and Evelyn easily envisaged the guest not being able to leave, just as it had struck him in the remoter parts of South America how completely the exploring traveller might find himself at the mercy of some gnarled and callous old man, as happened to Tony Last at the end of *A Handful of Dust*. Anyway, I declined the dedication of this *opusculum*, and so he dedicated it instead to my wife, which is the explanation of the Latin dedication: 'To the bolder wife of a more prudent husband'. But in the personal copy, he wrote more pungently, in his mother tongue, a dedication: 'To the lion wife of a church mouse husband'.

I incurred the same reproach a little later. He had paid a visit to Sweden on one of the rare occasions on which he accepted a literary invitation. He sent to *The Tablet* a probably somewhat improved version of the outpourings of a Swedish poet, rambling on in lacrymose inebriation, in the vein that Evelyn was not reciprocating his affection, that while he loved Evelyn, Evelyn loved only the Pope, and more to the same effect. Knowing that Pius XII, a great reader of Catholic journals, had been inculcated by Sir D'Arcy Osborne, our Minister to the Holy See during the War, into becoming a somewhat embarrassingly sedulous reader of *The Tablet*, without always knowing English as well as he hoped he did, this might have been very much misunderstood. But the refusal to print brought one of Evelyn's curt postcards, 'The Pop [*sic*] is an ass and so are you.'

As a novelist, he very much disliked anyone who went in for crude identifications of his fictional characters with living models. Not only did this detract from the appreciation due to the novelist's artistic skill in selecting and blending, taking one trait here and another there, but it could easily evoke needless enmities. The disclaimer which novelists put at the beginning of their novels, that all characters are fictitious, is not, I understand, a sufficient defence in law, since any novelist can put it at the beginning of a most photographically exact and libellous account of the people and place he is describing. Having recognised my own flat in Evelyn Mansions, Carlisle Place, as being described in *Unconditional Surrender* as 'Bourne Mansions', when I next wrote to him I headed my letter Bourne Mansions. Evelyn's riposte was to send to my wife an anonymous postcard, signed 'A Wellwisher', but in undisguised writing, saying: 'Your aged but incontinent husband is keeping a second establishment at Bourne Mansions, a name particularly distressing to those of us who knew and revered the late Cardinal.'

The only quarrel I had with him in these years was when the well-known Dominican Father Gerard Meath reviewed his *Helena* together with a book also on St Helena by Dorothy Sayers, the two clashing after decades without any book about that great figure in early Church history. One sentence gave the impression that whereas Dorothy Sayers was uninfluenced by any worldly consideration, Evelyn tended to confuse sanctity with being an Empress and an Emperor's mother. It was an unfortunate sentence, which Evelyn termed an 'odious imputation' but he also combined it with a pointless objection to having been called 'Evelyn Waugh' instead of Mr or Captain Waugh, and this caused me to tell Father Meath that I did not think he need take it seriously. Evelyn, however, did take it seriously, and threatened legal action; I have a postcard beginning 'Judge and Jury must decide', as well as a very long confession composed for my signature and publication in *The Tablet*. When a little later he published a slight work on the Holy Places which he had visited for the writing of *Helena*, I was able to take the occasion of noticing that book to do him justice on the point of St Helena, and at that time I was also lucky enough to find a little polychrome statue of her – they must be very uncommon – which I sent him and he liked.

When he went to Hollywood, expecting a large sum for the film rights of *Brideshead*, he asked me to draw up a list of deserving causes to which he should give some part of the expected proceed. But by a curious irony it was because of the Catholic Legion of Decency, or so I understand, for I have not checked on the details, that the film contract fell through. The producers wanted such changes in the plot as could meet the Legion of Decency's criteria and to this Evelyn would not agree. In consequence, the principal result of this Californian visit was *The Loved One*, when he became fascinated by Forest Lawn, and before its publication he contributed to *The Tablet* a foreshadowing article on 'Californian Burial Customs' as an anthropologist or archaeologist might have dealt with them. He would not take payment for contributions to *The Tablet*, whose straitened circumstances he was inclined very much to exaggerate, and to think that waiving payment entitled him to be as rude as he liked to *The Tablet* staff. His contributions were also sometimes lacking in that minimal charity which the world rightly expects in religious journalism. I thought also that from an apostolic point of view, it was preferable that his writings should appear in the general weeklies, notably *The Spectator*.

But *The Spectator* was a curious place in which to find his eloquent appeal, an appeal uttered, alas, quite in vain, to the English hierarchy, not to change the old rite of the Mass. It was headed 'The same again, please' and evoked a very wide response, and it remains a succinct and cogent account of the case against the changes, and also against the attempt to treat the very miscellaneous group of Catholics who go to any particular church as having on that account much else in common. In this part of his plea, Evelyn was helped by the new mood of ecumenism, for which otherwise he had little sympathy. It was difficult for the Catholic authorities, though they tried to do it, to say at one and the same time that Catholics should mix in more with their neighbours, join up with Anglicans and Nonconformists for joint social action, but also think of themselves as a group in a parish separated from the non-Catholic majority around them.

Evelyn had a great dislike of people foisting social intercourse upon him. When he met John Freeman in a television interview, and John Freeman went probing to find out why Evelyn chose to live in the depths of the country when he was not interested in country sports or rural pursuits, he was being truthful as well as neat in repartee when he said that it was 'to get away from people like you'. And he did not at all relish his attendance at Sunday Mass six miles away in Taunton, involving him in unwanted social contacts. I was successful in persuading him that as a well-known convert to the Church he had a duty to accept invitations from student bodies and other Catholic societies, because such societies can exist only if they arrange meetings which their members can look forward to, and he agreed to accept all such invitations for a year. Some of them he found very trying, as university student societies tend to be, because the officers are always inexperienced in the art of looking after their visitors. After a time, he began to flag and to call his natural inclinations into play to get out of the journeys and discomfort of visiting provincial universities. When the Catholic students at nearby Bristol invited him to address them, he replied that he would be glad to do so, and went on to fix the place as the lawn in front of his house as well as the day and the hour on which he would receive them. Afterwards, he had a card printed regretting that he could accept no engagements for the next five years, to prevent successive secretaries renewing their solicitations. At one time, he contemplated seeking leave to rewrite G. K. Chesterton's *Everlasting Man*, being greatly influenced by its argument but hating its fireworks style.

His friendship with Ronald Knox ripened in the last nine years of Knox's life when he had moved to Somerset. Ronald Knox greatly appreciated a public tribute which Evelyn paid him in *The Sunday Times* as the finest writer of English in our day. The dedication to *Enthusiasm* which Ronald had not originally intended to offer to anyone, was the prompt result. Evelyn was not really likely to appreciate the theme of *Enthusiasm*, which had been originally conceived as an apologetic work to show the need for authority in religion by tracing out in some detail the vagaries and eccentricities to which private judgment so easily leads. But as the work progressed, Knox became more and more impressed with the nobility of character which he so often found in conjunction with intellectual aberration, and the total impression of the work is very different from what he had originally in mind. He was aware of this, and when his last illness struck him, he had just embarked on a much more direct, large-scale apologetic work. He chose Evelyn to be his literary executor as well as his biographer. Some of their mutual friends thought that this was a skilful contrivance on Knox's part, feeling that Evelyn would be all the better for being brought into close association with the institutional life of the Church, but I think that the explanation was much simpler, that he felt sure that Evelyn would do him effective justice as a writer of English. Knox believed himself to be achieving in his translation, singlehanded, of the whole of the Old and New Testament, something that would endure, and it was a mercy that he died before seeing his translation faced with a great deal of competition and very rapidly displaced in favour of other versions like the Revised Standard Version or the Jerusalem Bible. For a man so genuinely imbued with the Oxford tradition, not talking about his own writings and referring deprecatingly to them if anyone else brought them up, Knox was very sensitive if anyone criticised even the most contentious of his renderings.

Evelyn embarked on the Knox biography with the greatest thoroughness and it involved research in quarters quite unfamiliar to him, like the Anglican episcopal background, or life at the Westminster seminary, St Edmund's College, Ware. When he invited me down to Combe Florey in the course of the work, he took me into the library after dinner and took out paper and pen, and then said

'I am sorry to make this so formal, but I find if I do not I take a lot of trouble for nothing.' He went on to relate that he had invited a principal witness for the St Edmund's period (it was Monsignor John Barton) to dine at the Hyde Park Hotel. They had dined well and talked long, but Evelyn had taken no notes, and when he awoke in the morning he realised that he did not remember any of the things he had been told, and while he was ruefully contemplating, a note was brought of warm thanks for a splendid evening in which Monsignor Barton went on to say 'I am afraid I talked much too much and much too indiscreetly. For Heaven's sake be careful what use you make of what I told you.'

Evelyn was incapable of bad or slovenly work, but the biography, though it sold very well, disappointed a good many of Ronald Knox's old friends, and some of the priests among them, in particular, felt that the whole picture was too sombre, that Evelyn had known his subject only in the last years of his life, and that this had coloured his outlook. Knox had an operation for cancer in February 1957, and Evelyn took him on a holiday in Sidmouth and elsewhere, during which it became slowly but clearly evident that he was not recovering, which was finally confirmed by Sir Horace Evans in June just before Ronald Knox made his last public appearance, giving the Romanes Lecture on Translation. Before Knox died, Evelyn had made an attempt to secure for his friend a Cardinal's hat, a rather crude gesture of friendship which may have played its part in causing Pius XII to send the distinguished English priest a relic of the recently beatified Pope Innocent XI, kindly meant and an unusual distinction. The irony of the gift was not lost on its recipient, for the Knoxes belonged to the Protestant Ascendancy in Northern Ireland, and Innocent XI was the Pope who had warmly approved of William of Orange taking the English throne, considering James II no more than a satellite king of the overbearing Gallican Louis XIV.

My review of the Knox life brought me a curious letter from Evelyn which said that many of Ronald's friends had thought it too critical but that he thought it just and wise, which I think was a way of telling me that he was not altogether pleased, but knew that authors should never complain of reviews. Afterwards he thought that because of my connection with Burns & Oates, the publishers of the Knox Bible but not of much else from Knox's pen, our ancient friendship might be clouded by the Knox estate. This happily did not occur, and he was a most reasonable executor.

What did overcloud his later years was the Second Vatican Council, and still more, all the people who tried to use it to push the Church in Protestant or liberal directions which they called, and for that matter still call, the spirit of Vatican II. He had become a Catholic thirty years earlier from a profound conviction of the essential need for authority in religion, and he saw those who should be upholding that authority apparently weakening before the spirit of the age, instead of realising that the spirit of the age, with its endemic anti-authoritarianism, made it more and not less necessary for the Church authorities to stand their ground. When I tried in *The Tablet* to bring some comfort to the bewildered and unhappy Catholics, particularly the elderly and the converts, by reminding them that in every century some sudden tempest of one kind or another had arisen to toss the bark of Peter, Evelyn pointed out that in Church history the response of the Church to these successive challenges had not been to give way to them, and that as a consequence of the exercise of her authority, most of the challenges had died away so that only scholars know about them. He had accepted the Church's discipline for himself at a time when it might have proved a severe and life-long burden.

The publisher was very discerning who spotted, after *Brideshead* and *Sword of Honour*, how deeply romantic Evelyn was, and commissioned him to write on the Crusades. I conjecture that that publisher was inspired by the opening pages of *Sword of Honour*, when Crouchback prays at the old crusader's tomb in Genoa. Evelyn accepted the commission, and as with previous commissions, turned to his friends for help in providing the raw material such as I had just provided for a highly lucrative study published in America of John XXIII, not a figure very congenial to Evelyn. But the Crusades book weighed on him. He could foresee how scholars like Steven Runciman might treat his amateur history, and yet he had not shirked the formidable historical challenge in writing about St Helena – but that had been more than ten years before. Certainly, when he renounced the project, a huge weight was lifted from his mind. His brother tells us that after his unsuccessful schoolmastering, it had been decided that he should do what he really liked, which would be making fine furniture, and Evelyn himself has recorded that writing never gave him the same intense satisfaction he found in working with wood. His love of the aristocratic world was in large part because of the possessions among which they moved, the eighteenth-century furniture of the cabinet-makers, the creators of masterpieces with which they proved their proficiency.

It always struck me what a heavy price Evelyn paid for the quickness and piercing quality of his perceptions. He was constantly suffering from *ennui*, which ought to be recognised as a major affliction more wearing and painful than most physical disabilities. He constantly found that reality fell short of anticipation and I remember him saying sadly one afternoon in White's, having called for champagne and looking gloomily at the bottle after it had arrived: 'It sounded as though it was going to be jolly, and then somehow it isn't.'

He could be capriciously and inexcusably rude, to women as well as to men. There were physical signs which showed themselves on such occasions, a boiled gooseberry eye and flushed features. I think that these came from internal tensions, a lack of relish for living, though life had treated him kindly; an absence of the note of joy on which the Church insists for sanctity. A great deal must stand to his credit, and he was full of surreptitious good deeds, not only the helping hand in a material sense, but the friendly push when he judged that a friend was ripe for the decisions he ought to take – which is an altogether rarer gift. But he also liked to say the disconcerting thing in the hopes of making something happen or getting a rise, or in some other way breaking the monotony of all too easily predictable social exchanges. He may be said to have been at the end of so many conversations before they began, knowing what the other person would say, and finding the encounter in consequence highly tedious; for in spite of many alleviations his life and circumstances brought him, that inner dreariness was never driven sufficiently far away, and remained the heavy price he paid for his eagle eye and lightning apprehension.

10

CAPTAIN WAUGH

Fitzroy Maclean

'**THE** trouble, you know', said Randolph confidentially, 'is that so few of your officers are my social or intellectual equals.' 'I don't mean you, of course', he added as an afterthought. It was in March 1944. We were in the mountains of Bosnia, snowbound and entirely surrounded by Germans, and it was not immediately obvious to me how I could satisfy Randolph's yearning for more glittering company or indeed my own feeling, after three months of Randolph at very close quarters, that my officers and I could perhaps also do with a change. The answer, as it turned out, was provided by the German High Command, who, when the weather got finer, suddenly launched a mass airborne attack against Tito's Headquarters, during which, incidentally, Randolph, as always in an emergency, behaved himself admirably and with great courage.

By mid-summer he and I found ourselves no longer in Bosnia, but installed in relative security on the off-shore island of Vis.

Randolph was never short of ideas. (He had even, I found, set about arranging a marriage for me.) And, now that he was temporarily in touch with the outside world, those ideas came bubbling up relentlessly. His latest thought was that it would be fun to have Evelyn Waugh with us. Shimi Lovat, he explained, on temporarily taking charge of Combined Operations, had at once got rid of Evelyn. This abrupt liquidation, arising from some obscure Roman Catholic vendetta, struck him as grossly unfair. All Evelyn wanted to do, after all, was to help fight the Germans. Could I not provide him with the opportunity to do so?

We needed officers at the time and this struck me as better than some of Randolph's ideas. Evelyn, I knew, had fought bravely under unpleasant circumstances in Crete. His early travels testified to enterprise and resilience. And, finally, looking around me, I saw no harm in having someone with us possessing his gifts as a writer.

I was also, I must admit, influenced by another consideration. Here, at last, was someone well qualified to contain Randolph, someone whom, with minor adjustments, he might even regard as his social and intellectual equal. I badly needed a new mission for Croatia, where the Germans were giving the Partisans a worse time than usual and could be counted on to keep anyone I sent there fully employed. Adding Freddy Birkenhead for good measure, I gave instructions for the three of them to be infiltrated, as the phrase went, soonest. With them, to leaven the mixture, I sent Stephen Clissold, an old Yugoslav hand, speaking the language fluently and possessing a calm temperament and amiable disposition. Rightly or wrongly, it seemed to me a well-balanced outfit and one in which the Partisans would find reflected many of their own qualities.

Not long afterwards, as a first step, Captain Evelyn Waugh reported for duty on Vis, wearing, I seem to recall, the uniform of an officer of the Royal Horse Guards. After the austerity of German-occupied Bosnia, life on Vis was almost luxurious. There was enough to eat and drink, and time for what Randolph used to call jolly jokes. One of Evelyn's favourite jokes was that Tito was a woman. She, he kept saying. Her body-guard. Her guerrilla forces. And we all laughed, I with vague forebodings.

A day or two later, before Randolph and his companions left for Croatia, Tito came down from the cave in which he was living on Mount Hum to visit me at my Headquarters by the shore. It was a hot day and we went for a swim. Tito was wearing nothing but a pair of exiguous and extremely close-fitting swimming pants. 'Captain Waugh', I said, producing Evelyn, 'of the Royal Horse Guards.' Tito shook him by the hand, looking at him through clear, steady, light-blue eyes. 'Ask Captain Waugh', he said, 'why he thinks I am a woman.' Impressed once again by Tito's universal awareness, I passed on the enquiry. Evelyn looked embarrassed; Tito smiled; and the introduction was over. They did not, as far as I know, meet again.

A week later, Randolph's party left for Croatia. A first-hand account of how they fared will be found elsewhere in this volume. The first report that I received of how things were going, apart from official signals, was brought to me a good deal later in Serbia by Stephen Clissold, who had walked through the German lines, partly, no doubt, in order to deliver it, but partly, I think also, as a rest cure.

11

FIERY PARTICLES

The Earl of Birkenhead

WHEN I look back on my first few months in enemy-occupied Yugoslavia, my memories seem to resolve themselves into a double biography of Evelyn Waugh and Randolph Churchill, as one might imagine one of Gladstone and Dizzy, and at this distance they have become inseparable in the mind. I had first met Evelyn shortly after he had gone down from Oxford, when he resembled an alert and malicious faun. I believed, perhaps with optimism, that he liked me, but our meetings over the years had been intermittent, and our service in Yugoslavia was the first time I had been continuously in his presence.

Evelyn seemed to me to belong in temper and sympathy to the school of aesthetes like Harold and William Acton who descended upon Oxford in the 1920s bringing a new and esoteric message. They did something to civilise a University long rooted in orthodox scholarship, politics and athletics, which also contained a fair leavening of eldest sons from aristocratic families who drank champagne at breakfast and were often to be found flourishing hunting-whips and breaking windows in Peckwater Quad. The Acton brothers brought to Oxford a wide knowledge of European, and particularly Florentine culture. Periodically debagged and cast by the Christ Church *magnificos* into the water-lilies of Mercury, they continued to propagate the aesthetic ideal boldly and with much success. They declaimed *The Waste Land* through megaphones from balconies to bemused passers-by and decorated their rooms in elaborate Victorian parody with an elegance hitherto unknown.

I formed the impression that their sophistication and passion for the arts appealed strongly to Evelyn's own instincts. These men were precious, outrageous and mature beyond their years. They had exalted folly into a kind of philosophy, and this too appealed to him. I heard Evelyn refer with amusement to Harold Acton's alleged declaration in an Italian accent: 'My dears, I want to go into the fields and *slap* raw meat with lilies.' It was also obvious that Evelyn had formed a withering contempt for the *jeunesse dorée* in the Bullingdon Club. He saw them as arrogant scions of noble or county families, like his character Sir Alastair Digby-Vane-Trumpington whom he pulverised in the superb opening chapter of *Decline and Fall*.

It was therefore not without amusement that one discovered, as his tastes matured, that when Evelyn began to find pleasure in aristocratic society and the houses these people inhabited, the Sir Alastairs, once objects of loathing and mauled in his writings, became numbered among his closest friends. He was indeed frequently to be found with them in their spiritual home, their *sanctum sanctorum*, White's Club, of which he also had significantly become a member. This change of heart can be attributed not, as some ill-wishers thought, to latent snobbishness, but to the fact that he had come to the conclusion that his earlier judgment had been wrong, and that although few of his friends could be described as intellectuals, there was an inherited ease in their manners and an elegance in their surroundings which made a strong appeal to one side of his nature.

His extraordinary love affair with the army was more difficult to fathom, and to me remained baffling to the end. No less probable conformist to the institutional life could have been imagined. One would have thought that his fastidious mind would have been repelled by enforced and continuous association with uncongenial people. I imagined also that as he never played games nor took any form of exercise, he must be physically unfit and would find the life hard and probably indecorous.

Yet no one could have embraced the new love with a greater ardour than Evelyn, and few can have been more courageous. He deliberately chose the branches of the service most likely to be exposed to extreme hazard – the Royal Marines and the Commandos. General Laycock, for a time Commander of the latter, told me that Evelyn and Randolph Churchill were two of the bravest officers he had ever known, although he qualified this tribute by adding that it was necessary to place them in special positions – Evelyn as Intelligence Officer – rather than as Troop leaders, as he suspected that otherwise both might be shot by their own men as soon as battle was joined. Even more surprising was Evelyn's complete acceptance of military life and his apparent absorption in it. In the early period of the war, when I saw him from time to time, the love affair was at its high noon of tenderness and passion. Having been ill at ease in army life, I pondered in amazement on the Oxford aesthetes.

It always seemed to me that Evelyn, like Max Beerbohm, but probably for different reasons, had decided to drop an iron visor over all his intimate feelings and serious beliefs and by so doing excluded one from any understanding of his true character. As a result of this frustrating device it was impossible for him ever to discuss such matters, or if occasionally he approached them, he could do so only with a frivolity which masked his inmost thoughts. This deep reticence detracted in a sense from his conversation, which was of the highest order, because however brilliant and witty, one always felt that he was playing some elaborate charade which demanded from him constant wariness and vigilance. Presumably he discarded this alien *persona* in his family circle, and as a devout Roman Catholic bared his soul to his priests. One had the impression that there was also a handful of friends of long standing with whom he might allow the mask to slip, but never far enough to give a full revelation. For the rest of us, it was as if he was embarrassed by his own emotions and felt that it would not only be grossly improper but also commonplace to give any hint of their nature, and would indeed be a form of indecent exposure. Those of my degree of acquaintance were thus precluded from any intimate or serious discussion, and my admiration for him did not blind me to the fact that his character included a strong element of *Schadenfreude*.

I had spent the first three years of the war in a Territorial Anti-Tank Regiment and after a course at the Staff College, found myself posted to the Political Intelligence Department of the Foreign Office, also known as the Political Warfare Executive, PWE.

It was while working in PWE that I was given the opportunity of joining one of the military liaison missions which, under the command of Brigadier Fitzroy Maclean, were dotted in small groups over enemy-occupied Yugoslavia and attached to the local headquarters of Tito's Partisan army. Maclean was an able member of the Foreign Office who had left it in order to join the army. He had fought with distinction in the Western Desert and other theatres, and apart from being a skilled diplomatist and fine writer, had shown himself to be equally impressive as a soldier, and a born leader of men. The Prime Minister, casting round to find a 'warrior-ambassador' to send to Tito, had picked Fitzroy Maclean, and he could not have made a better choice. After parachuting into Yugoslavia, he had had many desperate adventures, and had been successful in the forbidding task of winning the Partisan leader's confidence, even to the extent of becoming a personal friend.

Having no idea of the conditions to be expected in the part of Yugoslavia to which I would be posted, I made thorough preparations. I obtained from my doctor an ample medicine chest, and was given by the Birmingham Small Arms Company a superb folding sub-machine gun which they had recently developed. I had a feeling that being impractical and useless with my hands, I should need help, and the colonel of my Regiment, no doubt at considerable personal risk, provided me with a batman, a red-haired ex-coalminer from Durham who, he said, could turn his hand to anything and who proved to be imperturbable in any emergency.

After flying to neutral Lisbon and then Gibraltar, we reached Bari, the last staging post on the way to Yugoslavia. This town had been Mussolini's model seaport: now vanquished and decaying, it was a melancholy symbol of the transience and sterility of Fascism. How much Evelyn despised Bari and its residents can be clearly seen in the third volume of his war trilogy. The reason for his contempt was that he saw Bari as the refuge of disgracefully *embusqués* officers too cowardly to fight, who skulked there in ignoble safety.

Being less of a fire-eater than Evelyn and less impatient to get to grips with the enemy, I found it pleasant to spend a few weeks in Bari being briefed by Brigadier Maclean's headquarters and by my own department, and trying to master the complex and blood-mottled history of Yugoslavia. It was agreeable also to meet some old friends, particularly Lt Col William Deakin, who had been with me in the Oxfordshire Yeomanry, and who was the first British officer to be dropped to Tito's headquarters. He had arrived at the height of the Germans' Fifth Offensive in Montenegro, and had undergone a hideous experience with the Marshal's encircled army, being chased like animals for weeks in the mountains before they broke the ring.

I asked the officer in charge of PWE if I should go on a parachute course and was told that if this became necessary he would arrange it, but that the area of Yugoslavia for which I was first bound had a landing strip which, although often flooded, was at the moment in use. I learned that I was to be sent as second-in-command of a mission in Croatia, commanded by Randolph Churchill and of which Evelyn Waugh was the other member.

This news at once stimulated and disturbed me. My memories of Randolph extended to the mists of early childhood. Our families were closely linked, and our fathers intimate friends; at Christmas every year, we were taken to Blenheim. He was afterwards my fag at Eton – the only period in my life in which he had treated me with oily servility – and thenceforth we met frequently over the years. He was therefore my earliest friend, and although that brief authority at school had long been permanently lost, we found pleasure in one another's company, provided it was not too constant.

Randolph had been dropped into Yugoslavia to appear *deus ex machina* – the Prime Minister's son – a visible symbol, as he was paraded through stark and battered villages, of Great Britain's solidarity with Yugoslavia in the common cause. The springlike beauty of his youth which glows on the canvas of de László had faded, but although his face had coarsened, there were still traces of it. He was now a resolute and well set-up man who had fought with courage, survived a *pokrit* – one of those terrible forced retreats over the mountains – and an air accident in the wilds of Yugoslavia, when he was pulled from the flames in which many others had perished. He was a man essentially of the same tough calibre as the Partisan soldiers with whom his lot had been cast.

His adventures had thus been numerous and, like Evelyn, he was without fear. His almost insolent and contemptuous physical courage was indeed never disputed by even his worst enemies, whose numbers were not few. To me, the difference between him and Evelyn in this respect was that Randolph was liable to be stimulated by danger to a delicious excitement which accentuated a natural tendency to hysteria, while Evelyn remained calm, glacial and unmoved. But I was uneasily conscious that during all the years of our friendship I had never spent more than a few days in Randolph's company without some cosmic upheaval, and the idea of being for an indefinite period under his command in a small outpost was one for sombre reflection. Evelyn also, I thought, might prove a doubtful factor at close quarters, and the feline sorties that disturbingly broke his habitual charm, when he exchanged the velvet for the claw, might have a disruptive effect in a closed circle.

I met the officer who was to accompany me on the mission. This was Major Stephen Clissold, also a member of my department, whose charm and sanity were to ease many a grim situation. He had formerly been a lecturer at Zagreb University and was a fluent Serbo-Croat speaker. Clissold was an expert on the Partisan Movement and had written a standard work on the subject. Although some thought that he had viewed it through eyes too starry, he was recognised as the leading authority. I wondered what on earth he would make of us.

We left Bari on Friday, 13 November in an aged Dakota flown by a Russian pilot. It seemed an unhappy combination of chances. The pilot adjusted our parachutes, indicating in clumsy mime with guffaws and abrupt downward gestures that in case of use they were unlikely to open. We flew high in order to avoid enemy interception and it was bitterly cold. There were no riding-lights on the machine:

no stars or moon, and the night was of inky blackness. After two hours, we began our descent, and I saw a few dimly twinkling lights which we found afterwards to be feeble oil lanterns. Not unmindful of Randolph's disaster on the same flight, I watched our progress narrowly. It seemed to me improbable that the pilot could touch down in darkness with such pathetic illumination, but at the last moment he switched on powerful headlights and landed like thistle-down. It was plain, even if his sense of humour was macabre, that the Russian pilot understood his job.

After we landed, all lights were immediately doused, and when we left the machine our nostrils were immediately struck by an over-whelmingly sweet scent of new cut hay, as delicious as the whiff of a beanfield caught from a passing car. I could not understand how this could be at the time of year, and never discovered afterwards. We were at once surrounded by women Partisan soldiers, unlovely Amazons, as we were later to discover, who manhandled our heavy baggage like stevedores, tossing it from hand to hand. The last kitbag was scarcely out before the machine was again airborne, the sound of its engines slowly receding. Bundled into a jeep, we were driven a short distance and stopped before a small building outside which there was a strong smell of animals. On the threshold, his arms spread wide in ecstatic welcome, stood Randolph.

He greeted me with manic affection and shouts of joy, which would have been touching if one had not known from long experience how capricious his favour was. A shake of the kaleidoscope, and a new mood and temper were instantly revealed. Constant change was the breath of life to him and I had the perhaps unworthy suspicion that the warmth of his greeting owed much to the rigours of his enforced confinement with Evelyn, and the appearance of new faces and a fresh, unjaded captive audience. I introduced him to Clissold and the batman, explaining that Clissold was a fluent Serbo-Croat speaker

As we were talking, Evelyn, a demure figure in a brown woollen dressing-gown, joined us, summoned by Randolph's raucous bellows. 'There he is!' roared the Mission Commander – 'there's the little fellow in his camel-hair dressing-gown! Look at him standing there!' Evelyn directed on him a stare cold and hostile as the Arctic Ocean, and remarked with poisonous restraint: 'You've got drunk very quickly tonight. Don't send any more signals.'

Both were short but sturdy, and as I watched them standing there in angry and ridiculous confrontation I was reminded of a pair of belligerent robins, while Clissold, I thought, resembled a tall and elegant water-bird wading in the shallows. Having discharged his poisoned dart, Evelyn abruptly left us, while Randolph, still a trifle angry, explained that the farm building was his headquarters, and that it contained four rooms. Evelyn was in one, he told me; he had put Clissold in another, and 'since we are old friends', I was to share his own. This was a privilege of the most dubious kind and my heart sank.

Our humble dwelling had one notable distinction. It possessed the only indoor privy in Topusco, a dark and noisome hole with a bottomless pit from the top of which I once saw a large rat emerging, which did not encourage me to use it more often than was strictly necessary. This unique convenience reminded one that one was in the company of the Prime Minister's son, to salute whose indispensable presence unheard-of luxuries and indulgences must be provided. Some even claimed that it was the only privy in the whole village, and a later stroll through a nearby wood convinced me that this was no idle boast.

Although excited by the new surroundings, I was tired, but Randolph kept me up into the small hours, talking and drinking *rakie*, a local ardent spirit for which one all too readily acquired a taste. I have never drunk it since but I know that if I did, I should in its musty flavour at once, as by Proust's *madeleine*, recapture the *temps perdu* and be sitting again in the little cottage with Randolph and Evelyn exchanging disdainful glances, and catch a whiff of wood smoke and manure, and see our old cook, Zora, shuffling among the geese outside, the dignified peasants with their soft, courteous greetings, and a luminous sky over the unending fields of maize.

In the morning, we got our first glimpse of Topusco, the village in which the Mission was situated. It was also the GHQ of the Partisan army in Croatia. In happier days, Topusco had been a spa, although it was difficult to imagine where the visitors had lodged, as there was no conceivable building in the pathetic huddle of cottages which could have housed them. But the remains of formal gardens and borders preserved a forlorn and wistful elegance.

By a miracle, the pumping machinery which extracted the radioactive water from a spring had survived the fighting, as had the small building in which the baths were housed. In a few days, Evelyn and I, by bribing Partisan soldiers with cigarettes, induced them to put the pumps in working order. We were then able, on occasion, to indulge in a luxury fantastic in such a desolate place, and take baths which gave an indescribable tingling stimulation to the body, as though one had been reborn in a more radiant form.

On the morning after our arrival, Randolph took Clissold and me to meet the leading figures in the area. We met the Partisan General commanding in Croatia, who gave us to understand that he swayed the destinies of seventy thousand men, although we soon learned to accept such buoyant over-estimates with reserve, and to realise that his calculations were invariably inflated by an almost Herodotean fancy. He was thirty-three years old, and his Chief-of-Staff twenty-eight. Clissold had warned me that the political commissars exercised the real power in the Partisan army and it was obvious that the Commander-in-Chief stood in awe of the one to whom we were presented. This was a sinister and black-avized cut-throat with an oily Uriah Heep manner, who regarded the new arrivals with profound suspicion and during our service there was to use all the resources of an ingenious and well-trained mind to thwart our every effort to reach relations of trust with the senior officers.

We were afterwards to discover that a Cromwellian austerity prevailed in the Partisan army. There were many women in the ranks, and although their appearance was not of the sort that makes men forget themselves, there were severe penalties for sexual promiscuity, and also for drunkenness and hooliganism. The Partisans fought with Balkan courage and ferocity and took few prisoners – although they were believed to refrain from the more repulsive atrocities associated with this part of the world.

We were next taken to see two old devotees of the Cause who had fought for Tito in the hills and now, destined for portfolios in some future Communist Government, patiently awaited their hour. One was a decayed intellectual from Istria of more than seventy, with a grey beard, to whose cottage I would sometimes later ride on a borrowed horse; the other a former dentist, with gold teeth and a surly manner, to whom I would have hesitated to entrust my own molars. I learned from Randolph that, before Clissold's arrival, he and Evelyn had been dependent on a Yugoslav interpreter whom I will call M Pavelic, although that was not his name, who had been attached to the Mission, was seldom out of its building and for whom Evelyn had formed a particular distaste.

We were to see much of this man in the weeks to come. He clung to us in a manner which suggested that his duties were not confined to interpreting, but also included a certain element of espionage. He was always heavily armed and sometimes unshaven, and might have been taken for a caricature of a Balkan guerrilla. But his brain was sharp and alert, his English idiomatic, and although he was a Communist, his mind did not seem completely closed to reason nor his ears wholly blocked by the wax of dogma. He had previously been the only means of communication with the Yugoslavs for Randolph and Evelyn, but with the arrival of Clissold this situation changed. Although Clissold was recognised as an ardent admirer of the Partisan cause, one had the feeling that our hosts were not a little uneasy at his mastery of their language.

I had noticed that Evelyn did not accompany us on this *tour d'horizon*, and when I mentioned this to Randolph he said: 'He's sulking.' He explained that Evelyn was atoning for some obscure and unspecified lapse of behaviour. 'He refuses to drink, which makes him dull, and he has become petulant and censorious, as could be seen from his intolerable remark last night.' I replied soothingly that while I had known Evelyn on occasion to be petulant, I could not believe that he was ever dull.

I had gathered that the duties of the British missions in Yugoslavia were mainly to liaise with the Partisan military headquarters and the political commissars, and to spread with tact and care as much pro-British information as possible to counteract the passion for the great Slav Communist brother Russia to whom they were attached by political and historical association. We were expected also to attend air-drops of arms and supplies, and to deal with the various emergencies that arose. The Partisans' blind adoration of the Soviet Union was extremely irritating, as we soon discovered that the Russians were supplying practically no arms to them, whereas the British aid was immense and ever-increasing. It was our duty to point these facts out plainly to the commissars, and also to do our best to ensure that the weapons so lavishly bestowed were used for their proper purpose of fighting the enemy, and not simply stockpiled against an eventual post-war seizure of power in the state. This task proved to be beyond our powers.

Randolph added that this area was normally quiet, and that major German operations were not expected. There would probably, however, be local attacks from time to time by the Partisans, and it would be our duty to be present at these battles and to report to our department on morale and equipment.

We returned to the Mission, where Evelyn greeted Randolph with noticeable coolness, although his attitude to Clissold and myself was friendly and charming. Any sarcasm he might have been contemplating at my expense must have been frozen on his lips by the fact that I had brought him a pair of shoes and a box of Havana cigars entrusted to me by his wife. He was in desperate need of both. Evelyn smoked only cigars and had long been deprived of them, and he fell upon the box with joy. With a touching generosity, he offered me one which, in the circumstances, I thought it wise to refuse. He then suggested that I might like to see something of the countryside and that he would take me round it. During this walk, he conversed with delightful wit and freshness and gave every sign of friendship. He told me how pleased he was by our arrival, as relations between him and Randolph had become strained to breaking-point. He said that being confined with him in a small cottage had lacerated his nerves, and I did not fail to recall that Randolph had made exactly the same remark about him earlier in the day.

This led me to wonder again about the link that had for so long bound this incongruous pair in friendship. When one thought of Evelyn, that undoubted man of genius, one remembered his epicene subtlety of thought and his limpid prose, confined by so firm a discipline. There was at all times in him an intense fastidiousness. Randolph's character, on the other hand, although he was far from stupid or indifferent to words, contained an essential earthiness which one thought must be jarring to Evelyn. His preference in literature was for the set piece, the balanced melodious passage. He revered Macaulay (as his father had also done in his youth before reading that historian's estimate of his ancestor, the Duke of Marlborough), and was given to declaiming from his works in London restaurants in a rich penetrating baritone. When not in the grip of some sudden rage, when his soul boiled with causeless hatreds, Randolph was an entrancing companion, vibrant with an energy and warmth which seemed like an explosion of pagan mirth.

Another difference between them seemed to me to be that whereas Evelyn usually preceded his actions by a period of thought, not always wisely employed, Randolph more often seemed to be the mere sport of impulse, a stranger alike to the prudence of delay or the luxury of reflection. Again, one observed Evelyn's love of nature which at this time was completely lacking in Randolph. This could be seen when Evelyn later wrote in *Brideshead Revisited* with golden nostalgia of the Oxford of the 1920s. He made one think of the lilac and laburnum in the Banbury Road, of bergamot in the college gardens and dragonflies skimming the green waters of Parson's Pleasure. All this was, at the moment, *terra incognita* to Randolph. It was only in the evening of his days, when he developed an interest in gardening, that he began to be aware of his surroundings, and it is my conviction that this was the only period of unalloyed happiness in his whole angry life.

On our return, I was taken by Randolph to meet our Yugoslav cook, Zora, in the potting-shed in which she worked from dawn until late at night cooking for the Mission. She was a bent but friendly old crone with a few words of English, and Randolph told her that in all circumstances she must address me as 'Lord'. I was next introduced to two Partisan soldiers, Sergeant Stari and Private Mani, who were attached to the Mission. The sergeant was a richly comic figure, a character out of Shakespeare, who had lived for some years in America and spoke fluent English with a strong Brooklyn accent. Mani was a quiet young man who tended the china stove in the living-room.

When we returned to the Mission building, we found that our Communist interpreter was paying one of his all too frequent visits and that Evelyn was standing in a corner with a sullen expression. M. Pavelic was bristling with weapons, and a gold tooth gleamed luridly as he smiled. Randolph at once embarked upon what he conceived to be his duties as a British liaison officer, in a manner completely alien to his natural one. His approach was amiable, florid but a trifle patronising. He was hearty, bantering and facetious, and an element of embarrassing archness pervaded his words. As his confidence increased, he began roguish sallies about Communism, to which M. Pavelic responded with equally heavy badinage about capitalism. This was evidently a familiar ordeal for Evelyn, but the spectacle of Randolph ingratiating himself with Anti-Christ was beyond his endurance and his self-control was visibly wilting. When Randolph caressingly addressed our guest: 'Now M. Pavelic, as a good Communist you must surely admit . . .', Evelyn ostentatiously left the room.

I remembered then his detestation of Communism, which can be seen in his war novels when he describes with revulsion the consecration of the Sword of Stalingrad before it was offered to Stalin, whom he believed, with every reason, to be one of the arch-murderers of history. To Evelyn, our alliance with Russia completely deprived the war of the crusading element with which he had first invested it, and our Partisan colleagues' derogatory remarks about the Germans, at whose hands they had suffered hideously, were to him merely a particularly nauseating example of Satan rebuking Sin. One could not fail to recognise that holding these views so strongly, he could be of little, if any use as a liaison officer with Communist allies.

I imagine that his attitude was deepened by his faith. A convert to the Roman Catholic Church, his religion played a dominating part in his life. There was a Catholic church at no great distance, where Mass was still celebrated, although at all times the Angelus was silent. There Evelyn worshipped each Sunday in the company of a handful of devout but nervous peasants, for religion was regarded with disfavour by our godless allies, and a soldier with a slung sub-machine gun was stationed by the altar to catch any whisper of heresy against the Cause which might escape the priest's lips.

The days then, as we soon found, were busy and rewarding, but I came to regard with dread the approach of night, for Randolph proved an unnerving bedfellow, and his thunderous snores and other even less pleasing eructations precluded sleep. His extraordinary restlessness also compelled him to turn on every few hours at full volume the BBC Balkan News Service, so that even if one had at last fallen asleep, one was again brutally aroused. Its signature tune was *Lillabullero*, and the rollicking melody became associated in my mind with insomnia and despair. It was obvious that this purgatory could not last and there came a time towards a pallid dawn when we both rose and began shouting at each other. It was a disgraceful occasion when we almost came to blows, and I felt deeply ashamed of myself in the morning, as I knew that we had woken the whole Mission. Evelyn had heard us, but his remark to me at breakfast was commendably restrained: 'You were rather noisy last night.' Sergeant Stari heard us too, from some distant resting-place, and his comment, although insubordinate to an officer, was unquestionably true: 'Youse guys no good with our *rakie.*'

Fully occupied as we were during the day, there was an uneasiness in our relations in the evening when work was done. Evelyn, always least predictable when he twined vine-leaves in his hair, drank water. Unlike us, therefore, he was usually quiet and reasonable, asking only to be left in peace to read the many books he had brought with him. Sometimes he liked to discuss these, and on occasion his own work.

There was a night on which Evelyn and I found ourselves in strong agreement in dislike of Ruskin's wife, Effie, who coming from a bankrupt family, had done very well for herself by marrying a rich man and repaid him with vile ingratitude. 'I cannot bear her', said Evelyn. 'I cannot stand that horrible little pursed up rosebud of a mouth.' Such exploration of the gentler regions of literature caused Randolph to tap out boredom on the table, and he tried to draw Evelyn on to more familiar ground by referring to his father's *Life of Marlborough*, and asking him if he did not consider it a great work. He received the dustiest of answers: 'As history', Evelyn replied with unattractive vigour, 'it is beneath contempt, the special pleading of a defence lawyer. As literature it is worthless. It is written in a sham Augustan prose which could only have been achieved by a man who thought always in terms of public speech, and the antitheses clang like hammers in an arsenal.'

Randolph was not unnaturally outraged by this brutal and quite undeserved defilement of a shrine, and remarked angrily to me: 'Have you ever noticed that it is always the people who are most religious who are most mean and cruel?' Even the hungriest trout could hardly have risen to so heavily cast a fly, and I remained silent, but to my surprise Evelyn replied, not only without rancour but almost with vivacity: 'But my dear Randolph, you have no idea what I should be like if I wasn't.'

There was no doubt that while Evelyn remained polite to Clissold and myself, Randolph was getting increasingly on his nerves. My relations with Evelyn were happy but it was not in his nature to allow undisturbed tranquillity, although his occasional disloyalties to me were trivial and amusing. He put it about that I was having a homosexual affair with the bearded Istrian intellectual whom I occasionally visited, and later circulated a rumour that I had got at the morphia in my medicine chest and had become a drug addict.

Far more dangerous in its possible consequences was his obstinate insistence that Tito was a woman. He never referred to the Yugoslav leader except as 'Auntie', and claimed that the Marshal had been seen emerging from the sea off the island of Vis in a wet bathing dress and that there was no possible question about 'her' sex. So obsessed was he with his fantasy that he came almost to believe it and when, at a moment of particular intransigence on the part of Tito to the allied leaders, I remarked how tiresome the Marshal was being, Evelyn replied: 'I think she has come to a rather difficult age for women.' He had already spread the rumour in London and Bari and now repeated it in Croatia, never bothering to lower his voice, so that we became much concerned that the Yugoslav members of the staff would over-hear him and that our work might be seriously imperilled.

With this fear in mind I said to him: 'For God's sake stop this nonsense, Evelyn. Everyone knows that he's a man and a good looking one at that.' But Evelyn, with lips pursed, rather like the abhorred Effie's, merely replied obstinately: 'Her face is pretty, but her legs are *very* thick.'

A few weeks later, after a particularly hideous night, *Lillabullero* had made its last strident irruption and shortly before dawn I fell into a troubled sleep from which I was roused by a heavy kick in the ribs. Randolph was standing over me, his face transfigured by that mingled excitement and rage that so often possessed him at the approach of danger. 'Get up you fool', he shouted: 'The Germans are over, and they're trying to get me. They've got this house pinpointed – pinpointed, I tell you!' I followed him to the slit trench at the back of the Mission, into which the staff were already descending with a good deal more alacrity than they displayed in their normal duties. Randolph was obviously right in his belief that the Germans were trying to kill him, for they dropped a number of bombs near the Mission building, but although they blew the windows out, failed to register a direct hit.

I found my corner of the trench occupied by Zora, who pulled me down upon her with the anguished appeal: 'Cover me, cover me, Lord!' – a strange request, I had time to think even at a moment of tension. The Yugoslav peasants are sturdy and likeable people inured by centuries of experience to all the fouler aspects of war, but they have a great dislike of the *avioni* – the aeroplanes – which seem to them to bring an ungentlemanly element into the game.

The enemy, having failed to flatten the house, turned and made a low run on the position which they next sprayed with machine-gun fire. As we had no anti-aircraft weapons, we could not respond, and were fortunate to avoid casualties. In the middle of this attack, the small figure of Evelyn, somehow overlooked, emerged from the Mission, clad in a white duffle-coat which might have been designed to attract fire, and which gleamed in leprous prominence in the dawn. At this sight, Randolph's face, empurpled with rage, appeared over the trench and in tones verging on hysteria he screamed: 'You bloody little swine, take off that coat! TAKE OFF THAT ————— COAT! It's an order! It's a military order!' Evelyn did not seem to regard even this dire threat as binding, and without removing the coat lowered himself with leisurely dignity into the trench among the bullets, pausing only on his way to remark to Randolph: 'I'll tell you what I think of your repulsive manners when the bombardment is over.' Evelyn's behaviour was difficult to forgive, and we shared Randolph's annoyance. It seemed to us that Evelyn had either chosen this extremely hazardous method of irritating his friend, or else had been seized by some obscure death-wish. In either case, his action had endangered all of us.

The Germans dropped more bombs on the village which killed a number of villagers and destroyed the pumping-engines of the radium baths, after which, presumably short of petrol, they departed. The atmosphere in the Mission at breakfast was glacial. Evelyn sat in silence offering neither explanation nor apology, while Randolph's face wore an expression not only of rage but of martyrdom. Shunning Evelyn, he attached himself firmly to Clissold and me. As in some bygone essay in the balance of power, he seemed to realise that safety lay in numbers, but his brooding depression hung heavy over us all. Randolph's personality was so strong that his sustained anger became oppressive and intolerable and it was always advisable to attempt to lighten his mood.

With this object in mind, I related to him Zora's anguished appeal to me in the trench. As when the moon briefly illuminates some ravaged landscape, so did a wintry smile pass over Randolph's sullen features. 'I don't envy you that task, dear boy', he remarked. There was another way in which he could be mollified, although I refused to indulge this idiocy except in the absence of Evelyn and Clissold, and then only on one occasion. He had conceived the extraordinary idea that one of the most intelligent and hostile commissars would be impressed and encouraged to feel trust in us rather than suspicion, by listening to me declaiming Randolph's favourite passages of English prose. Once the preposterous idea had convinced him, he was eager to apply this rich public relations compost to an impoverished soil.

The commissar, polite but baffled, listened to Macaulay on Warren Hastings and Lecky on the place of the prostitute in society. I then made as if to stop, but Randolph, like an angry animal-trainer with a recalcitrant sea-lion, forced me to the floor for a further item, to declaim from a squatting position: 'For God's sake let us sit upon the ground, and tell sad stories of the death of kings . . .'. When this humiliating charade was over, Randolph, who of course had noticed nothing comic or bizarre in the scene, remarked complacently to the

His frontispiece to Labels, A Mediterranean Journey, *1929*.

'H. I. M. *Seth of Azania from the painting by a native
artist.' His frontispiece for* Black Mischief.

Illustration for Chapter Six of Black Mischief.
'Frightful hotel but Armenian proprietor v. obliging.'

ቅ ዴ ስ: ሚ ካኤ ል:

ም ስለ
ፍ ቁ ር ው
ዉ ፳:

ቅ ዴ ስ ገ ብ ር ኤ
ል:

ABYSSINIAN MADONNA
Presented by Evelyn Waugh

ሰ ማ ፈ: እ ግ ዚ አ: ጸ ሎ ቴ የ: ወ ዱ ብ የህ: ቅ ዱ ሜ ከ: ገ ኦ ር

38

*Presented to Campion Hall after his return from
Abyssinia as a war correspondent.*

His own collection of Abyssinian pictures.

In Kenya, 1930, on the travels described in Remote People.

With the Infanta Beatrice of Spain on a Hellenic
Cruise in 1935.

Waugh at War

In Palestine, Christmas 1935, describing himself as a war correspondent and a patriot.

On Military Mission in Croatia, with Randolph Churchill.

commissar: 'My friend has a wonderful memory. He has further treats in store for you.'

But Randolph soon began to yearn for a *détente* with Evelyn, and was restrained only by pride from seeking it. In time, he decided to throw even this to the winds and drawing Evelyn aside, apologised if his manners had been abrupt on the day of the attack, reminding him that as the Mission Commander he was responsible for the safety of all its members. Evelyn replied: 'My dear Randolph, it wasn't your manners I was complaining of: it was your cowardice.'

This devastating rejoinder caused a complete breach between the unquiet pair, and it was difficult this time to see how the severed bond could be spliced. It was at this moment that Randolph determined on revenge, and he showed both ingenuity and self-indulgence in devising it. He issued another 'military order', this time obeyed, that Evelyn should attach himself to the celebrations of a gruesome body called 'The League of Anti-Fascist Women', and join with them in the national dance. To keep him in countenance, I agreed to do so with him. These unsexed creatures, ferocious in appearance, were clad in battledress and wore girdles of live Mills bombs round their waists, which joggled up and down when they moved. Evelyn and I were not nimble upon the floor, and when during the dance our own stomachs were brought into brief contact with the leaping hand grenades, the moment was one of excruciating physical tension.

But Evelyn's strange friendship with Randolph survived even this penance, and a gradual reconciliation took place between them. The intense relief of their uneasy truce caused Randolph to talk more than at any time since our arrival, and his appalling garrulity preyed to such an extent on our nerves that we decided at all cost that he must be silenced. I had with me a Bible, given to me by my wife before I left England, and knowing that Randolph could never resist a wager, I suggested to Evelyn that we should each bet him £50 that he could not read the Bible in a fortnight and face reasonable questioning upon it afterwards. He accepted with a wolfish smile and took the Bible firmly, although seeming to gauge its bulk with misgiving. Evelyn watched him narrowly, and with a dawning hope.

It was soon apparent that such hopes would be disappointed, for not only did he read with devouring haste, but accompanied the reading with an incessant flow of comment. Genesis and Exodus were swallowed as by a ravenous panther on its kill. Leviticus and Numbers were soon far behind him, with the engulfing river of talk undammed.

It seemed that our pathetic stratagem already lay in shreds at our feet, and that we would not only lose our bet, but had utterly failed to establish the quiet for which we longed.

Randolph's behaviour had never been conspicuous for moral rectitude, but he now showed a shocked and uncharacteristic moral indignation at the turpitude of the Old Testament God, which gave him a further and ample field for comment. How well I remember that unquenchable eloquence, those ribald ecstasies – the premonitory rumbling, the rich eighteenth-century chuckles over salacious passages, the sudden explosions of moral outrage, of which: 'Christ, God is a ————!' lingers particularly in the mind. The pace at which he covered the ground merely deepened our dejection, and Evelyn made a gesture of despair. Randolph appeared strangely ignorant of the Bible, which came to him therefore with a delicious freshness: 'Why was I never told about this?' he would ask petulantly. 'Why was it never brought to my attention? It's *very well written!*'

But in spite of this headlong start, he lost his wager. Evelyn and I were saved by the providential arrival by parachute of an American Colonel in the OSS. Here was a new face and a new captive audience, and the Bible was forgotten in Randolph's ingenuous delight. He scrupulously paid his debts, and I still have his cheque which for some reason I forgot to cash.

From this time until I left Croatia, I was constantly in Evelyn's company. He was quiet, courteous and a trifle melancholy, and my affection for him deepened. There was only one period during which I did not see him, when I was absent for two days and nights at a battle at Cazin near Bihac. I asked Evelyn to accompany me, but he explained that Randolph was also to be absent, visiting another mission, and appealed to me to stay: 'You can't go away on a lovely Randolph-free day', he pleaded. So I went instead with a captain in the Secret Service, who was stationed in the neighbouring hamlet, Glina.

When I returned from the battle, Randolph and Evelyn were anxious to know how the Partisans had fought. I told them that I had seen Muslims in their ranks wearing the fez; that they had attacked with two Brigades and with resolution, but that they were pathetically young and in some cases barefoot. They had launched a terrific mortar bombardment on Cazin, supported by a battery of field guns, so that it was clear that not all their arms had been stockpiled. They had cleared the town after two days fighting and had killed twenty-two Gestapo in one pill-box. I advised Randolph and Evelyn to keep their distance as I suspected that I had become lousy after sleeping on the ground in the midst of Partisan soldiers.

Randolph then showed me signals from PWE urgently recalling Clissold and me to Bari. These orders were easier to issue than to fulfil, as the landing-strip was flooded and no aircraft could put down anywhere near Topusco. Randolph therefore arranged for an aeroplane to be sent to a remote map reference, and Clissold and I set out on a miserable and sometimes dangerous journey across Yugoslavia in an attempt to find it.

Our way lay through the grisly region of the Lika, and down flinty tracks winding through a boulder-strewn wilderness. At one point we met a band of allied airmen who had baled out of their machines weeks ago, and were still seeking escape from this horrible region. We were protected by Partisan patrols who alarmed more than they protected, leaping suddenly out of ditches in the darkness and warning us of the presence of the enemy. They told us at one moment that there were Ustachi nearby – the dreaded Croat quislings who were said to gouge out the eyes of their captives and take them in a basin to their leader in order to attest their zeal. While we waited for them to be dispersed, I remember the sound of some mighty waterfall in our ears.

Although our thoughts during this journey were naturally concentrated mainly on our own problems, I also reflected often and fondly on Evelyn. I wondered what sort of atmosphere would prevail in that little hovel in Topusco when he and Randolph were thrown again on their own resources.

I felt sure that they must separate if yet another murder in the Balkans was to be averted, but I realised from our own journey how difficult it would be for Evelyn to escape. As I thought of him at that moment with his nostalgia for the past, his hatred of the present, and his despair of the future, I saw him, in the words of Matthew Arnold, as one 'wandering between two worlds, one dead, the other powerless to be born'.

12

AMERICA AND THE COMIC VISION

Malcolm Bradbury

INTERVIEWER: Have you found any professional criticism of your work illuminating or helpful? Edmund Wilson, for example?

WAUGH: Is he an American?

INTERVIEWER: Yes.

WAUGH: I don't think what they have to say is of much interest, do you?

Waugh's Paris Review *interview, in Writers at Work: Third Series* (*1967*).

THE years after the Second World War saw a decided improvement in Anglo-American literary relations and contacts, and a decided change in their balance. In the postwar years, the image of America became obsessive in England and Europe, and preoccupation with the merits and harms of American civilisation, and increasingly Americanisation, grew. Many English writers, tempted by a variety of attractions, from the lure of a non-austerity economy to the pleasures of being a writer on campus, did the new Grand Tour, visiting America and writing about it. Sometimes – as with Dylan Thomas – their entire reputation changed as a result.

Among the less predictable of these new *ententes* was that between the United States and Evelyn Waugh. This arose partly because of a shift in the direction of Waugh's career; in 1945, he published *Brideshead Revisited*, a much more Catholic, much more romantic and in some ways rather more stylishly snobbish book than its predecessors. Though Edmund Wilson criticised the shift, the equation proved, in the States, to be very successful; the novel was chosen by the Book-of-the-Month club and sold three-quarters of a million copies. It aroused so much interest that Waugh – explaining that he did not believe in leaving letters unanswered – responded to his correspondents in an article in *Life* magazine. As he said, 'I have momentarily become an object of curiosity to Americans and I find that they believe that my friendship and confidence are included in the price of the book.' In the following year, 1947, Waugh was asked to go to Hollywood to discuss a film-version of *Brideshead*, and was offered 150,000 dollars for the rights. After seven weeks of discussion the arrangement finally collapsed, since Waugh was not to retain satisfactory control of the treatment to be given to the book. The visit was not entirely a success, which might have been predicted. Equally it might have been predicted that, while Waugh's outrageously aristocratic comedy and style might appeal to Americans, frequently charmed by the lordly, America would not entirely appeal to him. In fact, it was to acquire for him something of the fascination possessed by some of the milieux he had made his for his early novels, London's Metroland and Seth's Azania; it was a milieu of extravagances now sadly absent in austerity England. And it recreated for him, stimulated in him, those ambivalent responses of outrage and fascination which generated his best art.

In its dealings with Waugh, Hollywood, in fact, lived entirely up to type. He had already made good use of the absurdities and wiles of the film companies and the associated worlds of journalism and promotion in some of his earlier books. There was, in *Vile Bodies*, the Wonderfilm Company of Great Britain, hampered by lack of capital and the failure of the cameraman to put in a new roll of film. And in a delightful short story, *Excursion in Reality*, a young novelist named Simon Lent – known for his dialogue – is caught up by a film-company, asked to write the film scenario of *Hamlet*, constantly summoned from bed or meal to conferences which rarely take place and which, when they do, involve the gradual dismemberment of the original inspiration, granted an emotionless affair with a fellow scriptwriter, Miss Grits, and finally ejected back into a real world now sadly lacking in value, 'for' notes Simon Lent 'the first time in my life I have come into contact [in the film-world] with real life'.

The same surreal real life was available in southern California; Waugh's hunter's instinct was aroused to high pitch. He had given us glimpses of Americans and American life before, some of them ungenerous; there is Mrs Melrose Ape and Judge Skimp ('...that's an American...') in *Vile Bodies*, and the American 'Loot' in *Men at Arms*. In *Brideshead* itself, there is a brief American interlude in which Charles Ryder, returning from a rewarding withdrawal into the jungles of Central America, encounters, simultaneously, his wife and the 'civilisation' of New York City – 'in that city' he notes, 'there is neurosis in the air which the inhabitants mistake for energy' – before he undertakes the vulgarities of the Atlantic crossing home, decadence symbolised in the melting ice swan. The glimpses are not kind, but they are, perhaps, already engrossed; brief images of a larger fictional possibility. And for a writer who had claimed, in his travel-book *Ninety-Two Days*, and with justice, to be interested in 'distant and barbarous places, and particularly in the borderlands of conflicting cultures and states of development, where ideas, uprooted from their traditions, become oddly changed in transplantation', and who had also shown himself particularly obsessed by those special cultural frontiers at which barbarism and absolute modernity cross and interact, the United States – and above all southern California – was bound to have something to offer.

It is perhaps worth noting the special significance of southern California, an aberrant part of America which might also be thought of as in some sense its realisation, a land of sunshine and oranges placed on the cultural extremity at which the more extravagant forms of American dream and American fantasy are made manifest, not only on the stage-sets and in the studios of Hollywood, but in the surrounding environment. It is hard to write about it with balance and poise. A home of utopian experiments, novel religions, advanced forms of self-display, style-hunger and assertive identities, built upon desert and land-slippage, landscaped and bulldozed hills and an earthquake fault, on oil, gold, advanced technology, expectation and the promise of eternal youth followed by eternal salvation, it affords at times both horror and the ready promise of redemption. The salvation can seem more disturbing than the horror; 'You're angels, not a panto, see?' says Waugh's salvationist Mrs Melrose Ape to her religious troupe (Chastity, Faith, Creative Endeavour, etc.), who offer Love to the partygoers of a chaotic, declining, modern London in *Vile Bodies*. Mrs Ape is transparently related to the southern Californian Vaudevillean gospellist Aimée Semple McPherson, who made a million dollars with her message but fell into some discredit when, after a disappearance she blamed on kidnapping, she was found to have been tucked away in a 'love nest' in Carmel with one of her workers. The popular forms of American salvation appear to have interested Waugh greatly, and in Hollywood their presence is unmistakable.

Like most visitors there, Waugh, in the course of his abortive visit, was taken to see the Forest Lawn Memorial Park, the creation of another charismatic Californian personality, Dr Easton. A well-advertised cemetery, art centre and tourist attraction, Forest Lawn cannibalises and parodies Europe for its decor (Michelangelo's David, The Wee Kirk O' The Heather, the minor relics of Kipling) and the multiple religions of its own state for its eclectic, inter-denominational faith. The highlight of the tour through the gardens, past the carefully tended plots, is the biggest oil-painting in the world, the Crucifixion, painted on a canvas the size of a football field; along with Disneyland and Knott's Berry Farm, it is not to be missed. For a writer like Waugh, obsessed with the grim comedy of the *memento mori*, and fascinated by finding the relics of European civilisation abstracted from their cultural surroundings, this insight into Californian death practices was clearly of the greatest interest, the culmination of his American visit. Cemeteries, he announced, were 'the only real thing in Hollywood, – a deep mine of literary gold.'

Waugh's creative instincts were clearly roused. The experience immediately yielded another article for *Life* magazine, a savage, amusing, well-illustrated piece which sought to analyse from the standpoint of the future archaeologist the culture of southern California as revealed by its tombs, in which the traditional warnings of mortality associated with the graveyard are reversed: the body is prevented from decaying, the cemetery itself is earthquake-proof and images of eternal childhood are scattered everywhere. Dr Easton, Waugh observes, is 'the first man to offer eternal salvation at an inclusive charge as part of his undertaking service'. His response is part outrage and part comedy; his faith, but also his artistry, felt challenged. The article suggests that the park, multidenominational though economically and racially segregated, a necropolitan Arcadia with plots at a varied range of prices and with a varied range of cultural associations, a stage-set rather than a liturgical environment, eliminated almost all the theological meanings associated with the last things, rendered them bland and absurd and so offered a glossy and superficial death to round off a no less bland order of life.

More important still, the visit also yielded him his one novel with an American setting, *The Loved One* – subtitled *An Anglo-American Tragedy* – which appeared in 1948 and was perhaps the most success-ful of his postwar books, commercially and also artistically. It is a macabre, comic piece that draws on the tradition of the international novel, a great distilling of international images. In some ways, it can be taken as the last of a series, that line of books in which the bearer of European experience comes to expose American innocence and emptiness, as Dickens does in *Martin Chuzzlewit*. For shortly after, no doubt partly in response to the changing balance of power, the reaction against European association and the temptations of American openness, the fictional image of America appeared, for a spell, to improve, and the traditional plot to become reversed. In a number of novels (like Kingsley Amis's *One Fat Englishman*, my own *Stepping Westward*, Thomas Hinde's *High*), the image of America seems actually tempting, American experience promising, the Englishman rendered historically innocent. The experience Waugh treats coolly can become warm. But *The Loved One* is in fact far from being an aristocratic dismissal of American vulgarities; Waugh is clearly deeply involved in and immersed in American experience – just like his own hero, Dennis Barlow, who at the end of the book carries back 'the artist's load, a great shapeless chunk of experience; bearing it home to his ancient and comfortless shore . . .'.

The Loved One in fact involves a deep imaginative immersion on Waugh's part, which he enacts in the book, following out Dennis's experience as he 'goes native' under the instinctive pressures of his Muse. One reason for this is that Waugh's attitude to the United States in this novel is closely tied to his entire attitude toward the modern world; and that attitude was by no means simple. In the later years of his life, from the end of the war onward, Waugh's bitterness about social evolution and the movement toward equality, welfare and progress was considerable; it was a bitterness about the loss of civilisation and the hierarchy that maintained and ordered it, the devaluation of life, and individuality and privacy, the reducing of human nature to homogeneity and equivalence, the decline of complexity and form in social relationships and in the individual conduct of living, and the disappearance of serious and dedicated faith.

Waugh saw the historical processes at work in the times perfectly clearly and found little that was benevolent or beneficial in them. In the novel after *The Loved One, Scott-King's Modern Europe,* he exposes his hero, a classics master, to the world of modern European politics, of cold war power-struggle and the increasing politicisation of all human action, and puts him through its sufferings; it produces an obvious conclusion. 'I think it would be very wicked indeed to do anything to fit a boy for the modern world', Scott-King tells his headmaster, who wants him to teach economic history rather than classics, '. . . I think it the most long-sighted view it is possible to take.' As the ultimate egalitarian and materialist civilisation, committed to growth and technology, America's place in this was clear. Waugh's withdrawal from any complicity with the processes of modern history was ostensibly complete; it was a self-evidently disintegrating proceeding, a move from the greater to the lesser, an absurdist affair rhetorically disguised as betterment. The position he adopts is sometimes called conservatism; but by any conventional political standards it is idiosyncratic and strange – and what it generated was, of course, a complex comic posture. It was complex because, particularly, it clearly involved an investment in barbarism as well as in civilisation, and drew on an endless – and a delighted – comparison between the lost city of order and the wilderness forever encroaching further into it, compelling all human institutions and human nature, all progress and reform. That extravagant wilderness is the world of *The Loved One*.

Waugh's complicated attitude to it all is clearly given to us in *The Ordeal of Gilbert Pinfold*. Pinfold is presented to us as an idiosyncratic Tory, bored with the world, his strongest tastes all negative. 'The tiny kindling of charity which came to him through religion sufficed only to temper his disgust and change it to boredom. There was a phrase in the thirties: "It is later than you think," which was designed to cause uneasiness. It was never later than Mr Pinfold thought.' But Mr Pinfold's outrageousness is shown as a disguise for his modesty, which needs protection; and the action of the novel describes the intrusion into himself of the hostile, penetrative forces he fears. These become internal, and they give him both paranoia and his art. Pinfold thinks of his art as something external to himself to be used and judged by others; but the book is autobiographical and based on Waugh's own breakdown. Hence its art – which arises in part from the destructiveness applied by Waugh/Pinfold to his self-image – is precisely not external, but the product of irrationality and chaos within himself. Waugh's novels are very largely the product of these confrontations with a barbarism and anarchy that is not simply outside and to be resisted; it is also within and to be shaped and organised.

One figure that recurs in his work is that of the jungle or the desert, the dark places of the expanding wilderness; and if it is threatening to him, it is also decidedly attractive. The place without civilisation, beyond the orderly city, in which an odd glimpse of faith, or else a thrust of unregenerate human nature, is to be discerned, is his primary comic milieu. *The Loved One* begins by calling up this familiar figure; three expatriate Englishmen are talking on the edge of the desert, 'the counterparts of numberless fellow-countrymen exiled in the barbarous regions of the world', with an evening breeze shaking the palm-leaves and swelling 'the dry sounds of summer, the frog-voices, the grating cicadas, and the ever present pulse of music from the neighbouring native huts', and we read three pages before learning that this is Los Angeles.

Waugh is very much a novelist of the disillusioned Twenties, in that he shares the prevailing obsession of the decade with barbarism and vitalism as the alternative to rational civilisation; it is an essential part of his comic thrust and subject-matter. The portrait of Waugh which sees him as a very traditional novelist can be supported by instances; but what it does not satisfactorily explain is his comedy, and in fiction Waugh's vision is above all a comic vision. And his comic insight was devoted not simply to satirising the world of impermanence, insufficiency and change, the world of chaos and anarchy, but in many respects to celebrating it. He is, throughout his work, a devastating explorer and recorder of the frontiers of civilisation and barbarism, of the places that generate disintegration and the people who live by it; his great heroes and heroines, from Margot Metroland to Basil Seal and Trimmer, are people of change and high points of comic invention. His fiction is a fiction of the Big Wheel at Luna Park which, as Professor Silenus tells Paul Penny-feather, the ingénu hero of *Decline and Fall*, spins and spills the people off and 'that makes them laugh, and you laugh too'; with that spinning absurdity, and the people who hang on or fall off, his novels generally deal. In this respect, he diverges considerably from the tradition of moral or humanistic comedy; his world is contingent and arbitrary, and his position as a narrator strikingly well concealed, cool, hard, detached.

Like other writers who began in the 1920s – Aldous Huxley and, in America, Hemingway, Fitzgerald and Nathanael West – he is obsessed with the world of an irrevocable modernity, a world of psychological stress, dissolving relationships, new life-styles, novel technologies and environments; his creative energy takes him readily into encounters with such people and milieux, with a curiosity divorced from moral judgment and fascinated by extravagant behaviour. This gives his comic universe an aspect of vigorous, bleak chaos which both outrages and delights; an art from which many of the conventional human norms are abstracted. The result is a very modern form of comedy, and a great fascination with surreal modern milieux – like southern California, Hollywood and Forest Lawn.

In choosing that milieu, Waugh was to produce one of the best and purest examples of a genre which already existed and has gone on being important in American fiction, the southern California novel, the Hollywood novel. In the late 1930s, two major American writers had already tried their hands at the species; Scott Fitzgerald, working in his last years as a Hollywood scriptwriter, had produced the Pat

Hobby stories and had begun work on his extraordinary novel *The Last Tycoon*, left unfinished at his death, but published in incomplete form in a text edited by Edmund Wilson in 1941, the year after he died. Nathanael West, who died in the same month as Fitzgerald, and who also worked as a Hollywood scriptwriter, published in 1939 as his last book *The Day of the Locust*, another work set in Hollywood and focussed around the film-studios. In 1955 Norman Mailer was to produce his Hollywood novel, *The Deer Park*, and the genre was to persist. These are all profoundly apocalyptic novels, portraits of the American dream in disarray, catching not only at the spuriousness of the images and life-styles clustering around Hollywood, the great American dream-factory, but also at the extravagant possibilities for surreality in the material to be dealt with.

That Waugh should have produced what is surely one of the best of this species is significant; he based his book, after all, on a brief and unsympathetic glimpse of American life. His success lies partly in the fact that he had already learned, in Mayfair and in the 'remote places' he explored in the 1930s, the arts of black humour appropriate to his subject-matter. Of that tradition, which was to become of such significance in the United States in the 1950s and 1960s, Waugh was one of the great modern exponents; and his work is consonant with an entire tradition of macabre and apocalyptic writing, of bleak and black comedy, which has become one of the pre-eminent forms for dealing with the dehumanisations of a disintegrating world. The critics who have condemned Waugh for his anti-humanism have often not seen how much in tune he is with an entire body of modern artistic developments: indeed, when we survey the writers of the last twenty-five years or so, in England and the United States, we can sense a continuity of even a direct influence from Waugh to later work – on the brilliant, sharply intellectual and profoundly macabre performances of Muriel Spark, his co-religionist, in England, and on the outrageous comedy of cruelties and physical and metaphysical violations practised in America by latter-day black humorists like John Barth, Joseph Heller, Terry Southern, Bruce J. Friedman, James Purdy and Donald Barthelme. By comparison with some of these, certainly, Waugh is a very pure, controlled and reticent performer; but his form of oblique and morally anarchic comedy was a mode patently suited to the surreality of Hollywood life, and what that means for American life (of course, as I have perhaps failed to admit, it does not mean everything). Still, the comparison perhaps suggests why it is that, of modern novels by outsiders about America, *The Loved One* is so successful.

When *The Loved One* appeared, to win great esteem with the American public, it was reviewed by, among others, Edmund Wilson, who had been an admirer of Waugh's earlier work, but had been disappointed by the exoticism and Catholicism of *Brideshead*. He was disappointed by the new novel too, and particularly by what he assumed to be its primarily Catholic standpoint. 'To the non-religious reader . . . the patrons and proprietors of Whispering Glades seem more sensible than the priest-guided Evelyn Waugh', he observed, 'What the former are trying to do is, after all, to gloss over physical death with smooth lawns and soothing rites; but, for the Catholic, the fact of death is not to be feared at all; he is solaced with the fantasy of another world in which everyone who has died in the flesh is somehow supposed to be still alive and in which it is supposed to be possible to help souls advance themselves by buying candles to burn in churches.' Wilson was obviously dismayed that what in Waugh's earlier writing seemed like straightforward outrageousness now seemed to be consonant with and at the service of traditionalist religious and social attitudes. But he did note the affinity between Waugh and Nathanael West, saying that it lay not only with *The Day of the Locust* but also with West's novel about an advice-columnist anguished by the suffering of his correspondents, *Miss Lonelyhearts*. And though he seems to suggest that West managed things better, the comparison is not only fruitful, but a clue to the fact that it was as much Waugh's comic as his Catholic imagination that was stirred by his material.

West was a novelist who dealt in a world of suffering unmitigated by the traditional religious deliverances, of festering non-redemption. In *The Day of the Locust* there is, by coincidence, a scene in a funeral chapel; a recording of Bach's 'Come Redeemer, Our Saviour' is played on the electric organ, and to it the mourners, 'hoping for a dramatic incident of some sort' and drawn there only for that reason, respond only when, for a moment, the music hints at impatience at His absence. He deals, too, in a world in which the artist seems consequentially thrust toward grotesquerie and stoical indifference. The book centres around a painter with the emblematic name of Tod Hackett, who is brought into the studios as an illustrator but is, in his own work, in violent reaction against such glossy realism. He is, in fact, moving toward an extremist, 'Guernica'-like style; this he achieves by emotional withdrawal from others and by his prediction of and participation in disaster – the novel ends in a great urban riot, and that gives him his painting. Tod's uneasy response to the suffering with which he finds himself surrounded is patently shared by West, who of course creates that suffering, but also supports, in his act of creation, Tod's devotion to a grotesque art of 'Mystery and Decay'. West's novel is set on the fringes of the Hollywood studios, where the dream tarnishes: around its backlots and dream-dumps, its extras and cast-offs, its rejected and its discontented. Identities are both false and pathetically real, the crowd seethes, and in those who have come to California for leisure, sunshine and oranges there is generated the 'terrible boredom' of mob-bitterness: 'Every day of their lives they read the newspapers and went to the movies. Both fed them on lynch-ings, murder, sex crimes, explosions, wrecks, love nests, fires, miracles, revolutions, war. This diet made sophisticates of them. The sun is a joke. Oranges can't titillate their jaded palates. Nothing can ever be violent enough to make taut their slack minds and bodies.'

This is West's California; and it is presented by a method very cool, elliptical and rapid. He goes for a comedy of almost parodied agony, of distortion, perversion and misdirected desire, focussing this in strange images of the studios where acted battles suddenly turn real, where the faked scenery of the backlot matches the architectural realities of the Los Angeles urban scene, and where there exists an extraordinarily yearning yet also hostile relationship between the stars and the boiling and discontented crowd. 'It is hard', he notes, 'to laugh at the need for beauty and romance, no matter how tasteless, even horrible, the results of that need are. But it is easy to sigh. Few things are sadder than the truly monstrous.' West is an expert in the truly monstrous, and he sighs a little but in the end laughs more. The result is a quality of what Jonathan Raban has called 'aesthetic sadism' running through his treatment, forming his style.

The characters are object-like; they are made so not simply by their own inner distortions and the pressures of others and their environment, the conditions of the collapsed American dream, but also by the techniques of dehumanisation employed by West as his distinctive art-form. Each one of them – the dwarf Abe Kusich; Homer Simpson, who is like a poorly-made automaton: Faye Greener, the novel's sexual centre, whose invitation 'wasn't to pleasure, but to struggle, hard and sharp, closer to murder than to love' – is the invention of a sensibility given to seeing the human in a dehumanised and mechanical, and therefore in both a pathetic and a comic, light. Like Tod Hackett, whose greatest painting is the apocalyptic 'The Burning of Los Angeles', generated by the riot at the book's end, at which Homer Simpson is lynched for 'perversion', and depravity then runs wild, West too needs a sense of disaster, of physical distortion and emotional extremity, and a hard-won detachment to yield him form and art. It is the book of West's in which his matter and his manner come closest together; the vision of Hollywood and the style become consonant.

The pressure of Hollywood and southern California on form, a pressure toward grotesquerie and comedy, recurs in other treatments of the topic. By comparison, Scott Fitzgerald's *The Last Tycoon* is more restrained, its material more human, its mode more realistic; and it is not comic. And Fitzgerald is concerned, as West is not, with historical explanation, historical forces; he is concerned, in his story of Monroe Stahr, the movie mogul, with the transition from individualism to managerialism, with the economy and the power structure of the studios, the extent to which persons dominate or are subordinate to systems. But his theme, too, is extremity and collapse, the apocalyptic shaking of the world; and his sense of collapse leads him, too, into a sequence of surreal images – of the two girls floating down through the flood in the studio backlot on the head of the Goddess Siva, during the ominous opening earthquake; of Abe Lincoln in the studio cafeteria, eating a piece of pie, and the phone-call from the President of the United States, who turns out to be talking orang-outang; of the figures, like the Negro on the beach, who hint at the end of the power of Stahr's stories, and those, like the surrogates for his dead wife Minna, who hint at his own search for death. Images like these, grotesque figures given 'realism' by Hollywood itself, persist through into the overt apocalypticism of Mailer's *The Deer Park*, in which he presents a culture outrightly dead and then attempts, through a new politics of sexuality, to reconnect the broken circuits, the grotesque humour of Thomas Pynchon's *The Crying of Lot 49*, with its utterly technologised universe, and many another version of the new 'western' or anti-utopian novel.

The paradox of Hollywood is of course that it is a fulfilment as well as a negation – there are novels about that too, especially Harold Robbins's – and that its materialism is at the service of fantasy, its fantasy at the service of commerce; that it lives, through the lives of stars and the star-hungry, the dreams it creates. There are obvious reasons why southern California, like space, has its own fictional genre. The fact that Waugh was able to enter the genre with such eminent success has much to do with the way in which, in his earlier work, he had entered worlds like this, and with instruments and forms imaginatively consistent with those of American writers of his own generation. And he was also able to cross one body of images, those pertaining to California itself, with another, those arising from cultural comparison, to give an additional extension to his theme.

In February 1948, the readers of Cyril Connolly's magazine *Horizon* were able to have a sneak pre-view of *The Loved One*, together with an introduction from Connolly – noting that 'In its attitude to death, and death's stand-in, failure, Mr Waugh exposes a materialist society at its weakest spot, as would Swift and Donne if they were alive today' – and some comments by Waugh himself. Waugh 'anticipated ructions' with the book, because of its macabre treatment of two themes, death and Americans, and he explained the ideas and images which had generated his novel. 'The ideas I had in mind' he wrote 'were: 1. Quite predominantly, over-excitement with the scene. 2. The Anglo-American impasse – "never the twain shall meet". 3. There is no such thing as an "American". They are all exiles uprooted, transplanted and doomed to sterility. The ancestral gods they have abjured get them in the end. 4. The European raiders who come for the spoils and if they are lucky make for home with them. 5. *Memento mori*.' This suggests the particular images Waugh saw clustered in Whispering Glades – as he was to rename Forest Lawn – and something of their status. The images of Art and Death and Love are to be located in the Eden of Whispering Glades in a state of sterility and uprootedness, but also traced back to their transatlantic roots. And that in turn yields another theme, the contrast of American and European images and cultures. In the book, Dennis Barlow observes that he has become 'the protagonist of a Jamesian problem' and that his stories, about American innocence and European experience, are 'all tragedies one way or another'. In transferring the direction of that interchange, in letting the images of American innocence arise from America itself, Waugh converts it – as Nabokov was later to do in *Lolita* – into experience. And, like *Lolita*, *The Loved One* is one form of decadence seen from the standpoint of another.

This is why the book is more than a European comment on American sterility, an aristocratic come-uppance delivered to a simplistic and sterile world. That element is in the novel, but it is decisively con-

trolled. In *Vile Bodies*, it will be recalled, Mrs Melrose Ape receives her
come-uppance at Margot Metroland's party. She asks the company
to search their souls; a hush falls; 'What a damned impudent woman',
suddenly cries Lady Circumference, and the occasion collapses under
the weight of 'the organ voice of England, the hunting cry of the
ancien régime'. Waugh's novels are usually touched by this hunting
cry, and it is one of the application points, the angles of address, of his
comedy. It gives, as a persistent target, the world of culture transplanted and in the transplant parodied, which is one of the meanings
of Whispering Glades; it gives the world of plastics, homogeneity and
uniformity, which then seemed to be American matters only; it
gives the sparse furniture of Aimée Thanatogenos's mind. A certain
amount of the treatment of Whispering Glades is treatment in this
mode. Thus Dennis stands in the University Church there and listens
to this tape:

In 1935 Dr Kenworthy was in Europe seeking in that treasure house of
Art something worthy of Whispering Glades. His tour led him to Oxford and the
famous Norman church of St Peter. He found it dark. He found it full of conventional and depressing memorials. 'Why', asked Dr Kenworthy, 'do you call
it St Peter-without-the-walls?' and they told him it was because in the old
days the city wall had stood between it and the business centre. '*My* church,'
said Dr Kenworthy, 'shall have no walls.'

This is admirable buffoonery, and the visitor who has attended the
original can attest to its closeness to the truth; it has been and can
remain a staple of Anglo-American comedy. But Waugh, typically of
the book, goes on to dissipate the situation. 'I never was much good
at anything new', says Sir Francis Hinsley, one of the 'English titles
that abounded now in Hollywood, several of them authentic'; but it is
the essence of Dennis Barlow's function in the novel that he leaves
such standpoints and positions behind, going native, and so embarrassing the English colony, pressing on with a deeper if more indeter-
minate quest. He listens to the tape, its tones 'so often parodied yet
never rendered more absurd or more hypnotic than the original.
His interest was no longer purely satiric. . . . In that zone of insecurity
in the mind where none but the artist dare trespass, the tribes were
mustering. Dennis, the frontierman, could read the signs.'
  Much the same is true of the treatment of the bland emptinesses of
certain portions of American life which, like Kaiser's Stoneless
Peaches, taste when eaten 'like balls of damp, sweet cotton-wool'.
Uniformity, standardisation, mechanisation, the spirit of *Brave New*

World, is part of the matter here; it is a powerful, and not a new, image of America in Europe, and there are times at which, confronted with it, one understands the force of James Russell Lowell's complaint that 'for some reason or other, the European has rarely been able to see America except in caricature'. There are the eternal, interchangeable hostesses: 'American mothers, Dennis reflected, presumably know their daughters apart, as the Chinese were said subtly to distinguish one from another of their seemingly uniform race, but to the European eye the Mortuary Hostess was one with all her sisters of the air-liners and the reception-desks. . . . She was the standard product . . . but Dennis came of an earlier civilization with sharper needs.' The mechanisation of the human agent can go no further, and that gives comedy:

> Presently he heard steps approach and, without moving, could see that they were a woman's. Feet, ankles, calves came progressively into view. Like every pair in the country they were slim and neatly covered. Which came first in this strange civilization, he wondered, the foot or the shoe, the leg or the nylon stocking? Or were these uniform elegant limbs, from the stocking-top down, marketed in one cellophane envelope at the neighbourhood store? Did they clip by some labour-saving device to the sterilized rubber privacies above?

This is familiar matter in the European critique of America at this time; similar passages occur in Graham Greene, for example. But in Waugh's book, these passages build the way towards Dennis's distinguishing of the special, extraordinary, superbly created character of Aimée Thanatogenos – her name, frivolously translated, might be the title of Leslie Fiedler's book, *Love and Death in the American Novel* – who is to be Dennis's loved one, in both senses of the term that are used in the book. And she is 'unique. Not indefinably; the appropriate distinguishing epithet leapt to Dennis's mind the moment he saw her: sole Eve in a bustling hygienic Eden, this girl was a decadent.' She transcends the language of her upbringing:

> brain and body were scarcely distinguishable from the standard product, but the spirit – ah, the spirit was something apart; it had to be sought afar; not here in the musky orchards of the Hesperides, but in the mountain air of dawn, in the eagle-haunted passes of Hellas. An umbilical cord of cafés and fruit shops, of ancestral shady business (fencing and pimping) united Aimée, all unconscious, to the high places of her race. . . .

And divided as she is between her heart, 'a small inexpensive organ of local manufacture', and her ancestral instincts, her association with Alcestis and Antigone, so she is divided between the claims of Mr

Joyboy, Mom-centred embalmer at Whispering Glades, and Dennis, the European poet and employee of its four-legged rival, the Happier Hunting Ground pet cemetery. Both Mr Joyboy and Dennis speak to the objects of Aimée's contemplation, which are Art and Death; Joyboy with his elegant corpses, and Dennis with his plagiarised poems – 'in the dying world I come from', he explains, 'quotation is a national vice' – which plunder European romanticism along that dangerous borderline at which the love of love merges darkly with the love of easeful death. Aimée unconsciously, Dennis consciously, are explorers of this romantic and decadent disturbance, the disturbance and unease that underlies the beautified smoothness of Whispering Glades' deathly Arcadia.

It is in this way that Whispering Glades becomes a figure for the United States, for it is invested with the spirit, and the paradoxes, of that entire utopian disposition, that entire Arcadian and Edenic imagery, which is primary to the nature of America itself. Columbus, discovering America, was convinced that he had lighted upon 'the terrestrial paradise' about which so much had already been written and dreamed, in the notion of Atlantis, Avalon, the earthly wonderland, the Christian and Classical Arcadia which offered man a new start and restored to him the primaeval garden before sin was known. Michael Drayton, in his poem *To the Virginian Voyage*, represented that paradise as governed by the Natural Laws of the Golden Age. 'Behold, I dreamed a dream and I saw a New Earth sacred to HAPPI-NESS . . .', says the massive wall of marble at the entrance to Whispering Glades, signed Wilbur Kenworthy, Dreamer, on which its purposes and desires are made manifest. Of those desires, Mr Joyboy is the supreme agent, and Aimée his acolyte. But in this landscape of innocent romanticism, Dennis gains his experience, and it is an experience of the underside. Animals, we learn, are 'a headache in cemeteries'; Dennis, postlapsarian, European and the agent of the lower rituals of the animal cemetery, is the parodist of the dream. His quest is through it but also beyond it. Aimée, divided between her present and her past, Dennis and Joyboy, commits suicide in Joyboy's laboratory; Dennis appropriately assists his rival and appropriately celebrates the ancient spirit of his loved one by cremating her at the pets' cemetery. As the fire roars in the oven and Dennis arranges for an annual greeting card to go to Mr Joyboy – 'Your little Aimeé is wagging her tail in heaven tonight, thinking of you' – he sees the true end of his quest:

On the last evening in Los Angeles Dennis knew he was a favourite of Fortune. Others, better men than he, had foundered here and perished. The strand was littered with their bones. He was leaving it not only unravished but enriched. He was adding his bit to the wreckage; something that had long irked him, his young heart, and was carrying back instead the artist's load, a great, shapeless chunk of experience; bearing it home to his ancient and comfortless shore; to work on it hard and long, for God knew how long. For that moment of vision a lifetime is often too short.

He picked up the novel which Miss Poski had left on his desk and settled down to await his loved one's final combustion.

Dennis is, of course, the comic rogue, the successful centre of a plot in which Fortune does indeed work on his behalf and the grimmest misfortunes of others are to his advantage. He is also a spirit of postlapsarian decadence, and his end and purpose is the realisation of art. But it is an art of both distance and involvement. The message which the Muse who draws him is trying to convey is not, he realises, one of sentimental love: 'It was about Whispering Glades, but it was not, except quite indirectly, about Aimée. Sooner or later the Muse would have to be placated. She came first.' She is the spirit of macabre comedy, but it is a comedy in the service of a certain anarchic comprehension of experience. And what that involves is Dennis's realisation of experience in two different ways. One is experience as the antithesis to innocence, to Arcadia. The other is experience as the novelist uses the term, the shapeless chunk of experience which has in it the moment of vision. In both of these matters, Dennis is the consort of his author and the comic muse itself, a muse both detached and involved, 'over-excited with the scene', but also instinct with artistic purpose. It is a macabre comedy, but an intense realisation of two contrasting spirits of life: American innocence turned bland and mechanical, European experience turned anarchic, decadent and death-centred. But the symbiotic relation of the two gives macabre comedy at its best, a grotesquerie cooler and more controlled than West's, but decidedly in the same tradition.

The Loved One was not the end of Waugh's involvement with the States. In 1948, he returned to America with a more sober purpose, to lecture at the Catholic universities on converted English writers like himself. Thereafter, he was to retain a persistent interest in Catholic America, and the evolution of his faith there. In particular, he took great pleasure in the signs of a monastic revival which he detected in American Catholic life. As he said in his foreword to

Elected Silence, the title of the English edition of Thomas Merton's *The Seven Storey Mountain,* a powerful, very popular devotional work written 'in fresh, simple, colloquial American' by a Trappist monk: 'There is an ascetic tradition deep in the American heart which has sometimes taken odd and unlovable forms. Here in the historic Rules of the Church lies its proper fulfilment. In the natural order the modern world is rapidly being made uninhabitable by scientists and politicians. . . . As in the Dark Ages the cloister offers the sanest and most civilized way of life.' And he told Randolph Churchill in a letter that 'the best hope of the world is the remarkable increase of Cistercian vocations among the yanks'. This, perhaps, has helped critics to read *The Loved One* as pre-eminently a Catholic novel, and Catholic sensibility is inescapable from it; I am suggesting here, though, that it is pre-eminently a work of more complex interchanges, in which the comic muse is pursued and presides. It can scarcely be doubted, though, that Forest Lawn, with its suggestion that 'death is a form of infancy, a Wordsworthian return to innocence', had to do with his concern for the American Catholic revival and the form it took. It was, from the standpoint of his traditionalist faith, a threatening as well as a promising evolution; but it drew his high curiosity and attention.

The story does not quite end there. Waugh died in 1966; and there arose the question of what to do with his papers. They passed, in fact, to the vaults of the University of Texas, a form of interment typical enough of our age. It is not hard to guess what Waugh's own view might have been. It must bear some resemblance to his view of that institution which will, for future anthropologists, confound all the accepted generalisations, 'a necropolis of the age of the Pharaohs, created in the middle of the impious twentieth century, the vast structure of Forest Lawn Memorial Park'. 'To those of us too old-fashioned to listen respectfully,' he said of the Forest Lawn message, 'there is the hope that we may find ourselves, one day beyond time, standing at the balustrade of Heaven among the unrecognizably grown-up denizens of Forest Lawn, and, leaning there beside them, amicably gaze down on Southern California, and share with them the huge joke of what the Professors of Anthropology make of it all.' Perhaps the gaze may also shift to the professors of literature at Austin, Texas, not so many hundred miles away.

13

THE FUGITIVE
ART OF LETTERS

David Lodge

IN *A Little Learning* (1964), Evelyn Waugh described his father as 'a Man of Letters . . . a category, like the maiden aunt, that is now almost extinct'.* Evelyn himself was certainly never a Man of Letters in the ripe, fully resonant sense of the term, but he began his literary career in circumstances not unlike those of his father at the same age, and occasional journalistic writing was always a part of that career.

Arthur Waugh came down from Oxford in 1890 with a disappointing third-class degree, and took his chance in the world of London publishing and literary journalism. An opportune biography of Tennyson published a few weeks after the Laureate's death, and, later, an essay on 'Reticence in Literature' which attracted considerable attention by appearing incongruously but (it seemed to many) appositely in the first issue of *The Yellow Book*, brought him regular employment as a reviewer. He calculated that he noticed approximately six thousand books in the course of his life, mostly in his spare time as Managing Director of Chapman & Hall. 'Some of my earliest memories are of book-reviewing', Evelyn wrote in 1953:

> My father wrote a weekly literary article for the *Daily Telegraph*. . . . He greatly enjoyed this work, would read the book under review attentively and discuss it at table. Then on Saturday mornings a hush fell on the house while he wrote his article. My own first regular literary employment was reviewing for the *Observer* in the late '20s. I too enjoyed it. . . . Since then, off and on, I have done a good deal of such work, always with pleasure.†

Evelyn, too, came down from Oxford with a disappointing Third‡, and after several false-starts adopted the profession of letters: 'I realised that there was nothing for it but to write books; an occupation which I regarded as exacting but in which I felt fairly confident of my skill.'§ In his autobiography *One Man's Road* (1931), Arthur Waugh observed, 'When young men consult me . . . upon the best way of starting life as a reviewer or literary journalist, I can only give them the advice that comes of my own experience, and exhort them to write a book, and get their name upon a title-page. It is extraordinary what faith an editor, or even a publisher, seems to put in the judgment

---

* *A Little Learning*, p. 73.

† 'Mr Waugh Replies', *Spectator*, 3 July 1953.

‡ In *A Little Learning* Evelyn Waugh states that, though placed in the third class of the History Schools, he did not take the degree because he was not prepared to fulfil the necessary residence qualifications. He appears as a graduate of Oxford, however, in the University's own reference books.

§ 'My Father', *Sunday Telegraph*, 2 December 1962.

145, North End Road, N.W. 11.

Speedwell 2022.

Dear Patrick;

Thank you so much for the advertisement. As soon as I see any hope from my window in the Slough of Despond I will let you know.

As a matter of fact I think there will probably be an elopement quite soon.

Yours

Evelyn

A letter written from his parents' house; its envelope is postmarked
20 February 1928. 'Thank you so much for the advertisement. As soon as I
see any hope from my window in the Slough of Despond I will let you know.
As a matter of fact I think there will probably be an elopement quite soon.'
The last sentence refers to the end of his first marriage.

*Postcard from Abyssinia, 1930. 'I am just going to a
lake called Tanganyika where everyone dies of sleeping
sickness. I have also caught typhus in a prison, malaria
in a place called Hawash, and leprosy in a Catholic
church, so I am fairly sure not to come back.'*

3 S. M. le Négous TAFARI le jour de son couronnement

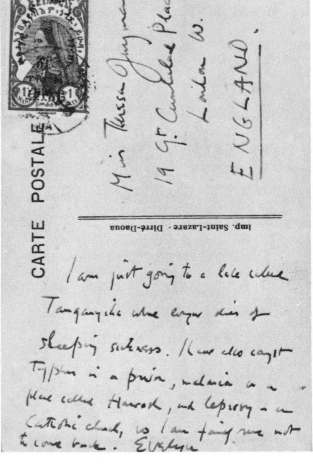

Three kinds of letterhead.

Piers Court
Stinchcombe Nr Dursley Glos.

Ascension Day 1956

Combe Florey House · Nr Taunton

31st December 1958

Dear Patrick

I hope you have a rollicking Hogmanay.

The major humiliations outlasted by Yorke after your luncheon do not directly involve Dame Rose. She, you may remember, was without water at her flat. Yorke claimed intimate acquaintance with a dignitary called 'Stop Cock' or 'Turn Cock'

FROM MR. EVELYN WAUGH
ETHIOPIA.

December 5th 1959

Dear Patrick

of someone other than himself.'* This seems to have been his son's experience also. The reviewing for the *Observer* in the late Twenties, mainly of art books, followed the publication of his own first book, *Rossetti: His Life and Works* (1928). His Mediterranean travel book *Labels*, his reporting of the coronation of Haile Selassie for the *Times* and the resulting book *Remote People* qualified him as a regular reviewer of travel books for the *Spectator* in the Thirties. And the success of *Decline and Fall* made him a fashionable commentator on the 'Younger Generation' – a phrase much in use at the time. 'The War and the Younger Generation' appeared in the *Spectator* of 13 April 1929. A little earlier, the *Evening Standard* printed a more racily titled piece, 'The Claim of Youth, or Too Young at Forty; Youth Calls to Peter Pans of Middle Age Who Block the Way'.†

The theme of the *Spectator* article overlaps the last chapter of Arthur Waugh's autobiography, which begins, 'The end of the War was the end of our generation. We did not realise it at the time, but it was the end all the same.' That whole chapter is a rueful, rather poignant attempt to come to terms with the violent upheaval in traditional values caused by the War, and with the particular strain thus laid upon parent-child relationships. The young Evelyn Waugh shared his father's view, but expressed it more coldly:

In the social subsidence that resulted from the War a double cleft appeared in the life of Europe, dividing it into three perfectly distinct classes between whom none but the most superficial sympathy can ever exist. There is (a) the wistful generation who grew up and formed their opinions before the War and who were too old for military service; (b) the stunted and mutilated generation who fought; and (c) the younger generation.

Especially interesting is the severity with which the author dissociates himself from 'this latter generation – the undiscriminating and in-effectual people we lament today'. The continuity of tone and attitude with the later Waugh is remarkable. When we read, 'Everything was a "substitute" for something else and there was barely enough even of that. The consequence is a generation . . . lacking in any sense of qualitative value', we may easily imagine that it is the children of the Second War who are being referred to. When we read, 'the restraint of a traditional culture tempers and directs creative impulses. Freedom produces sterility', we might be listening to Scott-King or Gilbert Pinfold.

* *One Man's Road*, p. 219.
† *Evening Standard*, 22 January 1929.

Opposite: Receiving the Hawthornden Prize, 1936, for his biography of Edmund Campion.

'There was nothing left for the younger generation to rebel against,' the article continues, 'except the widest conceptions of mere decency. Accordingly it was against these that it turned. The result in many cases is the perverse and aimless dissipation chronicled daily by the gossip-writer of the press.' One is not surprised to work out that Waugh must at this time have been preparing to write *Vile Bodies* (in which 'the topic of the Younger Generation spread like a yawn through the company' at Anchorage House), though the novel has a humour and compassion which the article lacks. It is worth noting that Waugh's disillusionment with contemporary society and 'Society' was emphatically stated before the break-up of his first marriage and his conversion to Catholicism. He seems already to have identified himself, in the spring of 1929, with 'a small group of young men and women [who] are breaking away from their generation and striving to regain the sense of values that should have been instinctive to them'.

At about the same time Waugh published 'Ronald Firbank',* in my opinion his best essay in 'pure' literary criticism, and a very useful key to an understanding of his own art. Everybody knows, of course, that Firbank 'influenced' Waugh, but the nature of the influence has not been analysed very deeply, perhaps because few critics have been prepared to take Firbank seriously, as Waugh did, as a technical innovator. His innovations, Waugh argued, were the result of a very specialised sense of humour seeking a means of expression, but they opened up possibilities for artists as different from Firbank in their values and aims as Ernest Hemingway.

> He is the first quite modern writer to achieve . . . a new, balanced interrelation of subject and form. Nineteenth-century novelists achieved a balance only by a complete submission to the idea of the succession of events in an arbitrarily limited period of time . . . [Firbank's] later novels are almost wholly devoid of any attributions of cause to effect; there is the barest minimum of direct description; his compositions are built up, intricately and with a balanced alternation of the wildest extravagance and the most austere economy, with conversational *nuances*. . . . His art is purely selective. From the fashionable chatter of his period, vapid and interminable, he has plucked, like tiny brilliant feathers from the breast of a bird, the particles of his design. . . . The talk goes on, delicate, chic, exquisitely humorous, and seemingly without point or plan. Then, quite gradually, the reader is aware that a casual reference on page one links up with some particular inflexion of phrase on another until there emerges a plot; usually a plot so outrageous that he distrusts his own inferences.

* *Life and Letters*, March 1929.

The examples Waugh gives show clearly how much the chronicler of the unlucky little Lord Tangent owed to the creator of Cardinal Pirelli. But he learned more than particular devices: Firbank offered the model of a kind of fiction that could be distinctively 'modern' in form and mood, quite liberated from the conventions of nineteenth-century fiction, without surrendering the classical literary virtues which Waugh valued or sacrificing the power to please. 'Other solutions are offered of the same problem, but in them the author has been forced into a subjective attitude to his material; Firbank remained objective and emphasised the fact which his contemporaries were neglecting, that the novel should be directed for entertainment. That is the debt which the present generation owes to him.'

Few of Waugh's essays and reviews of the Thirties, almost all of which were published in the *Spectator*, are as interesting or revealing as those two pieces of 1929. Really important books seldom seemed to come his way, and many that did, especially the travel books, were often very bad. On the whole, Waugh seems to have been a tolerant reviewer, more interested in praising merit than in punishing failure – or perhaps he had a lower motive for being kind: 'I used to have a rule when I reviewed books as a young man,' he recalled in an interview late in life, 'never to give an unfavourable notice to a book I hadn't read. I find even this simple rule is flagrantly broken now.'* He began a review of a book called *White, Brown and Black* with the ominous words, 'Very occasionally it is worth while noticing a bad book at some length, if only to give hitherto reputable publishers a reminder that they must not be insolent in what they try and put over on a public already stupified by literary over-production.'† This particular authoress was unfortunate enough to have recorded her impressions of a country Waugh knew well, Abyssinia:

> She claims to have seen a slave caravan and describes it with all the stereo-typed details of chinking chains, goads and whips and kicks, expressionless masks of faces, sockets of eyes, gaping mouths. This procession, she says, passed quite near her bed; she even saw one of the slave-drivers 'bury the point of his lance' in the back of one of the captives. I wonder how common these caravans are; I imagine they are pretty rare; she was in luck to run across one. Chain gangs of convicts are much more common in every part of Africa; she was clever to know the difference.

Waugh was always quick to pounce on any sign of pretentiousness.

* *Paris Review*, VIII (1963).
† *Spectator*, 26 July 1935.

Sacheverell Sitwell, whom he respected, was gently rebuked for 'melodramatically comparing the inhabitants of Fez to Dante's damned souls'.

> Those serene old men whom he saw jogging along the streets become extremely optimistic over their dinner; they are much richer than Mr Sitwell or me, and they have the jolliest ideas of how to employ their leisure; they can outface any race in the world in commercial negotiation; every year or so they travel down to Tangier, change into bowler hats and black suits and embark on a profitable but slightly lugubrious journey to Manchester; they return with their business completed and eagerly change back into their white robes; at home a shabby, scarcely noticeable door in a high white wall opens into a courtyard of light tiles and running water, and beyond it, in a cool drawing-room furnished with brass bedsteads and cuckoo-clocks, they can forget the inferno of Western life of which they have had a glimpse.*

Undoubtedly the best travel-book Waugh had for review was Graham Greene's *The Lawless Roads*, a work in which he acknowledged a special interest because 'It so happens that I arrived in Mexico last summer with ulterior literary motives a few weeks after Mr Greene had left with his notebooks full.'† Mingled with Waugh's sincere admiration for Greene's 'heroic' journey and vivid reporting there is a certain, sly humour:

> There is a great deal to be said for travelling poor . . . the chief disadvantage is that the physical exhaustion incurred in merely getting from place to place often makes one abnormally unresponsive to their interest. Mr Greene, particularly, suffered from this. He makes no disguise of the fact that Mexico disgusted him. In fairness it must be added that England disgusts him too.

This review was, I think, Waugh's first public comment on the work of Graham Greene, with whose name his own was to be so often coupled as a 'Catholic novelist'; and he must have been one of the earliest critics to remark the Jansenist flavour of Greene's Catholicism:

> Mr Greene is, I think, an Augustinian Christian, a believer of the dark age of Mediterranean decadence when the barbarians were pressing along the frontiers and the City of God seemed yearly more remote and unattainable. . . . Contemplation of the horrible ways in which men exercise their right of choice leads him into something very near a hatred of free-will.

* Spectator, 7 December 1934.
† *Spectator*, 10 March 1939. The allusion is to Evelyn Waugh's *Robbery Under Law: The Mexican Object Lesson* (1939).

Though their lives ran parallel at many points,* the attitudes and values of the two men were of course very different. Reviewing Greene's illustrated book *British Dramatists* in 1942, Waugh complained that Greene was excluded from sympathy with the larger part of his subject because of his subscription to 'the popular belief in "the People" . . . the new, complicated and stark crazy theory that only the poor are real and important and that the only live art is the art of the People'.† In this review, Waugh for the first time struck full and clear the militantly anti-democratic note for which he was to become increasingly notorious, quoting disdainfully the Henry Wallace phrase, 'the century of the Common Man', that recurs with almost obsessive frequency in his later journalism. But he describes Greene as 'a writer of outstanding imaginative power' and the ideological differences between the two men never prevented Waugh from expressing his admiration for Greene's fiction. He wrote, much later, appreciative and perceptive reviews of *The Heart of the Matter*‡ and *The End of the Affair*§ praising the latter, characteristically, for 'the variety and precision of the craftsmanship'.

Evelyn Waugh always had a great respect for literary craftsmanship, perhaps deriving from his early interest in graphics and his brief but enjoyable period as a student-carpenter (cabinet-making was the last vocation he tried before adopting that of letters). He was always happiest, as a critic, with writers whose technical skill and control was highly developed, whose individual and innovatory effects were obtained by a subtle modification rather than a radical readjustment of traditional forms. Firbank, Wodehouse, Belloc, Beerbohm, Knox

---

* Born within a year of each other, they were educated at public schools and at Oxford, where they both read history. After several false starts, they both made literature their profession, publishing their first novels within a year of each other. Both were received into the Roman Catholic Church, Greene in 1926, Waugh in 1930. Both travelled widely and wrote travel books about Africa and Central America. Both reviewed regularly for the *Spectator*. Both have recorded that they made half-serious attempts at suicide in youth, and both have complained of *ennui* and expressed a yearning for extinction. Mr Greene has described himself as manic-depressive and Evelyn Waugh manifested many similar symptoms. The two men were good enough friends for Waugh to have a joke at Greene's expense. Christopher Sykes recalled a meeting when Greene, describing his plans for *The Quiet American* exclaimed, ' "It will be a relief not to write about *God* for a change! " "Oh?" responded Evelyn with dangerous smoothness, "I wouldn't drop God, if I were you. Not at this stage anyway. It would be like P. G. Wodehouse dropping Jeeves halfway through the Wooster series." ' (*Sunday Times*, 17 April 1966)

† *Spectator*, 6 November 1942.

‡ *Commonweal*, 16 July 1948.

§ *Commonweal*, 17 August 1951; reprinted in *The Month*, September 1951.

– these were the writers, 'minor' by the standards of orthodox literary criticism, whom he delighted to praise.*

Style always obsessed him. 'Properly understood, style is not a seductive decoration added to a functional structure; it is of the essence of a work of art', he wrote. 'The necessary elements of style are lucidity, elegance and individuality; these three qualities combine to form a preservative which ensures the nearest approximation to permanence in the fugitive art of letters.'† This was said in a late essay, but he was applying the same criteria in his early reviews. 'The phrases are involved and slovenly, the metaphors mixed, the sentences in gross defiance of analysis', is a typical reproof of a travel-writer.‡ Malcolm Muggeridge, on the other hand, is praised for the correctness of his English:

It is a pleasure to welcome him into that very small company of writers whose work would escape the red ink of the Victorian governess. His new book gives the reader hope that no two words mean exactly the same to him; the punctuation, though not always orthodox . . . is usually consistent; with the exception of three painful conjunctival uses of 'like' there are no barbarities of grammar; there is an abundance of literary allusion and concealed quotation to flatter the reader's knowledge. It is, in fact, a highly unusual and welcome piece of workmanship.§

Christopher Isherwood earned similar praise for his contribution to *Journey to a War:* 'Not only does he seldom use a cliché, he never seems consciously to avoid one; a distinction due to a correct habit of thought.'‖

Isherwood was the only one of the Left-wing writers of the Thirties for whom Waugh had any respect. The same review is curtly dismissive of Auden, and one of the most savage reviews he ever wrote was of Stephen Spender's volume of autobiography, *World Within World* (1951). His resentment at the way in which these writers 'ganged up and captured the decade' had by no means exhausted itself in the portrayal of Parsnip and Pimpernell in *Put Out More Flags:*

* See: 'An Act of Homage and Reparation to P. G. Wodehouse', *Sunday Times*, 16 July 1961; 'Here's Richness' [review of Belloc's verse], *Spectator*, 21 May 1954 and 'Belloc Anadyomene', *Spectator*, 26 August 1955; 'Max Beerbohm: A Lesson in Manners', *Atlantic*, September 1956; 'Mgr Ronald Knox', *Horizon*, May 1948.
† 'Literary Style in England and America', *Books on Trial*, October 1955.
‡ *Spectator*, 7 December 1934.
§ Review of *In a Valley of This Restless Mind, Spectator*, 27 May 1938.
‖ *Spectator*, 24 March 1939.

What made them unlike any writers in English history except the early pre-Raphaelites was their chumminess. They clung together. They collaborated. It seemed always to take at least two of them to generate any literary work however modest. They praised one another tirelessly and an unfavourable review anywhere raised a babble of protest from the author's young friends . . . but the nuisance is past. At the first squeak of an air-raid warning the gang dispersed.*

The air-raid sirens of World War II reduced Waugh's own output of occasional journalism to a thin trickle, but he found time in 1941 to write (perhaps with official encouragement) an article for the American mass-circulation magazine *Life*, about the British Commandos with whom he himself was then serving. 'Commando Raid on Bardia',† thrillingly subtitled, 'Specially Trained British Bands Stealthily Attack Axis Strongholds in Libya at Night', and liberally illustrated with grainy monochrome photographs of British commandos in training – leaping out of landing barges, lighting smokeless fires and queasily watching a demonstration of how to kill, dress and cook wild game – makes fascinating reading for anyone acquainted with the *Sword of Honour* trilogy. The source material is common, but the difference in tone may be indicated by comparing the military journalist's first impressions of the commandos –

. . . the officers' mess was at a seaside hotel. I had come from the austerity and formality of the Royal Marines. I found a young troop leader wearing a military tunic and corduroy trousers. He was reclining in a comfortable chair, a large cigar in his mouth. Then I noticed above the pocket of his coat the ribbon of the Military Cross and later when I saw him with his troop I realised that his men would follow him anywhere

– with Guy Crouchback's arrival on the island of Mugg:

He was directed from the quay to the hotel. At three o'clock he found it empty except for a Captain of the Blues who reclined upon a sofa, his head enveloped in a turban of lint, his feet shod in narrow velvet slippers embroidered in gold thread with his monogram. He was nursing a white pekinese; beside him stood a glass of white liqueur . . . Guy recognized Ivor Claire, a young show jumper of repute . . .

(Claire, so far from inspiring his men with his leadership, deserts them at Crete.)
It is not surprising that the note of mock-heroic travesty and dis-

* *Tablet*, 5 May 1951.
† *Life*, 17 November 1941.

illusionment that permeates the war-trilogy is entirely absent from the *Life* article. The latter was published at a politically critical time when America was edging nearer and nearer to involvement in the war, and it was no doubt designed to interest the American public in the Allied cause. What is difficult to determine is Waugh's own attitude to the facts presented. The raid on Bardia is narrated in a completely straight, patriotic style – very much, indeed, in the 'Truslove spirit' so exquisitely parodied in *Men at Arms*. Did Waugh suppress his sense of humour in the interest of propaganda, or was he still in the honeymoon stage of his military service? And, in either case, how inspiring did he suppose his story was? The raid is described throughout as though it was a dangerous and successful mission, but to the dispassionate reader it seems to have had much in common with the fiasco at Dakar in *Men at Arms* and Trimmer's inglorious invasion of occupied France in *Officers and Gentlemen*. After a tense description of the assault party's climb up the escarpment from the beach, fearful of discovery at every moment, comes the anti-climatic revelation that the garrison at Bardia is completely deserted. The commandos proceed to blow up various installations and at last the enemy appears, in the form of two motorcyclists. 'Everyone near had a shot at them with Tommy guns and grenades but they somehow got through. They were not an easy target. It was lucky really that they did escape for it was through them that the enemy learned, as we particularly wanted them to learn, that a raid was taking place.'

The withdrawal was no more impressive than the marksmanship. The ramp of Waugh's landing-craft got jammed and it floated helplessly in the bay for half an hour until it was freed, so it was fortunate that the garrison was undefended. They caught up with the mother-ship only just in time; another landing craft missed the rendezvous completely and sailed back to Tobruch under its own steam; and a third boatload of men returned to the wrong beach and were apparently abandoned to death or captivity. Somehow, one doubts that this article was very reassuring to American supporters of the Allied cause, or that it struck much terror into the German High Command. Yet Waugh never indicates by so much as a flicker of an eyelid that he regarded the raid on Bardia with anything less than pride.

After the war, he wrote quite frequently for American magazines, attracted, no doubt, by the comparatively large financial rewards of such work, and rendered eligible for it by the popular success of

Opposite: His wedding to Laura Herbert, 1937.

Family

With his wife in St James's.

Mother, wife and first-born.

America

In Hollywood.
Seated in the centre, Sir Charles Mendl and extreme right Anna May Wong.

Return to Plymouth in the Ile de France.

rrival in New York, 31 January 1947, on
s America.

At Home

The garden at Piers Court.

With Alec Waugh.

On the steps of White's Club, St James's. Cartoon by
Osbert Lancaster.

Family and retainers at Piers Court.

Family group.

Right, *at Combe Florey.*

Left, *his eldest daughter Teresa reading.*

Mrs Waugh in the garden at Combe Florey, her son James in the centre.

Combe Florey

Wash-hand stand by William Burgess,
presented by John Betjeman,
and known as 'The Betjeman Benefaction'.

The library at Combe Florey, now removed to the
University of Texas.

The Pleasures of Travel, 1751,
1851, 1951. The first two are
by the Victorian artist Robert
Musgrave Joy. The third was
commissioned from
Richard Eurich.

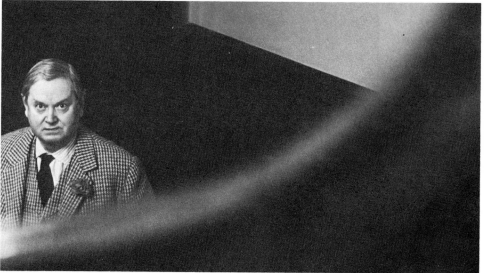

Top, *in the library, with the silver ash-tray known as
'The Glastonbury Bowl'.*
Above, *in the entrance hall of Combe Florey.*
Right, *the metal plaque on the wall says, 'No
Admittance On Business'.*

WAUGH
CLUB

EDINBURGH

UNIVERSITY

THE
RECTOR

EVELYN WAUGH

A hand-out to promote unsuccessfully,
his election as Rector
of Edinburgh University.

Right, *opening the house for a local fête*
attracted national publicity.

One of the Attractions of St. Dominic's Church
GARDEN FETE

WORKS OF ART
Paintings & Rare Books
at
PIERS COURT, STINCHCOMBE,
DURSLEY, Glos.
Saturday, August 14th
(Wet or Fine)
ADMISSION TO FETE 1/-. ADMISSION TO HOUSE 1/- More

Personally Conducted Tours by
MISS ROSE DONALDSON
every Twenty Minutes — 4 p.m. - 7 p.m. inclusive.

First (and possibly Last) Opportunity to see
Mr. Evelyn Waugh's Unique Collection
of Victorian Narrative Pictures
Victorian Illustrated Books
and other Items of interest.

(Buses from Gloucester and Bristol stop at Piers Court Gates)

F. Bailey & Son Ltd. (Printers) Dursley, Glos.

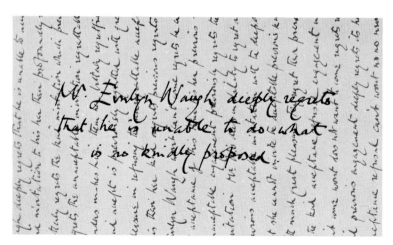

'Mr Evelyn Waugh deeply regrets that he is unable to do
what is so kindly proposed.' This specially printed
postcard was sent to those with untimely requests.

Brideshead Revisited (1945) in the United States. His second article for *Life*, 'Fan-fare', was, in fact, a droll open letter to the many American readers, mostly female, who had written to him about that novel.

> In a civilized age this unexpected moment of popularity would have endowed me with a competency for life. But perhaps in a civilized age I should not be so popular. As it is the politicians confiscate my earnings and I am left with the correspondence. This is something new to me, for English women do not write letters to men they do not know. . . . I have momentarily become an object of curiosity to Americans and I find that they believe that my friendship and confidence are included in the price of my book. My father taught me that it was flagitious to leave a letter of any kind unanswered. (Indeed his courtesy was somewhat extravagant. He would write and thank people who wrote to thank him for wedding presents and when he encountered anyone as punctilious as himself the correspondence ended only with death.) I therefore eagerly accept this chance of answering collectively all the cordial enquiries I have received.*

Like many an English writer before and after him, Evelyn Waugh found the differences and incongruities of American mores opened up fresh fields for satiric observation and gave a new zest to his own role-playing.

In the following spring, he visited Hollywood in connection with a projected film of *Brideshead*. He recorded his disenchantment in a cool but penetrating essay called 'Hollywood is a Term of Disparagement':† 'Each of the books purchased [by the studios] has had some individual quality, good or bad, that has made it remarkable. It is the work of a staff of "writers" to distinguish this quality, separate it and obliterate it.'

Waugh's last article for *Life* was 'The American Epoch in the Catholic Church',‡ a somewhat dull and circumspect piece in which even the commercialisation of devotional objects – 'a "rosary aid" which records each "Ave" on a dial with a sharp click, and a plastic crucifix which, I was assured, had the advantage that you could "throw it on the ground and stamp on it" ' provoke only the mildest satire. Waugh contemplated with surprising calm the possibility that American Catholicism might come to dominate the Universal Church. 'It may well be that Catholics of today, in their lifetime, may have

* *Life*, 8 April 1946.
† *New Directions in Prose and Poetry*, 1948.
‡ *Life*, 19 September 1949.

to make enormous adjustments in their conception of the temporal nature of the Church.' But when Vatican II asked him to accept doctrinal and liturgical change, Waugh jibbed.

In 1949, he had contributed to a symposium of Catholic converts a short piece entitled 'Come Inside' describing his loss of Christian faith as a schoolboy and his subsequent reception into the Church of Rome.* The appeal of Catholicism for him was, he suggests, historical in a way that an American might find difficult to understand. The spirit of *aggiornamento* released by the second Vatican Council, which most 'ghetto-Catholics' found liberating, seemed to Waugh to threaten the foundations of the Church's historic role and the grounds of his own faith.†

The core of that faith was, I feel, his sense of mankind exiled from a state of pre-lapsarian happiness, needing some providential guidance and institutional order. He has an eloquent passage praising Ronald Knox's rendering of the patriarchs of the Old Testament: 'They are precisely what they should be, men and women living in a fallen and unredeemed world, haunted by ancestral memories of a lost Eden, taught by hints and portents, punished by frightful dooms, people half lost waiting for something to happen.'‡ The theme recurs frequently in his writing, and if he went to religion for a saving idea of order, he often turned to literature for a fleeting recovery of lost innocence. In a lyrical celebration of Aldous Huxley's *Antic Hay*, a book that exhilarated his youth, he says, 'It is Henry James' London possessed by carnival. A chain of brilliant young people linked and interlaced winds past the burnished front doors in pursuit of happiness. Happiness is growing wild for anyone to pick. . . .'§ And his enthusiasm for P.G. Wodehouse becomes easier to understand when we read in 'An Act of Homage and Reparation': 'For Mr Wodehouse there has been no fall of Man . . . the gardens of Blandings Castle are that original garden from which we are all exiled.'||

There is much more variety in Evelyn Waugh's occasional writing after the war than before it, in both content and places of publication. He renewed his association with the *Spectator*, but also wrote for *Time*

* *The Road to Damascus*, ed. John A. O'Brien.
† *See:* 'The Same Again Please: A Layman's Hopes of the Vatican Council', *Spectator*, 23 November 1962 and correspondence between Waugh and Abbot Butler in the *Tablet* between 31 August and 19 October 1963.
‡ 'A Literary Opinion', *The Month*, July 1949.
§ 'Youth at the Helm and Pleasure at the Prow', *London Magazine*, August 1955.
|| *Sunday Times*, 16 July 1961.

and Tide, for the Catholic weekly *The Tablet* and for the Jesuit periodical *The Month*; towards the end of his life he reviewed occasionally for the *Sunday Times*. In America, *Life, Esquire,* the *Atlantic, Commonweal* and even *Playboy** published his work. Over the same period, he indulged in polemics of various kinds, not only in his frequent letters to the Press, but sometimes in full-length articles. One of the earliest of these was 'Palinurus in Never-never-land',† an effective satire on a Utopian manifesto printed in *Horizon* by Cyril Connolly, in which we may detect the germ of *Love Among the Ruins*. In 1953, he was given the opportunity, in a *Spectator* series, to review the reviewers of that story, but his only serious complaint was of the treatment he had received in the Beaverbrook Press.‡ He continued this feud in 1955 with 'Awake my Soul! It is a Lord!'§ the ironical account of an unsolicited and successfully repelled visit to his home by Nancy Spain of the *Daily Express* and Lord Noel-Buxton – an unchivalrous but effective broadside, which provoked some amusing correspondence in the *Spectator*.

In 1956, Waugh leaped to the defence of P. G. Wodehouse against an allegedly 'caddish' and ill-informed review by John Wain, who was made to stand for a new, university-nurtured cultural barbarism which was to be the subject of frequent complaint thereafter.‖ In the same year appeared his celebrated 'Open Letter to the Honble Mrs Peter Rodd (Nancy Mitford) on A Very Serious Subject',¶ a witty intervention into a rather laboured current debate about U (Upper-class) and Non-U speech and behaviour. Waugh argued brilliantly that 'there are no classes in England; there is only precedence. . . . There is a single line extending from Windsor to Wormwood Scrubs, of individuals all justly and precisely graded (no one knows this order of precedence: it is a Platonic idea)!' This letter is a very characteristic piece of late Waugh, full of outrageously provocative anti-democratic sentiment ('Mr Butler in his Education Act . . . provided for the free distribution of university degrees to the deserving poor') and at the same time subtly subversive of upper-class pride and prejudice.

Of the occasional prose which Evelyn Waugh published in the last

---

* 'The Death of Painting', *Playboy*, August 1956. (Reprint of a review originally published in *Time and Tide*.)

† *Tablet*, 27 July 1946.

‡ 'Mr Waugh Replies', *Spectator*, 3 July 1953.

§ *Spectator*, 8 July 1955.

‖ 'Mr Wodehouse and Mr Wain'', *Spectator*, 24 February 1956.

¶ *Encounter*, December 1955.

years of his life, two pieces of 1962 stand out for their high literary quality and autobiographical interest. The first of these is 'Sloth', commissioned by the *Sunday Times* for a series on the Seven Deadly Sins.* Waugh begins by quoting St Thomas Aquinas's definition, '*tristitia de bono spirituali*, sadness in the face of spiritual good. Man is made for joy in the love of God, a love which he expresses in service. If he deliberately turns away from that joy, he is denying the purpose of his existence.' No one who has read *The Ordeal of Gilbert Pinfold*, or the memoirs of Waugh's friends, can doubt that this was the sin that tempted him in later years – as indeed he all but openly confesses in his conclusion: 'It is in that last undesired decade, when passion is cold, appetites feeble, curiosity dulled, and experience has begotten cynicism, that *accidia* lies in wait as the final temptation to destruction.' In between these sombre passages, Waugh forcefully examines the deleterious effect of secular sloth upon civilisation, especially in his own field of literature.

The second essay is 'My Father', also commissioned for a series in a Sunday newspaper.† Though the same ground is covered in *A Little Learning*, the article is quite distinct, and in some ways is more revealing. What it reveals above all is the profound and painful alienation of father and son, which was aggravated by Evelyn's apparent aimlessness and irresponsibility as a young man, and healed only by his successful start as a writer. 'Immediately the whole relationship with my father was changed. Here at last I was engaged in an activity he fully understood. Moreover he was himself the publisher of my novels, so that he had a double satisfaction in my prosperity. He read my reviews with keener interest than I felt myself. The cheques bearing his signature were now sent with a light heart.' But it was too late for a total reconciliation. 'We were never intimate in the sense of my coming to him with confidences or seeking advice. Our relationship was rather that of host and guest.' It is poignant to set these words beside Arthur Waugh's, thirty years earlier:

Perhaps . . . the greatest mistake our own generation made lay in its effort to keep on equal terms with its successor, to be brother and sister to its boys and girls. . . . We saw the limitation of the Victorian home . . . the lack of confidence between father and son. . . . We would be young with the young. . . . It

* *Sunday Times*, 7 January 1962.
† *Sunday Telegraph*, 2 December 1962.

cannot be done. It never has been done and it never will. . . . Youth and age can never keep on terms together.*

My survey, which began by juxtaposing one of Evelyn Waugh's earliest pieces, on the Generation Gap, with his father's autobiography has thus come full circle, or should one say, cycle? 'My Father' ends:

I am now the father of three sons, two at school, the eldest already embarked on the family trade of writing. I have very little knowledge, or curiosity, about what they think of me. They are always polite. I have tried to fulfil the same duties to them and provide the same amusements as my father did to me. I lack his gift of reading poetry and his liveliness. I think I am less good company to them than he was to me, but I think I am kinder than my grandfather. Perhaps host and guest is really the happiest relation for father and son.

* *One Man's Road*, pp. 373–4.

14

HIS BOOKSELLER'S VIEW

Handasyde Buchanan

I became a bookseller in March 1930, so that I sold Evelyn Waugh's novels more or less from the moment at which they first began to come out. No one ever seemed to buy any books then or perhaps I was not a very good bookseller, but we always sold Evelyn's books in respectable quantities and from the first time (out of probably, by now, fifty times) that I read *Decline and Fall*, I recognised what a great writer he was. But I met him only once before the war, when he came into my shop and bought two prints from Dr Thornton's Temple of Flora. 'My name's Waugh, E. Waugh' he said. I thought this remarkably modest, as this was just after *Black Mischief* had been published.

It is relevant at this moment to remember that *Decline and Fall* was turned down by Evelyn's original publishers, Duckworths, because they found it improper and was then published slightly bowdlerised by Chapman & Hall. A year or two ago, I bought a first edition of this book given by Evelyn to Tom Balston, then head of Duckworths (in which Anthony Powell worked and found the material for his novel *What's become of Waring?*), with the inscription 'To Tom Balston – the stone that the Builder rejected'.

In 1938, *Scoop* appeared and while this may not be everyone's favourite, it is to me a vintage work. *Vile Bodies* read again recently seems slightly dated and I never loved *A Handful of Dust* in the way that most of my friends have. *Brideshead* is unique but somehow it always reads to me like Evelyn's Apologia. Possibly his war books, the *Sword of Honour* series, are his greatest achievement. *Pinfold* is a *tour de force*, and I am only sorry that our libel laws prevented his autobiography from being expanded. If on a desert island and severely rationed for reading, I should take *Decline and Fall* and *Scoop* in the same little drawer as *The Diary of a Nobody* and *The Wrong Box*, to be read when I really wanted to enjoy myself.

After the war, when I got back to bookselling in Curzon Street, Nancy Mitford was working in Heywood Hill, and so at last I got to know Evelyn apart from his books. It is hard to remember exactly how we got on all those years ago but get on we did and seemed to do it pretty quickly. Possibly we came together because we neither of us could suffer fools gladly, possibly because he wrote in English – very few people do – and because I tried to, almost always making one word do the work of two, not using long words needlessly, nor jargon nor clichés, but most of all perhaps it was because we both could see what I have always called THE JOKE. This means the Joke of Life and if you cannot see it, life is not worth living.

*With the Duchess of Devonshire at Foyle's Literary
Lunch to launch* The Ordeal of Gilbert Pinfold, *1957*.

Overleaf, *an interview on the 'Face to Face' programme
of the* BBC *with John Freeman (back to camera)'
26 June 1962*.

Fairly early on – in 1948 – I went to stay with Evelyn to start making a list of his books. He was a great collector of Victorian illustrated and illuminated books, from Owen Jones downwards, all now so fashionable and I was about to write what must have been one of the first articles about them. Just before this, we had sold Evelyn a barrel-organ which he had taken all the way to his home in Gloucestershire strapped to the back of a taxi. As I got into the car at the station, he said 'A curious thing has happened, Handy; five postcards have arrived for you all posted in different parts of London, in assumed handwritings, but looking much the same, *what* does it mean?' 'It means it's my birthday, Evelyn!' 'Ah, CHAMPERS.' And champers it was. He played the barrel-organ during dinner and the butler showed no surprise. Finally we went up to bed. 'Would you like a book?' 'Yes I'll take up the best book you ever wrote, *Decline and Fall*.' 'Jolly good news for an author to be told that his first book is his best. Good night.'

I have about a hundred and fifty letters and postcards from Evelyn, and from now till the final round up it will be him speaking. I cannot give the dates since he hardly ever dated any letter or postcard except to put, for instance, 'St Bartholomew's day'. But I do not think the consequent arrangement matters, as he was entertaining at all times and in his own special way.

'Why were you not at Laski's cremation?' It is well known that I am a socialist, and had met and liked Laski. 'Greatly encouraged that Agnostic socialist can find interest in KNOX, thanks awfully for telling me.' This was, of course, a reference to his new (1959) book on Father Ronald Knox. Evelyn, alone of authors as far as I know, used to have about twelve extra special copies of his books bound up and gave them to selected people. I was lucky enough to get *Knox* and *The Ordeal of Gilbert Pinfold*, inscribed 'For Handy, a warning'. Clearly a reference to my enjoyment of drink. Next, 'N. Rodd says heavenly 1948. God help her. I can't.' 'Thank you for your second postcard. The first was confiscated in the post. Very sorry you have influenza. So have Sangorski and Sutcliffe.' This refers to the world-famous binders who had kept Evelyn waiting too long for a book!

One postcard just states 'GRAVE COMPLAINTS'. But perhaps better is the one which says 'Very sorry to learn that LOVE AMONG THE RUINS bored you. It seems to have had the same effect on the Beaverbrook Press. Rest assured that my regard for my friends is not measured by their enjoyment of my writing.'

Opposite: At the wedding of his son, Auberon.

Evelyn was the only famous writer I have ever known who received criticism objectively. In 1961, I ventured to say, mistakenly as I now think, that *Unconditional Surrender* was not as good as *Men at Arms* and *Officers and Gentlemen*. 'Really', was all he said. And a little later I got a copy of it inscribed 'To Handy to reread patiently and at leisure when unsuspected beauties will emerge.' No one else could have behaved like this.

I have a piece of wrapping-paper returning a book that he had disliked addressed to 'The Secretary, West London Pornophilic Society, c/o H. Buchanan Esq'. I have also a card which says 'It is intolerable to use your distinguished shop as a circulating library, but may I please return this? I have dipped into it and find it wretched trash. Could you not have a BWT (Bought when Tight) column in your ledger?'

And on another occasion: 'I think you have a customer with a taste for pornography. An American Jew wrongly supposes that I have this taste and has sent me CANDY. Ripe for confiscation and destruction in this more civilized country. Any offers?' It was followed shortly afterwards with a bit about this book from the newspaper and saying 'Will not this bit in the *Sunday Times* excite your pornophiles to fancy prices?' And as the last of this particular series: 'May I please return this absolutely awful book. I can't read it myself and I don't want to leave it lying about to corrupt my children.' But dare I add a postscript, 'I have an American copy of P. Quennell's smutty "F. Hill". What offers if suppressed. It is not the kind of thing I like to have in the house.'

Next I had been helping with the possible sale of his manuscripts once, and did sell the MS of *Scoop*. In the course of writing about this he says 'Talking of manuscripts I hope we shall have our bills in Molly's [my wife who sent and sends the bills] fine hand on good paper instead of those nasty typed chits.' We had tried typing the bills, but we took Evelyn's advice and to this day they are still sent out in 'Molly's fine hand'!

More astringent was 'What is happening in your shop? Has it mutinied like the Force Publique and are NCO's in command? Many days ago I ordered Elizabeth Bowen's TIME IN ROME and have not received it.' But more cheerfully: 'My brother Alec is elated by, and slavering in admiration of, your treatise on cricket.' I had edited a cricket anthology which was quite a success and Evelyn had given his brother a copy.

I hope that after all these years Peter Quennell will not mind these two little jokes. 'Dinner at the Garrick: Quennells of sole on the menu.' And 'Thank you for excerpt from Beeton describing the construction of the farce Quennell.' Evelyn had always, as appears often in his books, a true schoolboy sense of humour and so perhaps have I.

Now last about his autobiography: the first quote is 'I fiddle away at my autobiography – very flat.' Followed by 'My autobiography will not be out this year. I toiled away at it.' But it did come out finally, as *A Little Learning*, and I have a letter, dated for once, 13 April, which says

Thanks awfully for your exhilarating letter. I am delighted that you like my biography [sic] and that you find some similarities between my youth and your own.

Thank you also for pointing out corrigenda [I had of course been reading a very early proof] I am a hopeless proof reader and printers, deprived of the supply of unfrocked clergy, seem not to employ readers at all.

The succeeding volumes will be much harder to write as I have used almost all adult experience already in one form or another.

And finally not long before his death: 'Answer to enquiries about second vol autobiography that since it will deal with younger and more identifiable people I shall have to wait until they die off.' I too cannot give some of the bits in his letters for the same reason.

I must end with my own idea of Evelyn's place as a writer. Dr Watson says in *The Valley of Fear*, 'Mediocrity knows nothing higher than itself but talent instantly recognizes genius.' For me, the most talented writer of my contemporaries is Anthony Powell, and no single piece of his writing falls below this very high level. At his worst, Evelyn is well below Tony, but at his best, and this to me is *very* often, he is a genius, with no reservations.

It remains only to say that he was a friend with whom I never had a row (and if anyone finds this hard to believe, it is true), and someone who rubbed into me, without his knowing it, the lesson that I had begun to learn at Rugby: that is, the unique importance of mental discipline.

15

WHAT'S IN A NAME?

John Jolliffe

PSYCHOLOGISTS of the more

plausible kind have begun to announce with increasing confidence that human aggression does not spring from some arbitrary reservoir implanted in us all, but from threats, real or imagined, to the esteem in which we are held by others, and to the obviously related esteem which we feel for ourselves. It would be only of minor significance to suggest that Evelyn Waugh's often gratuitous pugnacity arose out of compensation against a Christian name which, as he tells us in *A Little Learning*, from time to time caused confusion as to his sex. If Evelyn sounded girlish, it became clear at an early stage that Waugh was made of sterner stuff, under no circumstances to be trifled with.

Whatever his feelings about his own name, his powers of imagination and his highly developed, if erratic, sense of what was fitting enabled him to people his novels with characters of complete plausibility, whether on a realistic or on a fantastic level, often with interesting and apt names of their own. The inspiration of two other novelists whom he admired, Dickens and Ronald Firbank, are at once noticeable: on the one hand Sniggs, Beaver, the Reverend Mr Tendril, Professor Jellaby, Mr Joyboy, Colonel Sproggin (though he is perhaps nearer to Surtees than to Dickens); on the other, the Runcibles and Malpractices, Lady Anchorage and the Duke of Stayle, the Flytes themselves and Mrs Beste-Chetwynde – though the suggestion that her name should be pronounced Beast-Chained must surely be fanciful.

Another and more particular source of inspiration, of course, came from people whom he knew in real life. More often than any other, the name of Cruttwell (the Dean of Hertford College, Oxford, in Waugh's day, and later its Principal) is singled out for hatred, ridicule and contempt. The kindest reference to him in Waugh's own autobiography is that he was 'not at all the kind of don for whom I had been prepared by stories of Jowett'. His name is given to a character, either ludicrous or loathsome, in all of Waugh's first five novels, and it was not until 1942 that he composed one without dragging in the name of a man whose form of immortality is perhaps not much to be envied.

Other references to real life were not hostile: his friend for forty years, Lady Mary Lygon, had a Pekinese dog called Grainger, whose name is perpetuated in *Black Mischief*, *Scoop*, the short story *Incident in Azania*, *Put out More Flags* and *Work Suspended*, in which, appropriately, its owner has become Old Grainger. Places as well as people provide clues: by the time of *Unconditional Surrender*, the Waughs had settled in West Somerset, and the deleterious, parlour-pink diplomat Sir Ralph Brompton owes his name to the harmless Exmoor village of Brompton Ralph. Less recondite is the use of the name Connolly. *The Loved One* originally appeared as a complete issue of *Horizon* in February 1948, and an imaginary magazine called *The Ivory Tower* had featured in *Put Out More Flags*. It is impossible to identify its editor, Ambrose Silk, with the editor of *Horizon*, but, in a spirit of impish teasing, the horrific refugee children in that novel are called the Connollys. (Earlier, in *Black Mischief*, in the same spirit, General Connolly and his wife, Black Bitch, had been ennobled as the Duke and Duchess of Ukaka.)

The publication of *Black Mischief* had aroused fierce criticism, not least in the pages of *The Tablet*, in which, in an editorial notice of 7 January 1933, Mr E. J. Oldmeadow announced that 'in case he is still so regarded [*ie* as a Catholic] by booksellers, librarians, and novel-readers in general, we hereby state that his latest novel would be a disgrace to anyone professing the Catholic name'. This charge roused Waugh to indicate for the first time the infinite pains – sometimes associated with genius – that he took in the construction and execution of books which have often deceived the casual reader into regarding them as superficial, or satirical only in an artless and heartless fashion. One passage that was attacked was that in which Basil Seal is informed that his friend Prudence has just been consumed at a cannibal feast in which he has taken part. Waugh replied in an open letter to the Cardinal Archbishop of Westminster (at that time the legal owner of *The Tablet*) dated May 1933, not yet published, but referred to in Dr F. W. Stopp's thorough and interesting book *Evelyn Waugh – Portrait of an Artist*: 'Several writers whose opinion I respect', Waugh wrote, 'have told me that they regard this as a disagreeable incident. It was meant to be. *The story deals with the conflict of civilization, with all its attendant and deplorable ills, and barbarism.*' The italics are mine, but the subject remained his.

The conflict, indeed, is almost the same as the one that at many different levels gave him the material for the masterpiece of his maturity, the *Sword of Honour* trilogy, though the crux of those novels is of course the disillusionment of the idealist when he becomes acquainted with the day to day nature of his crusade. The letter went on:

The plan of my book throughout was to keep the darker aspects of barbarism continually and unobtrusively present, a black and mischievous background against which the civilized and semi-civilized characters performed their parts. I wished it to be like the continuous, remote throbbing of the hand drums, constantly audible, never visible, which any traveller in Africa will remember as one of his most haunting impressions . . . hoping to prepare the reader for the sudden tragedy when barbarism at last emerges from the shadows and usurps the stage. It is not unlikely that I failed in this; that the transition was too rapid, the catastrophe too large.

This is the artist speaking (and foreshadowing, incidentally, Trimmer's rendering of *Night and Day*), not, of course, the moralist, but the letter contains by implication a crushing rebuke for those of his hostile critics who make the foolish mistake of ignoring or distorting his avowed intent in writing novels.

This intent, by the way, is nowhere better summed up than in the well-digested interview with Mr Julian Jebb in the *Paris Review* in 1963, only three years before Waugh's death: 'I regard writing', he said, 'not as investigation of character, but as an exercise in the use of language, and with this I am obsessed. I have no technical psychological interest. It is drama, speech and events that interest me.' Few authors have chosen their ground so carefully, and are less open to attack on it; few have made sparer claims for their works, or have described them with such precision or such sharply perceptive self-criticism. Of *Vile Bodies*, for example, he observed in the same interview: 'It was a bad book, I think, not so carefully constructed as the first. Separate scenes tended to go on far too long – the conversation on the train between those two women, the film shows of the dotty father. . . . It was second-hand too. I cribbed much of the scene at the customs from Firbank. I popularized a fashionable language, like the Beatnik writers today, and the book caught on.' This delightful detachment was again to be observed when a friend sympathised with Waugh on the illness and hallucinations that he had plainly undergone himself before writing *The Ordeal of Gilbert Pinfold* (a name he borrowed, incidentally, from an earlier owner of Piers Court, and therefore in a sense a prototype of himself. One wonders what the original Pinfold would have thought of his bizarre reincarnation). Waugh disclaimed the sympathy, and pointed out what a stroke of luck it was for an ageing novelist, not taking much part in general life, suddenly to be provided with a rich vein of new material for a story.

If he did not spare himself, he notoriously failed to spare others. In this respect, the example of his comrade-in-arms Randolph

Churchill, whose courage he admired, was perhaps unfortunate. Many and tedious are the stories of his rudeness, some of them of the most disagreeable variety of all, cruelly directed against those who were too young, too unsure of themselves, or for some other reason unable to answer back. But one of his most curious if silent outbursts occurred when an old friend of his, a prominent man of letters, brought a visitor, of whom Waugh disapproved, to lunch at their club. When they had sat down, he sent over a series of notes offering larger and larger bribes to secure the departure of the offending guest. The recipient of them coolly allowed the sum to rise to £15 before beating a retreat, and no doubt entertained his guest still more lavishly and in greater tranquillity elsewhere.

Why Waugh was a victim of these transports of rudeness and hostility remains a mystery. Was it because of the threats, real or imagined, to his sense of security, mentioned already? He cannot have liked it when the *Corriere della Sera*, in a series of articles on English writers described him as *modestamente borghese in apparenza*. Yet it exposed him to no ridicule in his own country – those deafening tweeds needed no external reinforcement. Perhaps a general resentment at being misunderstood, at being estimated incorrectly – as opposed to not highly enough – was intolerable for an artist for whom nothing was too much trouble to get right, and who was, as I have already quoted him, obsessed with the use of language, and whose interest in the vagaries of general life became, perhaps, largely professional.

But if he could be pointlessly cruel, he could be not only genial and good-humoured with old friends and cronies of either sex, but also handsomely generous to his juniors. To a recent Oxford graduate whose fortunes had fallen from a respectable level to one of bewildered unease, the following words in a letter from Waugh were greatly comforting, and needless to say in sharp contrast to the reactions of others. They can have been prompted only by the most genuine if little deserved sympathy: 'I hope you are not cast down by your result in Schools', he wrote. 'Of my contemporaries, those who achieved any success in after life nearly all got thirds or were sent down. To have achieved both sounds to me like a good omen.' And a friend of his eldest daughter's, who had had the temerity to avail herself of the gentlemen's downstairs lavatory at Combe Florey, only drew the cheeriest rebuke: Waugh inscribed the words 'SWEET ALICE KEEP OUT' on a large sheet of paper and pinned it to the violated door.

16

YOURS AFFEC: EVELYN

Anne Fleming

EVELYN

EVELYN became a friend in March 1952, when I left Esmond Rothermere and married Ian Fleming. Though obeying the dictates of the heart, I had that shaky feeling which must accompany the breaking of laws and vows. Support and encouragement were welcome. Evelyn's was remarkable and unexpected. A letter arrived. It contained a sheet of Victorian Valentine writing paper liberally decorated with bells, doves and cherubs, and one short sentence, 'I rejoice in your escape from the arms of Esmond.' Mystified, I requested clarification. Apparently, since Esmond had a wife, though divorced (or die-vorced, as Evelyn always pronounced it), I had been living in sin and was now in a state of grace. Heartened by this news, friendship and correspondence ensued and did not cease till his death. It was a relationship giving nothing but joy.

Evelyn affected a grave demeanour of manner, he seldom laughed aloud, and a smile was very rewarding. He was a great comedian, and at moments one was reminded of Charlie Chaplin, the little man, the figure of fun. It is difficult for me to understand why so many feared him – perhaps he could not resist attacking pretension and all forms of cowardice. And it must be admitted that sometimes he just liked to attack.

In one letter, he describes a country sale of furniture: elegant pieces were beyond his means but he had a penchant for elephantine Victoriana and bid thirty shillings for, and secured, a sideboard so mammoth that the auctioneer got crusty and said he could get more for it as firewood. The crowd took Evelyn's side and shouted, 'Give it to the little guy, let the little guy have it.'

Evelyn did not know what fear meant, and he worshipped the sort of physical courage epitomised by Bob Laycock. When the war trilogy appeared, I pretended to identify the caddish Ivor Claire with Bob, and his response was violent indeed but not wholly simulated. Much of the abuse and disdain in his correspondence was devoted to my friends, Peter Quennell, Lucian Freud, Stephen Spender, Alistair Forbes. Except for Cyril Connolly for whom there were undertones of affection, they were known collectively as the 'Fuddy Duddies'. He deplored both their war and their matrimonial records. War could not apply to Lucian for he was too young for it, but 'his inability to put a tiara on a lay figure' was an unkind comment on Lucian's portrait of me. Catholics like Graham Greene, Christopher Sykes and assorted clergy, were preferred to all of us.

It was difficult to distinguish his attitudes from his convictions.

'Country gentry' played a large part in his mythology. He loved his
wife and children, though his profound melancholy and fits of 'aggro'
cannot have made him the easiest of husbands or fathers. He and
Laura spent a weekend in the house which Ian and I had built; he
was persistently critical of all we had done and Laura bade him write
an apology. It starts: 'I am apt to pick holes.' On one occasion, the
Waughs called upon me to commiserate on a child of mine who had
recently died at the age of six weeks. Advance news from White's
Club informed me that Evelyn was saying, 'I shall make funny faces
at her to console her.' This news was ill-received, and Laura, seeing
that something was amiss, said, 'When Evelyn is in one of his bad
moods, we send him to a witch in Somerset who spits at him.'

'Marble Halls' denoted the Ritz, which was his favourite restaurant.
He could not abide small and smoky eating-places and deplored the
fact that Diana Cooper, his favourite woman, liked snacks and cheap
meals. Clothes had to be formal, though in the Fifties he occasionally
wore a pale grey suit and a pale grey half-melon bowler. It looked
decidedly eccentric.

Twice Evelyn provoked me to physical violence. The first time was
when he was sporting a National Health deaf-aid as part of his psychological warfare for dinner-parties; it resembled a small aluminium
saucepan and would be stuck in his ear when he said something specially
provocative and was waiting for the reaction. It was so outrageous
that I hit the saucepan sharply with my soup spoon, and it set up
terrible reverberations in his ear-drum. He claimed to have a headache
for weeks as a result of a malicious attack.

The next bout of fisticuffs was in the sepulchrally silent tea-room
of the Grand Hotel, Folkestone. Evelyn was annoyed that I had
brought my three-year-old son, who was perched on my knee; so
he put his face close to the child's dragging down the corners of eyes
and mouth with forefingers and thumbs, producing an effect of such
unbelievable malignity that the child shrieked with terror and fell to
the floor. I gave Evelyn's face a hard slap, overturning a plate of
éclairs, and presently had my revenge by driving over a cart-track so
bumpy that he swallowed half his cigar.

Never a good sleeper, in the last years of his life he increased his
intake of paraldehyde, a harmless but evil-smelling sedative. He
indignantly denied that he smelled of it, until he was sharing a sofa
with Evangeline Bruce in my house when she asked, 'Should we tell
Anne the gas is escaping?' His problems of sleeplessness and boredom

became as real to Ian and me as to him when he spent two weeks with us in Jamaica. A promise had been made to Peter Quennell who was also our guest that Evelyn would not arrive until Peter was due to leave. Probably with a view to torturing Quennell, Evelyn appeared long before he was due. Ian suspected that we should interrupt his work on the current 'Bond' and despatched the three of us to raft on the Rio Grande. A motor drive and a night in a hotel preceded a day spent on long narrow bamboo rafts poled by grinning Negroes over stretches of wide calm water alternating with moments of bouncing and slithering through rapids. It was a treat usually memorable for silence and nice water noises, tropical flowering trees and exciting birds. But Evelyn would not let things be. He had delegated to Peter the role of head boy on a safari, and Peter did not protest.

'Peter', Evelyn said, 'shall walk five paces behind us and carry the luncheon basket. We will travel on the advance raft, and he will travel on the second, seeing that the comestibles do not become damp.'

Once afloat, Evelyn sadly confided that he got no pleasure from natural beauty. Unsympathetically, I requested silence for bird-watching. We were passing a flock of wading egrets. 'Owls!' cried Evelyn loudly, frightening them all away. Argument followed but abruptly ended, for we were tumbling about in the first rapid, and the raft slowly and surprisingly disintegrated. Peter sailed by dry and triumphant, and he said it had been like watching an old-fashioned carriage accident. We swam for the shore, Evelyn doing a slow breast stroke, blue eyes blazing and mood much improved, for he liked things to go wrong.

On the return journey to Goldeneye, stops at petrol stations were punctuated by Quennell being told 'Gentlemen always pay for the petrol.' Gravely they divided the price between them.

Peter departed, Ian wrote and I tried to entertain our entertaining but exigeant guest. Danger was the best stimulant; alarming trips in the very small rubber boat on or over the edge of the reef where it was always possible that a jagged coral rock would sink us. The bows sank low with Evelyn's weight, he looked solemn and hopeful, wearing a large Panama hat borrowed from Lord Brownlow. Then one day his hopes were realised. A gust of wind blew the Panama out to a rough sea, and into barracuda-infested water. Evelyn said that it was not his property and we must retrieve it. I flung him the oars and swam ashore. His was a far from safe adventure, but he returned gleeful and heaped reproaches on my head for cowardice, though promising never to tell my friends of my true nature.

It was Lent, and the morning task was to spear a lobster not less or more than two and a half pounds in weight, a suitable luncheon which did not break the rules of Evelyn's Catholic fasting. Apparently the evening meal is called a 'Coena' and it appeared to our heathen eyes that one ate a very great deal of everything. Alcohol was not abandoned, 'because', we were told, 'water was a great health risk when the Church was founded'.

Despite our efforts, boredom set in for Goldeneye afforded little of the human material so necessary to the author. He was sent to Kingston, to an acquaintance whose living-room was furnished with a bar adorned with tall glasses which were engraved with doubtful jokes. The visit was a happy idea. A Catholic bishop was lured to cocktails, he became very drunk, fell off the bar stool and lost his ring. Evelyn returned to Goldeneye much stimulated by the horrors of Kingston.

For the remaining days he spent with us, he amused himself by forcing Ian to rewrite all the current Bond love scenes over and over again. 'An author', he decreed, 'must be in a state of lustful excitement when writing of love.' Ian was not allowed a drink until he was judged to have been in the right mood.

Some may have been permitted to telephone Evelyn, to me it was forbidden, though I once broke the rule. Some hours after he had left our house in Kent for a hotel nearby, a telegram arrived for him; it seemed to me urgent, for it gave the hour on the following day at which he was to be sponsor to Dame Edith Sitwell at her reception into the Catholic Church. An epic involving such formidable human beings was not negligible, I telephoned and was crushed. 'Your manservant should have delivered it', he said reproachfully and rang off. He knew perfectly well that I had no manservant, though these obsolete and useful persons were part of his act. He declared that Nancy Mitford should not dictate on U and non-U because her parents had not employed a manservant.

Cut-throat razors, 'concs' and catemites played a large part in his letters – concs being concubines, and catemites being homosexuals: references are of course all libellous. It was regarded as cowardly not to use a cut-throat razor, and he was awfully cross when three little holes appeared in the bathrooms of the Hyde Park Hotel and the cowards all went electric. Cyril Connolly was among the first to own one. They were staying with Patrick Kinross who had no facilities for this invention, so Cyril drove to a neighbouring hotel, shaved in the public bar and returned with 'his poor little face all blue'.

I preferred lunching in Marble Halls with Evelyn to entertaining him at home. The Ritz mellowed him, he tucked into caviar and drank his chablis, and then we would go hunting for Pre-Raphaelite paintings. He had once found lipstick on a napkin in our house, and worse, paper napkins. Then there was the hazard of my delinquent friends. 'Still time to go to Marble Halls', he would say in a loud aside, staring horribly at them. The round blue eyes would grow rounder, the stare more intense. I wondered if it had been perfected before a mirror, and was amazed at the success of so simple a device to disconcert. But perhaps it was natural to him, for fellow-pupils at his first day-school still complain of it. Cecil Beaton still remembers fear.

When Ian died, Evelyn's letters showed compassion and understanding; a more sensitive and kinder friend one could not wish for. If any of our acquaintance became a widower, however unlikely a suitor, a postcard would arrive, advising against matrimony. One reads, 'I see Osbert Lancaster is bereaved, it would be most imprudent to marry him.' It is tempting to dwell on the comedy but alas, Evelyn's health was inexorably declining. He had great misery with his teeth and generally was feeling ill. The change in the Mass upset him dreadfully, and so did the Pope's visit to America. With a return to the old levity, knowing that my son Caspar has a weakness for fire-arms, he wrote offering him a bribe if he would go to New York to shoot the Pope.

Visits to Marble Halls became less frequent. The last time he attended Brian Frank's Christmas luncheon banquet at the Hyde Park Hotel, he had no appetite. We usually dined after the banquet, but on this occasion he was low in spirit and we stayed in his suite. The bathroom was without sponge or toothbrush, furnished only with aids to sleep. He wanted Laura, who had taken some of the children to the cinema, and could not be found. I stayed with him till Laura's arrival was imminent, and was very sad to find him so changed.

Here is a letter he wrote to me in May 1960 which seems typical of the last years:

I am slowly composing a third volume of the War novels – not bad, so far. All about the 'Sword of Stalingrad'. Do you remember that? does anyone? It is the theme of the first part of the book and it will fall pretty flat if it is quite forgotten. Ask representative younger people such as O'Neill [my son] if they have heard of it. Well I suppose the young don't read my books anyhow.

Did I tell you Bron has a bizarre book appearing shortly? Very funny, I thought when I read it but I can't remember anything about it now. It is very pleasant losing one's memory. One can read old favourites with breathless curiosity. I have just reread all G. Greene and A. Powell.

I spent a weekend in London with Margaret [his second daughter] – and came near death from exhaustion – Soane Museum, St Paul's Cathedral, a play about buggery called Ross (a visit to [Sir Alec] Guinness in dressing room) much champagne with Maimie, Royal Academy to see Stanley Spencers, huge very expensive meals in marble halls of which I could eat nothing. An odd attack of Pinfold. I had planned to come home on Sunday. On Saturday, dead sober, I told the hall porter to look up a train for me to Gloucester – a station I never used in my life. I had the time firm in my mind. Margaret came to see me off and I went to the booking office and asked for a train to Gloucester. She corrected me. Dazed I asked for Taunton. Last train had gone. Had to spend another night in London and give Margaret another enormous dinner (St James' Club). Why in heaven's name Gloucester? it was always Kemble or Stroud when I lived in Stinkers.

I don't expect you know today is Ascension Day. This day 1917 was the most unhappy of my life. My first term, first month at Lancing. I had never heard about Ascension Day before. It was not observed in my home or at my prep school. Well, I overheard boys talking of this mysterious day, and when it came they all disappeared. It was a whole holiday. I had nowhere to go and no friends. The steward gave me some ghastly galantine (first war food was worse than second) and I ate it alone on the downs near Chanctonbury Ring. So every Ascension Day since I have felt that things can never be as bad as that.

Now say you are out, and don't take telephone calls, and write me a letter.

Yours affec:

Evelyn.

Index

Abyssinia: EW reviews book on, 191; EW visits (1930), 83–6; war in, EW covers (1935), 90, 122; *156–7, 186*
Acropolis, the, 83
Acton, Harold, 4, 35, 138; Catholicism of, 62; EW's caricature of, *32*; *Memoirs of an Aesthete*, 40; *More Memoirs of an Aesthete*, 77; on Olivia Plunket-Greene, 40; *118, 119*
Acton, William, 138
Addis Ababa, 84, 85, 92
Aden, 84, 87
Alba, Duke of, *120*
Allingham, William, 16
Amis, Kingsley: *One Fat Englishman*, 169
Antic Hay (Huxley), EW praises, 214
Antrim, Lord, *119*
'Ape, Mrs Melrose', 61, 167, 168, 178
'Apthorpe', 91, 93
Arnold, Matthew, 11
Asquith family, EW's friendship with, 77
Asquith, Mrs Raymond, *120*
Atlantic, the, 194n, 215
Auden, W. H., 194
Authors Take Sides on the Spanish War, 2–3

Baldwin, of Bewdley, Lord ('Bloggs'), 51
Balfour, the Honourable Patrick *see* Kinross, Lord
Balliol College, Oxford, 24, 33, 36
Balston, Tom, 220
Bardia, Commando raid on, 195–6
Bari, 53, 55, 142, 163; EW despises, 141
Barth, John, 173
Barthelme, Donald, 173
Barton, Mgr John, 130
Bath, Lord, *118, 119*
Beaton, Cecil, 240; drawing of Nancy Mitford, *116*
Beatrice, Infanta of Spain, 159
Beauchamp, Lord ('Boom'), 13, 52n, 53
Beaverbrook Press, 91, 215, 225
Beerbohm, Max, 139, 193, 194n
Belloc, Hilaire, 193, 194n
Bendir, Mrs Arthur, 14, 53
Berkhamsted, 24
Berkhamsted School, 24
Berners, Lord, *115*

'Beste-Chetwynde, Mrs', 230
Betjeman, John: 2, 98, 99, 100; on *Brideshead Revisited*, 2; marriage to Penelope Chetwode, 98, 99; *208*
Bevan, Emlyn, 18n
Birkenhead, Frederick, 2nd Earl, 3; in Yugoslavia with EW and Randolph Churchill, 55, 134, 138–63
Bisley, 16
'Blanche, Anthony', 35, 36
Blenheim Palace, 141
Boa Vista, 89
Books on Trial, 194n
'Boot, William', 91, 92
Boothby, Robert, baron, 119
Bosnia, 134, 135
Bowen, Elizabeth: *Time in Rome*, 226
Bowlby, Henry, Headmaster of Lancing, 16, 20
Bowra, Maurice, 11; on EW and women, 40; at Penelope Chetwode's confirmation, 101
Boy Scouts, Aden troop of, 87–8
Bracken, Brendan, 93
Brave New World (Huxley), 187–9
Brent-Smith, master at Lancing, 16
Brick-Tops, nightclub, 82
'Bright Young People', 40
Bristol Grammar School, 128
British Broadcasting Corporation, 55, 149 *and see Face to Face*
British Dramatists (Greene), 192
British Guiana, 89–90
Browning, Robert, 11
Bruce, Evangeline, 237
Buck's Club, 124
Bullingdon Club, Oxford, 24, 36, 138
Burns and Oates, publishers, 130
Butler, Abbot, 214n
Byron, Robert, 83

Cabell, James Branch, 44
Cairo, 82
California, 167, 168, 172, 175, 176, 177, 182
Campion Hall, Oxford, 77, 99, 100, 121; *120*
Canonbury Square, the Waugh's house at, *106*
Capetown, 88, 94
Carew, Dudley: friendship with EW, 3–4, 19, 40–7; introduces Evelyn Gardner to EW, 41–2; marriage to Anthea Gamble, 43, 47

Cartland, Barbara: *Follow My Leader*, 40
Carlyle, Thomas, 16
Catholic Church: EW received into (1930), 74,
    120, 214; *and see* Catholicism, Vatican Council,
    Second
Catholic Legion of Decency, 127
Catholicism: Alfred Duggan and, 36; and
    ecumenism, 128, 131; EW and, 51, 60–79,
    100–2, 104–30 *passim*, 149, 190, 213–14, 236,
    239, 240; and EW's work, 53, 62–3, 64–5, 73–4,
    78, 87, 127–8, 166, 174, 186, 227; in EW's
    family, 10; Frank Pakenham and, 51, 62; of
    Graham Greene, 192–3; Penelope Chetwode
    and, 100–101; the Plunket-Greene's and, 61–2;
    in the USA, EW's interest in, 181–2, 213–14
Cecil, Lord David, *120*
Chagford, Devon, 124
Chaplin, Charles, 236
Chapman and Hall, publishers, 8, 44, 47, 184, 220
Chesterton, G. K., 64; *Everlasting Man*, 129
Chetwode, Penelope (Lady Betjeman), friendship
    with EW, 3, 98–102
Christ Church, Oxford, 11, 32, 36, 138
Church of England, 10, 61, 63, 104, 128
Churchill, Randolph, 182; in Bosnia, 134; EW's
    relationship with, 77, 232–3; with EW in
    Yugoslavia, 55, 135, 138–63; *160*; and
    identity of 'Buttocks', 18n
Churchill, Winston S., 140, 147; *Life of
    Marlborough*, 150; *My Early Life*, 62
Circular Saws (Wolfe), EW's jacket for, *68*
Clissold, Major Stephen, 134–5, 142, 143–4, 145,
    146, 147, 150, 152, 163
Clonmore, Lord, 35
Cocteau, Jean, 82
Combe Florey, Somerset, the Waughs' home, 79,
    100, 129, 233; *204, 205, 207–8, 210–11*
Commandos, EW in, 52, 123–4, 139, 195
Commonweal, 193n, 215
Communism, 145, 146; EW's detestation of, 3,
    148–9
Connolly, Cyril, 2, 3, 4, 177, 215, 231, 236, 239–
    40; *119*
Constantine, Emperor, 78
Cooper, Lady Diana, 4, 237
Corriere della Sera, 233
Corsley, 10
Coward, Noel, 51; *Private Lives*, 51
Cowfold, 19
Crease, Francis, 19
Crete, 94, 124, 134
Croatia, EW in 94, 134–5, 141–63; *160*
'Crouchback, Guy', 73, 88, 93–4, 123, 195
Crusades, the, 131
Cruttwell, C. R. M. F., Dean of Hertford College,
    Oxford, 33–4, 76, 230
Crying of Lot 49, The (Pynchon), 176
Curzon, Lord, 36

Daily Mail, The, 122
Daily Telegraph, The, 184
Dakar, 196
Daphne, 83
D'Arcy, Father Martin: and EW, 3, 51, 121, 122;
    on EW's Catholicism, 60–79; *120*
Dawkins, Prof., R. M., 11
Day of the Locust, The (West), 173, 174–6
Deakin, Col William F. W. D., 141
Deal, EW stationed at, 123

Deer Park, The (Mailer), 173, 176
Diaghilev, Sergei, 44
Diary of a Nobody (Grossmiths), 220
Dickens, Charles, 11, 89; EW admires, 230;
    Little Dorrit, 20; *Martin Chuzzlewit*, 169
Djibouti, 84
Dominican Order, 100–101, 125
Donaldson, Mrs Frances: *Evelyn Waugh,
    Portrait of a Country Neighbour*, 60, 75, 76
drawings by EW, 11, 12, 50; *26, 32, 65–72, 153–5*
Drayton, Michael: *To the Virginian Voyage*, 180
Driberg, Tom, friendship with EW, 19
Drury Lowe, John, *118*
Dubrovnik, 55, 83
Duckworth, publishers, 44, 220
Duggan, Alfred, 36–7
Duggan, Hubert, friendship with EW, 24, 36, 56;
    death of, 76; *111*
Dunne, Philip, 52
Dursley, 123, 124

Easton, Dr, creator of Forest Lawn, 168, 169
Egg, Augustus, 123
Elected Silence (Merton), 182
Eliot, T. S.: *The Wasteland*, 45, 138
Elmley, Lord, 35
Encounter, 18n, 215n
End of the Affair, The (Greene), EW reviews,
    193
Enthusiasm (Knox), 129
Erskine, Hamish St Clair, 56; *111*
Ervine, St John, 44
Esquire, EW writes for, 215
Etna, Mount, 83
Eton College, 16, 141
Eurich, Richard, *209*
Evans, Sir Horace, 130
Evelyn Waugh, Portrait of a Country Neighbour
    (Donaldson), 60, 75, 76
Evelyn Waugh – Portrait of an Artist (Stopp), 231
Evening Standard, The, 189
Everlasting Man (Chesterton), 129
Eyston, Agnes, 101

Face to Face, TV programme (1962), 2; *222–3*
Fiedler, Leslie: *Love and Death in the American
    Novel*, 179
Firbank, Ronald, EW on, 190–1, 193; influence
    on EW, 190–1, 230, 232
Fitzgerald, F. Scott, 172–3; *The Last Tycoon*,
    173, 176
Fitzherbert, Giles, *119*
Fleming, Anne, friendship with EW, 4, 236–41;
    marriage to Ian Fleming, 236
Fleming, Caspar, 240
Fleming, Ian, 93; death, 240; friendship with EW
    237, 238, 239; marriage, 236
Follow My Leader (Cartland), 40
Fonthill Abbey, 10
Forbes, Alistair, 236
Forest Lawn Memorial Park, 63, 127, 168–9, 172,
    177, 182; as 'Whispering Glades', 177, 178–81
Forster, E. M.: *A Passage to India*, 54
Foujita, 82
Fox, Adam, master at Lancing, 16
Franco, General, 2–3, 125
Frank, Brian, 240
Freeman, John, 128; *221*
Freud, Lucian, 236

Friedman, Bruce J., 173
Fulford, Roger, 4, 16–21

Gamble, Anthea (Mrs Dudley Carew), 43, 47
Gardner, the Honourable Evelyn, 41–2, 46–7; *105*
Gibbon, Edward, 62
Gibraltar, 141; EW's loathing for, 83
Gifford, Barry, 41
Glen, Sir Alexander, 51
Gloucester, Duke of, 85–6
Golders Green, EW's youth in, 8–11, 12
Gordon, E. B., House-master at Lancing, 16
Gosse, Edmund, 10
Gosse, Sylvia, 44
Graham, Alastair ('Hamish Lennox'), 12, 83; *114*
Greece, 83
Greene, Charles, Headmaster of Berkhamsted, 24
Greene, Graham, 179, 236, 241; *British Dramatists*, 193; *The End of the Affair*, 193; *The Heart of the Matter*, 193; *The Lawless Roads*, 192; *The Quiet American*, 193*n*
Greenidge, Terence, 35
'Grimes, Captain', 36
Grossmith, George and Weedon: *Diary of a Nobody*, 220
Grotius, Hugo, 125
Guiness, Sir Alec, 241
Guiness, Desmond, *119*

Haile Selassie, Emperor of Abyssinia, 83, 85, 86, 122
Hampstead, 8, 9, 44
Hance, Captain, 13, 50, 56, 98
Harris, 'Dick', House-master at Lancing, 16
Harrod, Dominic, *119*
Harrod, Henry, *119*
Harrod, Sir Roy, *118, 119*
Hay, Ian (Maj-Gen. Sir John Hay Beith), 93
Heart of the Matter, The (Greene), EW reviews, 193
Heller, Joseph, 173
Hemingway, Ernest, 172, 190
Herbert, Aubrey, (EW's father-in-law), 74, 77
Herbert, Laura, *see* Waugh, Mrs Evelyn
Herbert, Mary (EW's mother-in-law), 74, 77; *120*
Hertford College, Oxford, 11, 33, 37, 61, 76, 104, 230
Hinde, Thomas: *High*, 169
Hollis, Christopher, 62
Hollywood, EW visits, 127, 166, 168–9, 213; *199*; EW writes on, 169–74, 213; novels of, 172–3, 175–7; *and see* Forest Lawn Memorial Park
Horizon, 177, 194*n*, 215, 231
Horner, Lady, *120*
Howard, Brian, 35; *118*
Hügel, Baron Friedrich von, 60, 61
Huxley, Aldous, 172; *Antic Hay*, 214; *Brave New World*, 182–3
Hyde Park Hotel, 124, 130, 239, 240
Hypocrites' Club, Oxford, 35, 38

In a Valley of this Restless Mind (Muggeridge), 194*n*
Innocent XI, Pope, 130
International Lawyers, Congress of, 125
Isherwood, Christopher: *Journey to a War*, 194
Italy, 53, 57; EW's honeymoon in, 52; invasion of Abyssinia, 122

Jacobs, W. W., 24–33
Jamaica, EW visits, 238–9
Jebb, Julian, 232
John XXIII, Pope, 131
Jones, Owen, 225
Jordan, Philip, 53
Journey to a War (Isherwood), 194
Joy, Robert Musgrave, *209*
Jungman, Teresa, 51

Keble, Lady, 34
Kennedy, Margaret: *The Outlaw on Parnassus*, 54
Kenya, EW in, 88; *158*
Kinross, Lord (formerly Patrick Balfour), 240; *108–9, 118*
Knox, Mgr Ronald: dedicates *Enthusiasm* to EW, 129; death of, 130; EW's biography of, 129–30, 225; EW's friendship with, 77, 129; sleeps during own lecture, 102; as a writer, 129, 193, 194*n*, 214; *120*

Lamb, Henry, 42, 43, 104; *31*
Lancaster, Osbert, 124, 240; *201*
Lancing School, 11, 16–21, 33, 43, 60–1, 62, 241; *28–9*
Laski, Harold, 225
'Last, Tony', 62, 126
Last Tycoon, The (Fitzgerald), 173, 176
Laurencin, Marie, 82
Lawless Roads, The (Greene), EW reviews, 192
Lawrence Gertrude, 51
Laycock, Colonel Robert (later Maj.-Gen. Sir Robert), 52, 94, 124, 236
League of Anti-Fascist Women, 161
League of Nations, 122
Lecky, William, 62, 152
Lej Yasu, Abyssinian claimant, 85
'Lennox, Hamish', *see* Graham, Alastair
Life, 166, 169, 195–6, 213, 215
Life and Letters, 190
Life of Marlborough (Churchill), 150
Little Dorritt (Dickens), 20
Lolita (Nabokov), 177
London Mercury, The, 8
Longford, Christine and Edward, 98
Longford, Lord *see* Pakenham, Frank
Loom of Youth, The (Alec Waugh), 10–11, 18, 33
Loose Ends (Lunn), 61
Lovat, Lord ('Shimi'), 93, 134
Love and Death in the American Novel (Fiedler), 179
Lowell, James Russell, 179
Lucas, Audrey, 46
Lucy, EW's Nanny, 9
Lunn, Arnold: *Loose Ends*, 61
Lutyens, Sir Edwin, 76; *120*
Lyford Grange, 99, 121–2
Lygon, The Hon. Lady Dorothy, friendship with EW, 4, 50–7; *110, 111, 112*
Lygon, Hugh, friendship with EW, 13, 35, 51, 53; *118*
Lygon, Lady Lettice, 35
Lygon, Lady Mary ('Maimie', 'Blondie'), 51, 53, 56, 230, 241; *110, 112*

Macaulay, Thomas Babington, 125, 147, 152
Mackie, Dr, 57
Maclean, Sir Fitzroy, 3, 134–5, 140
McPherson, Aimée Semple, 168

Madresfield Court: EW's visits to, 50–1, 57, 98; as source for *Brideshead Revisited*, 53–4; *110–11, 113*
Mahon, Theodosia (EW's great-grandmother), 10
Mailer, Norman: *The Deer Park*, 173, 176
Malvern, 50, 56
Manchester University, 76
Mani, Private, Yugoslav Partisan, 148
Martin Chuzzlewit (Dickens), 169
Meath, Father Gerard, 127
Memoirs of an Aesthete (Acton), 40
Mendl, Sir Charles, *199*
Merton, Father Thomas, 2; *The Seven Storey Mountain* (*Elected Silence*), 182
Messina, 82
'Metroland, Margot', 8, 172, 178
Mexico, 90, 192
Midsomer Norton, 9
Mihailovic, Draga, 124
Miss Lonelyhearts (West), 174
Mitford, Jessica, 2
Mitford, Nancy (Mrs Peter Rodd), 215, 220, 225, 239; *116–17*
Molson, Hugh, 19
Mombasa, 88
Monte Carlo, 82
Montenegro, 83, 141
Month, The, EW contributes to, 193*n*, 215
More Memoirs of an Aesthete (Acton), 77
Morrell, Lady Ottoline, 34
Moulungetta, Commander-in-Chief of Abyssinian Army, 86
Muggeridge, Malcolm: *In a Valley of This Restless Mind*, 194
Murray, Basil, 36
Mussolini, Benito, 141

Nabokov, Vladimir: *Lolita*, 177
Nairobi, EW visits, 88
New Directions in Prose and Poetry, 213*n*
New Statesman, The, 3
New York City, 167
Noel-Buxton, Lord, 215
Northcote, Lewis Stafford, 99

O'Brien, John A. (ed.): *The Road to Damascus*, 63, 214
Observer, The, EW reviews for, 184, 189
Ogilvie-Grant, Mark, 83; *110, 118*
Old Mortality (Scott), 54
Oldmeadow, E. J., 231
One Fat Englishman (Amis), 169
One Man's Road (Arthur Waugh), 13, 184–9, 216–17
Osborne, Sir D'Arcy, 126
Outlaw on Parnassus, The (Kennedy), 54
Oxford, 100–101; Acton brothers' influence on, 138; EW at, 11, 16, 24–38, 40, 61, 62, 104, 184; *30–2*; EW's description of in *Brideshead Revisited*, 147–8
Oxford Union (1920s), 104; *32*

Pakenham, Elizabeth, 51, 101
Pakenham, Frank (later Lord Longford), 51, 62
Pakenham Hall, 98
Pakenham, Lady Pansy, 42, 43
Palestine, EW visits, 63, 73, 82
Paris, EW visits, 82

Paris Review, 166, 191, 232
Pascal, Blaise, 62
Passage to India, A (Forster), 54
'Pavelic, M', Yugoslav interpreter, 145–6, 148
Pavlova, Anna, 44
'Pennyfeather, Paul', 34, 62, 172
Peters, A. D., 4
Piers Court, Stinchcombe, the Waugh's home at, 100, 232; *187, 200, 202–3, 212*
'Pinfold, Gilbert', 13, 38, 75–6, 189
Pius XII, Pope, 126, 130
Pixton Park, Somerset, 74–5, 100
Playboy, EW writer for, 215
Plunket-Greene, David, 40; *118*
Plunket-Greene family, EW's friendship with, 61–2, 77
Plunket-Greene, Gwen, 40, 61–2
Plunket-Greene, Olivia: EW and, 40–1, 42, 61; religion of, 40, 61–2
Plunket-Greene, Richard, 40
Pope, Alexander, 60
Powell, Anthony, 227, 241; *What's Become of Waring?*, 220
Priestley, J. B., 3
Private Lives (Coward), 51
Proust, Marcel, 36, 144
Pryce-Jones, Alan, 8–14; *110*
Purdy, James, 173
Pynchon, Thomas: *The Crying of Lot 49*, 176

Quennell, Peter; with EW at Oxford, 32–8; EW's subsequent dislike of, 3, 32, 226, 227, 236, 237, 238
Quiet American, The (Greene), 193*n*

Raban, Catherine Charlotte, *see* Waugh, Mrs Arthur
Raban, Jonathan, 175
Railway Club, Oxford, *118–19*
Rattigan, Terence: *Ross*, 241
Ravensdale, Baroness Irene, 85, 122
Reade, Winwood, 62
Rickett, F. W., 91–2
'Ritchie-Hook, Brigadier', 94
Ritz Hotel, 121, 237, 240
Road to Damascus, The (ed. O'Brien), 63, 214
Robbins, Harold, 176
Rodd, Peter, 36
Rodd, Mrs Peter *see* Mitford, Nancy
Rome, 53, 54; and annulment of EW's marriage, 74
'Rothschild, Father, S.J.', 61
Rosebery, Lady, *115*
Ross (Rattigan), 241
Rosse, Lord, *118*
Rothermere, Esmond, Viscount, 236
Roxburgh, J. F., EW's form-master at Lancing, 11, 16, 19, 61, 62
Royal Marines, EW in, 52, 94, 123, 139, 195
Rugby School, 16, 227
Runciman, Sir Steven, 131
Ruskin, Mrs John (Effie), 150
Russian Ballet, 44
'Ryder, Charles', 64, 82, 167

'St Cloud, Reggie', 52
St Edmund Campion, 73, 77, 99, *121–2*
St Edmund's College, Ware, 129–30
St Helena, 78, 79, 127, 131

St James's Club, 93, 241
St Joan (Shaw), 40
St John's Gospel, 64
St Peter, 64
St Thomas Aquinas, 216
Salisbury, EW's cottage at, 104
Sarawak, White Rajah of, 41; Ranee of, 42
Sayers, Dorothy L., 127
Scott, Sir Walter: *Old Mortality*, 54
'Seal, Basil', 36, 86, 89, 93, 172, 231
Selfridge's, 40
Serbia, 124, 135
Seven Storey Mountain, The (Merton), 182
Shaw, George Bernard: *St Joan*, 40
Sherborne School, 11
'Silk, Ambrose', 36, 231
Sitwell, Dame Edith, 239
Sitwell, Osbert, 83; *120*
Sitwell, Sacheverell, 83, 192
Somerset, 92, 128, 129, 227 *and see* Combe Florey
South America, EW visits, 89–90
Southern, Terry, 173
Soviet Union, 146, 148
Spain, EW visits (1947), 125–6; *and see* Spanish Civil War
Spain, Nancy, 215
Spanish Civil War, 2–3, 122
Spark, Muriel, 2, 173
Sparrow, John, *119*
Spectator, The, EW's contributions to, 2, 128, 184, 189, 190, 191, 192, 193, 194, 214, 215
Spencer, Sir Stanley, 241
Spender, Stephen, 236; *World Within World*, 194
Spitzbergen, EW visits, 51
Squire, J. C., 8
Stalin, Joseph, 148
Stalingrad, Sword of, 148, 240
Stari, Sergeant, Yugoslav Partisan, 148, 149
Stavordale, Lord, *118*
Stella Polaris, the, 82
Stepping Westward (Bradbury), 169
Stern, G. B., 44
Stinchcombe, Glos., 57, 100, *and see* Piers Court
Stonyhurst, EW attends retreat at, 121
Stopp, Dr F. W.: *Evelyn Waugh – Portrait of an Artist*, 231
Strachey, Isobel, *110*
Sunday Telegraph, The, EW writes for, 184, 216–17
Sunday Times, The, 226; EW writes for, 2, 129, 193*n*, 194*n*, 216
Sutro, John, 36; *118*, *119*
Sweden, EW visits, 126
Swift, Dean Jonathan, 60, 74, 177
Sykes, Christopher, 4, 102, 193*n*, 236; *119*
'Symes, Adam', 62

Tablet, The, 131; criticism of *Black Mischief in*, 231; EW contributes to, 126, 127–8, 214*n*, 215
Tanganyka, EW visits, 88
Tatler, The, *108*, *110*, *113*
Tennyson, Alfred Lord, 11, 184
Texas, University of, 4, 182
'Thanatogenos, Aimeé', 178, 179–81
Thomas, Dylan, 166
Time and Tide, 214–15
Time in Rome (Bowen), 226
Time-machine, The (Wells), 20
Times, The, EW reports for, 122, 189

Times Literary Supplement, The, 47
Tito, Marshal, 124, 134, 140, 141, 145; EW insists is a woman, 135, 150–1; EW meets, 135
To the Virginian Voyage (Drayton), 180
Tobruk, 196
Topusco, Yugoslavia, 144–5, 163
Trevelyan, George Macaulay, 24
Trollope, Anthony, 11, 55, 56
Turkey, EW visits, 83
Tutankhamun, EW sees treasures of, 82

Udine, Prince, 86
United States of America: EW lectures in, 181–2; EW's view of, 3, 167–74, 177–81, 213; EW visits, 127, 166, 168–9, 213; *199*; EW writes for, 196–213, 215, *and see Life*; the Pope's visit to, 240; and World War II, 196; writers of, 172–3, 175–7
Urquhart, 'Sligger', Dean of Balliol, 11, 37, 38

Vatican Council, Second, 78, 131, 214
Venice, 57, 83
Villefranche, EW at, *108*, *114*
Vis, Yugoslavia, 134–5, 150
Vittoria, Francisco de, 125

Wain, John, 215
Wallace, Henry, 193
Wasteland, The (Eliot), 45, 138
Waugh, Alec (EW's brother), 104, 226; and birth of EW, 12; caricature of, *65*; on EW's attitude to Golders Green, 8; on EW's choice of career, 131; engagement, 33; *The Loom of Youth*, 10–11, 18, 33; school years, 9, 11; *114*, *200*, *212*
Waugh, Dr Alexander (EW's grandfather), character of, 9–10, 60
Waugh, Arthur (EW's father), 8, 43, 47; attitude to EW's writing, 13, 216; character of, 9; courtesy of, 213; literary activities of, 10, 184–5; and publication of *Decline and Fall*, 44; *One Man's Road* (autobiography), 9, 13, 184, 216–17; relationship with EW, 9–10, 216–17; relationship with his own father, 9; *25*
Waugh, Mrs Arthur (EW's mother), *nee* Catherine Charlotte Raban, 8, 43; *25*, *27*, *198*
Waugh, Auberon (EW's son), 123; *119*
Waugh, Evelyn Arthur St John (1903–66): *26–7*, *28*, *29*, *30*, *31*, *108–13*, *119–20*, *158–60*, *188*, *197–207*, *210–11*, *221–4*
  character and tastes of: aggressiveness, 45, 47, 75, 230; belief in divine guidance, 78; bitterness about social evolution, 170–1, 189–90; boredom in later life, 75, 132, 193*n*, 237–8; Catholicism of, 60–79, 100–101, 104–30 *passim*, 149, 181–2, 213–14, 236, 239, 240; courage, 94, 134, 236; dandyism, 33, 37, 237; depressions, 38, 75–6, 193*n*, 216, 237, 240–1; dislike of music, 44; dislike of strangers, 10, 12, 75, 128–9; drawing abilities, 11, 12, 50; *26*, *32*, *65–72*, *153–5*; drinking habits, 34, 40, 45–6, 123; as a father, 60, 124, 217; generosity, 37–8, 60, 76–7, 100, 132; good-naturedness in youth, 37–8, 43; literary tastes, 44–5; love of the army, 139; love of nature, 147–8; love of wood-carving, 131–2, 193; loyalty to friends, 11–12, 37–8, 130; offensiveness, 4, 60, 76, 93, 123, 132, 150, 233, 237, 239; opinion of Dominicans, 100–101; personae of, 3, 13, 76,

Waugh, Evelyn Arthur St John (1903–66)—*cont.*:
124, 139–40; political views, 2–3, 104, 122,
148–9; pride in tradition, 77–8; puritanism,
14, 120, 239; reactions to criticism, 127, 130,
226; relationship with Alec Waugh, 13;
relationship with his father, 9–10, 216–17;
relationship with his grandfather, 9, 12, 13;
relationship with his mother, 9; reticence,
139–40; snobbery, 13, 34, 77, 131, 138–9,
239; taste for Victoriana, 2, 100, 123, 225,
236; *209*; views on exercise, 124–5, 139; wit,
18, 20, 50, 193*n*, 227; and women, 40
life of: antecedents, 10, 60; boyhood in
Golders Green, 9, 10–11, 12, 63; *26–7*; home
background, 8–11; at Lancing College
(1917–21), 11, 16–21, 33, 43, 241; *28–9*; loses
religious faith, 60–1, 214; at Oxford (1922),
11, 16, 24–8, 104, 138, 184; *30–1*; drinking
habits at, 34, 37, 40; social life at, 34–8;
attitude to religion at, 61, 62; and Olivia
Plunket-Greene, 40–1, 42, 61; at Welsh prep
school, 41, 43; suicide attempt, 14, 45, 193*n*;
meets Evelyn Gardner (1927), 41–2;
engagement, 43; *Rossetti* published (1928),
43, 189; reviews books, 184–9; writes
Decline and Fall (1927–8), 43–4; difficulties
of publishing, 43–4, 45, 46, 220; *Decline and
Fall* published (1928) 220; success of, 12, 46,
104; social life in 1920s, 14, 41, 45–6, 104;
travels in Mediterranean, 82–3; success of
Vile Bodies (1929), 46; marriage breaks up
(1929), 82–3; *Labels* published (1930), 82,
189; received into Catholic Church (Sept.
1930), 74, 120, 214; travels to Abyssinia and
Africa (Oct. 1930), 83–8, 122; *156–8, 186*;
Remote People published (1931), 83; reviews
travel books, 189; retreat at Stonyhurst
(1932), 121; visits South America, (1932),
89–90; visits to the Lygons at Madresfield,
50–1, 53, 57, 98; *110–13*; learns riding at
Captain Hance's Academy, 50, 98; *112*;
writes *Black Mischief* (1931), 50, 84; *Black
Mischief* published (1932), 231–2; visits the
Betjemans, 99; writes biography of *Edmund
Campion* (1934), 99; awarded Hawthornden
prize for, 121; *188*; covers Abyssinian War
(1935), 90–1, 122; delays in getting marriage
annulled, 52, 74, 120–1; engagement to
Laura Herbert, 74–5; marries Laura Herbert
(1937), 52, 100, 122–3; *197*; buys Piers
Court, 100, 123; *Scoop* published (1938), 220;
efforts to enlist in war, 52, 92–3; in Royal
Marines, 52, 94, 123, 139; *160*; in
Commandos, 51, 123–4, 139, 195; drinking
habits and the army, 123; in Crete (1941),
94, 124, 134; in Yugoslavia (1944–5), 53,
54–6, 138–65; writes *Brideshead Revisited*
(1944), 53–4; *Brideshead Revisited*
published (1945), 166; moves to Combe
Florey, 100, 123; visits Hollywood and
writes *The Loved One* (1947), 127, 166,
168–9, 213; visits Spain (1947), 125–6;
writes *Scott-King's Modern Europe*, 125;
lectures in USA (1948), 181; friendship with
Knox, 77, 102, 129; visits Palestine and
writes *Holy Places* (1952), 63, 73; *Love
Among the Ruins* published (1953), 215, 225;
depressions and insomnia in later life, 3, 38,
60, 75, 216, 232, 237–8, 240–1; writes *Ordeal

of Gilbert Pinfold* (1958), 232; writes life of
Knox (1959), 129–30, 225; TV interview
with John Freeman (1962), 2, 128; *221*;
death (April, 1966), 79, 182;
Works referred to in text:
'Act of Homage and Reparation to P. G.
Wodehouse, An' (Sunday Times), 2, 194*n*,
214
'Awake My Soul! It is a Lord!' (*Spectator*),
215
'American Epoch in the Catholic Church,
The' (*Life*), 213
'Belloc Anadyomene' (*Spectator*), 194*n*
Black Mischief, 50, 89–90, 99, 220, 230;
criticism of, 231–2; illustrations, 50;
154–5; sources, 84–7, 92, 122
Brideshead Revisited, 2, 64, 78, 82, 83, 90,
124, 131, 147–8, 220; film of discussed,
127, 166; sources, 35, 53–4, 123, 167;
success in USA, 166, 215
'Californian Burial Customs' (*The Tablet*),
127
'Claim of Youth, The' (*Evening Standard*),
189
'Come Inside' (*The Road to Damascus*), 63,
214
'Commando Raid on Bardia' (*Life*), 195–6
'Death of Painting, The' (*Playboy*), 215
Decline and Fall, 62, 98, 172, 225; difficulties
of publishing, 43–4, 45, 46, 220;
illustrations, 11; *66*; sources, 11, 16, 19,
34–5, 138; success of, 12, 46, 104, 189
Edmund Campion, 73, 77, 99, 100, 121–2
Excursion in Reality, 167
'Fan-fare' (*Life*), 213
Handful of Dust, A, 2, 52, 62, 89, 120, 126,
220
Helena, 73, 77, 78, 127, 131
'Here's Richness' (*Spectator*), 194*n*
'Hollywood is a Term of Disparagement'
(*Life*), 213
Holy Places, The, 63, 73, 77–8
Incident in Azania, 230
Labels, 73, 82, 83, 189; *153*
Life of Ronald Knox, The, 129–30, 225
'Literary Style in England and America'
(*Books on Trial*), 194*n*
Little Learning, A, 9, 14, 18*n*, 20, 24, 33, 40,
44, 45–6, 60, 76, 184, 227, 230
Love Among the Ruins, 215, 225; *72*
Loved One, The, 62–3, 89, 127, 169–74,
177–82, 231
'Max Beerbohm: A Lesson in Manners'
(*Atlantic*), 194*n*
Men at Arms, 38, 91, 123, 167, 195–6, 226
'Mgr Ronald Knox' (*Horizon*), 194*n*
'Mr Waugh Replies' (*Spectator*), 184
'Mr Wodehouse and Mr Wain' (*Spectator*),
215
'My Father' (*Sunday Telegraph*), 184, 216–7
Ninety-Two Days, 89, 167
Officers and Gentlemen, 12, 88, 94, 196, 226
'Open Letter to the Honble Mrs Peter Rodd'
(*Encounter*), 215
Work Suspended, 230
Ordeal of Gilbert Pinfold, The, 3, 13, 220, 225;
as self-portrait, 38, 60, 75–6, 171, 216, 232
Put Out More Flags, 62, 92–3, 194–5, 230,
231

Waugh, Evelyn Arthur St John (1903–66)—*cont.*:
    Remote People, 83–9, 189
    Robbery Under Law, 90, 192*n*
    'Ronald Firbank' (*Life & Letters*), 190–1
    Rossetti: His Life and Works, 43, 44, 46, 47,
      62, 104, 189
    'Same again, please, The' (*Spectator*), 128,
      214
    Scoop, 47, 220, 226, 230; sources of, 90–2, 122
    Scott-King's Modern Europe, 125, 170;
      dedication of, 126
    'Sloth' (*Sunday Times*), 216
    Sword of Honour trilogy, 2, 78, 123–4, 131,
      195–6, 220, 231, 236, 240–1
    Tourist in Africa, A, 92
    Unconditional Surrender, 78, 94, 124, 126,
      141, 226, 231
    Vile Bodies, 47, 61, 62, 178, 220; *71*; EW
      criticizes, 232; sources, 3, 11, 167, 168,
      190; success of, 46, 104
    Waugh in Abyssinia, 90–2
    'War and the Younger Generation, The'
      (*Spectator*), 189–90
Waugh, Mrs Evelyn (EW's first wife) *see*
    Gardner, the Honourable Evelyn
Waugh, Mrs Evelyn (*nee* Laura Herbert, EW's
    second wife): engagement, 74–5; EW's
    marriage to, 52, 53, 55, 60, 147, 236, 240;
    farming abilities, 100; *197–9, 204–5, 207*
Waugh family: in nineteenth century, 10; social
    life of, 44
Waugh, James, (EW's son), *207*
Waugh, James Hay, Rector of Corsley (EW's
    great-grandfather), 10, 14

Waugh, Margaret (EW's daughter), 241
Waugh, Teresa (EW's eldest daughter), 4; *206*
Wavell, Archibald, 1st Earl, 94
West, Nathaniel, 172, 173; *The Day of the Locust*,
    173, 174–6; *Miss Lonelyhearts*, 174
What's Become of Waring? (Powell), 220
White's Club, 102, 124, 132, 139, 237; *201*
Wicklow, Lord, 62
Wilson, Angus, 2
Wilson, Edmund, 2, 166, 173, 174
Windsor, 95
Wodehouse, P. G., 2, 193, 194*n*, 214, 215
Wolfe, Humbert: *Circular Saws*, 68
Woodruff, Douglas, 62, 99; friendship with EW,
    3, 120–31
Woodruff, Mrs Douglas (Mea), 99, 126
World War I, 17, 124, 189
World War II, 2, 3, 52–7, 92–5, 123–4, 134–5,
    138–63, 195–6
World Within World (Spender), 194
Wrong Box, The (Stevenson), 220

Yellow Book, The, 10, 184
Yorke, Henry (Henry Green), *118*
Yugoslavia, EW in, 4, 53, 94, 134–5, 138–63;
    Partisan army of, 143, 144, 145–6, 148–9,
    152–3, 162–3

Zagreb University, 142
Zanzibar, EW visits, 88
Zoroastrianism, 101